ECONOMICS OF ARMS REDUCTION AND THE PEACE PROCESS

Contributions from Peace Economics and Peace Science

ECONOMICS OF ARMS REDUCTION AND THE PEACE PROCESS

Contributions from Peace Economics and Peace Science

Edited by

Walter ISARD

Cornell University
Ithaca, N.Y., U.S.A.

Charles H. ANDERTON

College of the Holy Cross
Worcester, M.A., U.S.A.

1992

NORTH-HOLLAND
AMSTERDAM · LONDON · NEW YORK · TOKYO

ELSEVIER SCIENCE PUBLISHERS B.V.
Sara Burgerhartstraat 25
P.O. Box 211, 1000 AE Amsterdam, The Netherlands

Distributors for the United States and Canada:

ELSEVIER SCIENCE PUBLISHING COMPANY INC.
655 Avenue of the Americas
New York, N.Y. 10010, U.S.A.

```
Library of Congress Cataloging-in-Publication Data


Economics of arms reduction and the peace process : contributions from
  peace economics and peace science / edited by Walter Isard, Charles
H. Anderton.
      p.   cm.
   "Jointly sponsored by ECAAR (Economists against the Arms Race) and
PSS(I) (the Peace Science Society, International)"--Pref.
   Includes bibliographical references.
   ISBN 0-444-88848-9
   1. Arms control--Economic aspects.  2. Disarmament--Economic
aspects.  3. Peace.  4. Armed Forces--Appropriations and
expenditures.  5. War, Cost of.  6. Defense industries.   I. Isard,
Walter.  II. Anderton, Charles H.
JX1974.E33  1992
338.4'76234--dc20                                            91-47631
                                                                 CIP
```

ISBN: 0 444 88848 9

Printed in The Netherlands

Contents

List of Illustrations

List of Tables

Preface

This book is jointly sponsored by ECAAR (Economists Against the Arms Race) and PSS(I) (The Peace Science Society, International). ECAAR is a recently organized group of economists (including a number of Nobel Laureates in economics and others of world renown) concerned with research and policy development aimed at controlling the arms race and the reduction of military expenditures.

The PSS(I) is a group of quantitative political scientists, sociologists, psychologists, geographers, regional scientists, and a limited umber of economists and other social scientists and professionals who conduct basic research on conflict and the peace process. The findings of the non-economists in this group are essential for economists to consider in adapting their theoretical and applied research to the complex world of reality.

At a recent meeting of Trustees and Directors of ECAAR it was urged that (1) the various findings of economists pertaining to conflict, arms escalation, disarmament and related topics published in diverse and scattered journals and books be summarized in a literature survey, and (2) there be brought together some of the basic research by leading economists on selected topics of critical importance to the field. Accordingly, this book. It contains a summary of the peace economics literature by the editors, and selected seminal contributions to the field of peace economics largely drawn from papers presented at recent conferences and joint meetings of ECAAR and PSS(I). In selecting papers for this book, along with the survey, the editors sought to achieve a fairly comprehensive coverage of the newly emerging peace economics field as well as a presentation of its nature and scope. In line with the objectives of ECAAR they have tried to put out a product that would have considerable value for economists and other scholars, in particular those entering the field and concerned with the impacts of arms reduction and conversion by the major powers and the escalation of military expenditures elsewhere.

We wish to acknowledge the excellent typing and graphics of our secretaries, Helena Wood, Pamela Allain and Beverly Bylund. We also are grateful for the many suggestions from members of ECAAR and PSS(I) on topics to be covered in this volume, and in particular to Robert Schwartz, founder of ECAAR, for encouragement.

WALTER ISARD
Cornell University

CHARLES H. ANDERTON
College of the Holy Cross

Economics of Arms Reduction and the Peace Process
W. Isard and C.H. Anderton (Editors)
© 1992 Elsevier Science Publishers B.V. All rights reserved.

Chapter 1

A SURVEY OF THE PEACE ECONOMICS LITERATURE

Walter Isard and Charles H. Anderton

Cornell University

and

College of the Holy Cross

1.1 Introduction

In this chapter we wish to present a short, but compact survey of the main strands of thought in the literature on peace economics. A more detailed and thorough survey requires a book-length manuscript currently being written.

There are many ways in which this survey can be organized. One way would address first the question of why there is conflict, proceed to the identification of specific economic factors generating or lying behind conflicts, hone into the consequent phenomena of military expenditures and arms races, perhaps then investigate the interplay of economic factors in specific conflicts (including those leading to major unrest, wars, revolutions and terrorism), examine the basis for arms control, and finally at all stages probe into the manifold direct and indirect effects (the impact) of arms escalation, control and disarmament.

To proceed in this way, however, is not very useful. The literature on peace economics is helter skelter, appearing in diverse journals and books without adhering to any semblance of organization. Hence we choose to present first some general conceptual materials to help identify the myriad of forces and problems that have been encountered. Then we proceed to survey the literature, for the most part on operational models and hypothesis testing, following the four approaches suggested by economic reasoning that Arrow (chapter 2) uses in treating the economic effects of arms reduction. These are: standard resource allocation theory, macroeconomic stability analysis, modern growth theory, and political economy thinking. We find examination of the literature in this manner at least as good if not better than any other that has been proposed. However, we discuss writings on arms race models and arms control which are the outgrowth of the standard resource allocation problem in a separate section. Also since there are extensive writings on sectoral and regional impacts of military expenditures which employ models derived from both standard resource allocation theory and macroeconomic stability analysis, we add a section on these impacts after the discussion of macroeconomic stability analysis. Finally, we end up with a section on conflict management analysis and procedures, a topic of concern to all social sciences and many professions, and one on which economists have made notable contributions.

2.1 The General Conceptual Framework and Some Basic Issues

In setting forth a general conceptual framework, we need to broaden the economist's traditional study of cooperation, rivalry and conflict among economic behaving units and organizations to cover the study of *peace and war,* as Hirshleifer (1988) has proposed. Hirshleifer calls for a general equilibrium framework to embrace within economics the full variety of conflicts. To understand the operation of the world economy and most national economies, "peaceful" production and exchange ways of generating income and utility need to be complemented by appropriative-type ways and efforts. These efforts, associated with military expenditures, weaponry accumulation and conflict that can lead to physical violence, are designed to secure resources of others or to defend against loss of resources to others. In a real sense, most national economies are geared simultaneously to war and peace -- each being typically located along a spectrum whose extremes are "absolute peace and total war". "Individuals and groups can choose between two main ways of acquiring income: (1) producing economic goods, versus (2) seizing what other parties have produced....It is the fact that intrusive efforts (and defending against them) can be as renumerative as production or exchange that makes conflict a permanent feature of life" (p. 202). Accordingly, Hirshleifer sets up a model involving a resource partition function, a contestable-income production function, a combat power function and an income distribution function.[1]

In a vein more consistent with arms race modelling, other scholars have developed general conceptual frameworks. For example, for nation J (opposing nation L) the societal resource allocation problem at a given point of time can be stated in a highly simplified manner as:

$$\text{Max } W^J = W^J(C^J, S_e^J) \tag{1.1}$$

subject to:

$$T^J(C^J, M^J, K^J, L^J) = 0 \tag{1.2}$$

$$S^J_e = f^J(S^J, S^L, \phi) \tag{1.3}$$

$$S^J = (1-\alpha)S^J_{-1} + M^J \tag{1.4}$$

where:

W^J = social welfare (utility) of J.

C^J = J's production of civilian (consumption and investment) goods.

S^J_e = J's perceived level of national security.

T^J = J's transformation function (production possibility frontier).

M^J = J's production of military goods, to be viewed as additions to J's stock of these
goods.

K^J, L^J = J's stock of capital and labor, each defined broadly to include all of J's
resources.

S^J, S^L = J's and L's stock of military goods, respectively.

ϕ = parameter reflecting the quality of military goods in J and L, the state of the
international environment, and other exogenous factors affecting J's security.

α = rate of depreciation (covering obsolescence) of military goods.

S^J_{-1} = J's stock of military goods at the previous point of time.

Nation L faces a similar economic-choice problem, although the specific form of J's and L's functions will differ. The link that gives rise to the arms race is the assumed negative externality of each nation's stock of military goods on its adversary's security.

Explicit treatment of security as a variable addresses Hirshleifer's defense against invasion or appropriation by another nation (behaving unit) of one's resources. It less adequately addresses Hirshleifer's appropriative efforts to acquire resources, since acquisition and accumulation of power and other noneconomic commodities[2] tend to loom much larger in governing such efforts. Nonetheless, the recent Iraq invasion of Kuwait may be interpreted by some as basically economically motivated to possess and control more oil resources; and the subsequent repossession of these oil resources and reassignment of them to a restored Kuwait government represents an economically based appropriation (reappropriation) effort to maintain oil resources for trade in a "free world".

The basic framework of eqs. 1.1-1.4 has been used by Dumas (1972) and Anderton (1990a) to illustrate the fundamental economic nature of arms rivalry. Many of the relationships have been developed in a more in-depth fashion by a number of scholars. For example, McGuire (1965) embodied many of the relationships when he considered the role of secrecy in the arms race. Isard (1988, ch. 13) presented a very general mathematical statement in an attempt at synthesis of arms race models. Wolfson (1991, ch. 9) has moved forward in the construction of a dynamic two period general disequilibrium model.   An earlier dynamic equilibrium model is presented in Brito (1972).

1.3 Standard Resource Allocation Analysis and Strategic Behavior

General conceptual frameworks need to be simplified and modified through the injection of assumptions, sometimes very strong, to yield magnitudes and directions of change of variables useful for projecting behavior, attacking problems and identifying appropriate policies. In this section, we look at ways standard resource allocation theory has been employed to do so.

In a direct and simple manner, the general problem of resource allocation is well posed by the famous Samuelson guns and butter diagram. On Figure 1.1 production of butter (civilian goods) and guns (military weapons) are measured along the vertical and horizontal axes, respectively. Society's production possibility frontier is given by the curve PP' indicating that an efficiently operating society can only produce guns at the expense of butter, or vice versa. (For the moment, ignore the other curves and numbers thereon presented). The basic questions are: (1) how much of each good should be produced, that is what point on the curve PP' should be chosen; and (2) if society is operating inefficiently, say at a point Q, inside the curve PP' (the set of all efficient points) because of non-economic factors or poor economic decisions, how can society reach a point on the curve or move toward such a point while increasing production of both goods? Moreover, if there are several paths from Q to a point on the curve allowing increasing production of both goods, which should be chosen?

Society's decisions on where to produce and how to move to the frontier if inside are dependent on the desires of its behaving units -- individuals, organizations, interest groups and so forth -- desires which generally are conflicting because of the different utility or welfare functions of these units.

In his classic 1962 book, *Conflict and Defense,* Boulding has examined this problem, as well as many others on which economists have subsequently worked, extending Boulding's analysis in many directions. In examining the behavior of two units, A and B, each say a leader of a political party, Boulding might have added to a diagram such as Figure 1.1 the two sets of indifference curves thereon depicted, the upper left set for A and the lower right for B. Combinations of butter and guns represented by points a* and b* are the most preferred by A and B, respectively. For a system that will be operating efficiently, the arc a*b* represents the conflict set (the negotiation or bargaining set), requiring the use of a conflict management procedure, rule or other device (discussed in Section 1.9 below) in order to reach an agreement by the two parties on which combination to produce.

However, if society is operating at an inefficient point Q, then the interior area Qcd represents the trading or improvement set. Given the combination of guns and butter that any point in that set represents, there is at least one point within the arc cd which would represent an improvement for both participants, and so suggests a trade within their demands.

Many procedures have been suggested for the parties to use to reach an argreement in cases where the initial demands are defined by a* and b*, or when a society is operating at a point Q and greater efficiency is desired. See for example the early work of Zeuthen (1930) and Bishop (1960, 1963, 1964), and the more general analysis in Isard (1988, ch. 10).

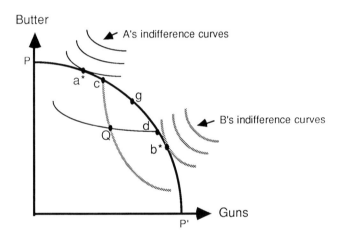

Figure 1.1: Society's Production Possibility Frontier and Parties' Indifference Curves

The resource allocation problem, as posed with a continuous production possibility frontier and well-behaved indifference curves, may constitute a theoretical economist's perception of reality, but not that of a typical political leader. To such a behaving unit, both his and his opponent's set of possible actions is much more limited. An extreme case consists of only two possible actions by each participant in a situation where symmetry obtains, and where each simultaneously chooses an action once and for all. One possible action, a *cooperative* one, is when a leader, say A, publicly admits there is some validity to the resource allocation which his opponent most prefers. He knows that if his opponent B chooses the other possible action, the *noncooperative* (highly competitive) one, and denounces his (the first leader's) action as folly, B will win out, resource allocation b* will be realized and he (A) will end up on a low ranking indifference curve, say with the low, *ordinal rank* of 2. He also knows that if B chooses a cooperative action and recognizes publicly some validity to the resource allocation A most prefers, then they are likely to end up in a 50-50 type of split like that represented by point g (a median point along the frontier), at which the ordinal ranking of his indifference curve is say 5. Finally, he knows that if B chooses a cooperative action and he chooses the noncooperative one, and thus wins, resource allocation a* will be realized, at which the ordinal ranking of his indifference curve is say 10. This situation of symmetry can be represented by the matrix in Figure 1.2 where the first number in each cell represents A's ranking of the outcome of the joint action represented by that cell, and the second number, B's ranking.

B's actions

	cooperate	noncoop.
cooperate	5, 5	1, 10
noncoop.	10, 1	2, 2

A's actions

Figure 1.2: The Prisoner's Dilemma Game

Figure 1.2 is the classic PD (Prisoner's Dilemma) game, which has been discussed *ad infinitum* for an arms race situation involving two nations, where the noncooperation action involves an increase in military expenditures (an escalation), sometimes designated defection, and the cooperation action, no increase or even a decrease in military expenditures.

According to some scholars, rational myopic players would choose their unconditionally best of the two actions, namely noncooperation, and the Pareto-inferior Nash equilibrium (2,2) would result. It is stable; no player is motivated to depart from non-cooperation; and clearly if the joint cooperation were in effect leading to the outcome (5,5), such would be unstable since each player would be tempted to depart from it. If the rules of the game are changed, so that sequential action is possible, the second mover has the advantage.

The literature on this game, on the game of Chicken (where the payoff of rank 1 is replaced by a rank between 2 and 5, say 4)[3] and on many other one-shot games is extensive. (See Shubik, 1982; Brams and Kilgour, 1988). The one-shot aspect disqualifies these games for most conflict situations encountered in reality. However, many of these games have been extended to many-period cases (see Shubik, 1982; Fraser and Hipel, 1984; Friedman, 1990).

The restricted-action game framework has led to innumerable studies of strategy. In his pioneering 1960 work, *The Strategy of Conflict*, Schelling is not concerned with conflict as a pathological state or as a consequence of irrational or unconscious behavior. Rather, he focusses on the more rational, conscious and artful kind of behavior. To him, most conflict situations are essentially bargaining situations which usually involve both conflict and cooperation, and where the behavior of each party significantly influences the outcome possibilities and thus courses of action of the other parties. The actions of the parties often involve commitments, threats, promises, concerns about reputation and credibility, and deceptions of many types. Schelling has illustrated various bargaining situations. For example, where *enforceable promises* are possible in an appropriate revision of the PD game, the Pareto efficient outcome (5,5) becomes stable. Another bargaining situation that has been of considerable interest has centered around deterrent threat. Suppose the ordinal ranks are as in the matrix of Figure 1.3:

The status quo is the joint cooperation outcome (5,10). Let A plan to defect (leading to 10,5) with B threatening subsequently to defect (leading to 2,1). The payoff matrix points up the tradeoff between the effectiveness and credibility of B's deterrent threat. B's threat to defect (to be noncooperative) is effective because it takes A down to an outcome of rank 2 only. But is the threat credible. Were B to carry out the threat, he would impose a cost to himself, a fall in an outcome ranked 5 to an outcome ranked 1. Whether B carries out the threat depends on many factors including whether the play of future games depends on this one (reputation effects). See Brams and Kilgour (1988) for extensive analysis of deterrent threat games.

In his studies, Schelling has examined many other topics including a theory of tacit bargaining, problems of communication and coordination, strategic moves, randomized threats and promises, surprise attack, optimal choice of weapons systems, the diplomacy of violence, the art of commitment, and the manipulation of risk (see Schelling, 1960, 1966a, 1966b. For a recent in-depth theoretical treatment of tacit bargaining based on Schelling's foundation, see Downs and Rocke, 1990).

B's actions

	cooperate	defect.
cooperate	5, 10	1, 2
defect	10, 5	2, 1

A's
actions

Figure 1.3: Deterrent Threat

There have been many important advances in game analysis since Schelling's pioneering works. One of the more recent developments has been Hirshleifer's concept of evolutionary equilibrium. In a 1987 study he assumes that people are members of a homogeneous population meeting randomly in pairwise interactions. The people can play cooperative, non-cooperative or mixed strategies in their dynamic encounters with one another. The idea of evolutionary equilibrium is that over time, some strategies will be "defeated" by others and eventually driven out, if they yield lower average returns than other strategies. Since conflict is generally inefficient, won't cooperative strategies generally emerge in society? Not necessarily. The average returns of cooperative, non-cooperative and mixed strategies "will be a function of the proportions of the population choosing each of the strategies." (p. 224). Human nature and social/legal institutions significantly affect the types of games and the associated returns that emerge in dyadic encounters. There is no guarantee that these variables will give rise to cooperative strategies driving out non-cooperative ones.

In particular, in a Prisoner's Dilemma with cardinal payoffs in Figure 1.4a, the average returns α and β for cooperation and defection are:

$$\alpha = (p)(-1) + (1-p)(-20) \tag{1.5}$$

$$\beta = (p)0 + (1-p)(-10) \tag{1.6}$$

where p is the proportion of people playing the cooperative strategy. For the whole range of p, $\alpha < \beta$, i.e., the average return for the cooperative strategy is always less than the average return for the non-cooperative strategy. The evolutionary equilibrium occurs at p=0 in Figure 1.4b. Cooperative play is weeded out in PD social structures.

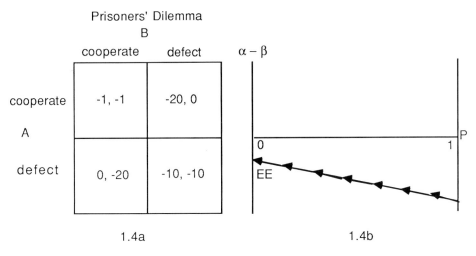

Figure 1.4: A Case of Evolutionary Equilibrium

Of course, social scientists have explored ways to escape from the PD. We will not examine that literature here but see Axelrod (1984), Hirshleifer (1987:231-248), Dixit and Nalebuff (1991: ch.4), and Brams (1985:chs. 3 and 4).

Finally, we should note some of the conclusions of Shubik (1968, 1982, 1984, 1987) in his classic works on game theory. Shubik contends that at the two person tactical level in zero-sum games, considerable game-theoretic analysis is available and relevant. But at the strategic level in two-or-more-person nonconstant-sum games of reality there are substantial obstacles to application of game-theoretic analysis. Among others, there are the following questions: (1) *who are the players?* and if players are aggregated, what are and how do we describe these preferences? (2) *how is utility evaluated?* are the preferences merely those of a nation's political leader over the limited number of outcomes he perceives, or do the "preferences" of the public, however defined, enter in some way? (3) *how is uncertainty treated?*; especially when dealing with nations, group behavior with risk and uncertainty is involved along with individual risk and uncertainty, and we know so little about the former; (4) *how is information, communication and coding handled?* that is, what is the context in which information is generated, spread (coded) and received (retrieved and understood) by the participants? Shubik concludes: "Gaming experiments are needed to study the differences and causes of differences in situations where the game theoretic model is the same, but the briefing or setting of context, the players (their training and background) and organizational structure and time pressures are varied" (1987, p. 80).

1.4 Arms Race Models and Arms Control

Strategic behavior of two or more political leaders of nations on occasion lead to war, and frequently to arms races and the desire for arms control. On the initiation of war and its probability there have been a number of notable contributions by economists, of which we can briefly mention only a few. Boulding (1962) has examined the effect of distances separating nations on their spheres of influence and viability, the greater the distances from others, the more viable a nation, *ceteris paribus*. Tullock (1974) develops a microeconomic choice model of the decision to abstain from or engage in war, indicating with reaction functions (such as in Figure 1.5 below) how nation A's probability of victory relates to its allocation of resources to arms and that of its opponent B. He speaks of the present discounted value of peace, the expected discounted value of war, and sets up a gain-loss relationship which takes into account the consideration that if A conquers B, in the future it will be unnecessary for A to put as much resources into arms. He also points out that under certain circumstances mutual disarmament may increase the probability of war. Wittman (1979) develops an expected utility model of war termination to study the impact of changes in variables on the feasibility of settlement, reaching such results as (1) a reduction in the intensity of fighting (i.e. a partial settlement) may *decrease* the probability of a full settlement, and (2) settlement is more likely to take place when the countries are risk-averse as opposed to risk-loving. See also the excellent study by the political scientist Bueno de Mesquita (1981).

Some of the most recent and advanced analysis of peace economists has centered around arms control and deterrence and attack capability in a nuclear weaponry Cold War world. Analysis frequently starts using Cournot-Edgeworth concepts in one form or another to point up inefficiency of arms rivalries. For example, in Figure 1.5, measure country L's weapons stock along the horizontal from point 0 to the right (movement to the right representing increases in weapons; movement to the left representing disarmament). Country J's weapons stock is measured vertically from point 0 (a vertical upward movement representing increases; downward movement representing decreases). For both J and L, their set of indifference curves are indicated by one complete indifference curve and segments of others. Each one's reaction functions are also shown. If myopic Cournot behavior is assumed, the arms race settles at point e. The Pareto-efficient points are shown along the contract curve L*J*, L* and J* being the most preferred position of L and J, respectively. Thus, point e represents a Pareto-inefficient use of resources. All points such that one or both nations are better off and neither is worse off relative to e is the set of Pareto improvement points (the football-shaped region in Figure 1.5). The segment CD of the contract curve is the core.

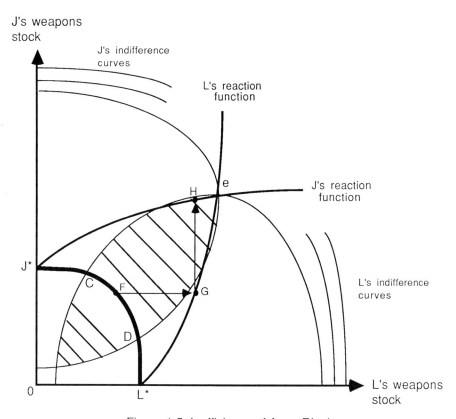

Figure 1.5: Inefficiency of Arms Rivalry

Arms-control efforts are a recognition of the Pareto inefficiency of the arms race. Arms control is designed to move nations J and L away from point e into the cigar-shaped region of mutual gains. Only when the weapons point is on the core (in between, but not including, the end points of the core) can it be said that both J and L have gained relative to e and neither nation can gain from further arms control efforts without worsening the position of the other nation (see Anderton, 1990a).

The mutual gains from arms control depicted in Figure 1.5 do not depend on the goodwill of the parties toward one another. An arms race is a variable sum game, exhibiting elements of both competition and cooperation, such that it is not true that whatever one side gains the other must lose (McGuire, 1965:213-214). Purely selfish and extremely intense rivals can gain from arms control.

Even if arms control efforts move nations J and L to the core, however, there is still the problem of defection (cheating). Assume that the joint efforts of J and L move them to point F in Figure 1.5. Nation L can make itself better off by cheating and moving to point G which then induces nation J to defect and increase its armaments, and so on. Only if arms-control cheating can be easily detected and punished (via some enforcement mechanism or resumption of a mutually detrimental arms rivalry) will the nations have an incentive not to cheat. This is why inspection of adversary weapons sites and verification of arms control agreements are such important issues in arms-control debates.

These issues have been examined in a number of studies. Tullock (1974) examined a prisoner's dilemma situation, employing cardinal payoffs and in one case involving cheating probabilities. He reached the conclusion that nations who intend to abide by arms control treaties will be reluctant to enter them, while nations who plan to cheat will be eager to enter them. In a similar study, McGuire (1965) develops a missile war scenario where the war is a sequence of counterforce strikes first by one side, then by the second side, then by the first again, and so on-- taking the position that "to understand why a nation amasses the tools of war, one must reflect upon war itself" (p. 47). McGuire then develops a body of arms race/arms control theory for exploring secrecy, verification and the cheating problem.

One of the more important and controversial models relating to arms control is that of Intriligator and Brito (1976) which focusses upon the use of arms for both attack and deterrence purposes. There are two basic terms in determining the level of missiles necessary for deterrence for, say, nation J. One term specifies the number of J's missiles that L can destroy with its stock S^L. In oversimplified fashion, this number is derived by multiplying S^L by a factor f^L (indicating the destructive effectiveness of one L missile) yielding the term $f^L S^L$. The second term specifies the number of J's missiles that must remain intact (after L in an attack has used up its entire stock S^L) in order for J to inflict what it estimates to be an unacceptable number, at least $\bar{C}^L$, of civilian casualties on L. In oversimplified fashion, if each of J's missiles can cause υ^J of such casualties, then $\bar{C}^L/\upsilon^J$ must be the number of J's missiles that must remain intact. Thus, in oversimplified fashion the amount S^J of missiles that J must have for deterrence purposes is given by:

$$S^J \geq f^L S^L + \bar{C}^L/\upsilon^J \qquad\qquad (1.7)$$

A proper statement of this relationship recognizes that there is a time delay before J can retaliate after a missile attack and that there would be a time period during which retaliation would occur.[4]

On the other hand, J may contemplate the use of arms for a potential attack. Where f^J is the effectiveness of one of J's missiles in destroying L's missiles, $f^J S^J$ is the number of L's missiles J can destroy with its stock S^J. Then J must consider the number of L's missiles, $S^L - f^J S^J$, left intact after its (J's) attack. Nation J must find acceptable the number of civilian casualties in J's country that this left-over number can inflict. If v^L is the number of J's casualties an L missile can inflict, then for J to attack it must be that (in oversimplied terms):

$$v^L(S^L - f^J S^J) \leq \hat{C}^J \tag{1.8}$$

where $\hat{C}^J$ is the maximum number of civilian casualties that J considers acceptable. By reordering terms in Eq. (1.8), we obtain[5]

$$S^J \leq \frac{1}{f^J}(S^L - \frac{\hat{C}^J}{v^L}) \tag{1.9}$$

Assuming L's reactions are similar in nature to those of J, we have two similar equations for L. When the equality sign holds and when we graph these four relations, we obtain the familiar Intriligator-Brito figure presented here as Figure 1.6. Those combinations of S^J and S^L that lie on the line "J deters" and in the areas to its right (1, 2J and 4J) are combinations where the stock S^J is sufficient to deter L from attacking. Likewise, combinations of S^J and S^L on and above the line "L deters" (in the areas 1, 2L and 4L) are combinations where the stock S^L is large enough to deter J from attacking. The dashed area (1) in the upper right can then be clearly designated the cone of mutual deterrence.

Those combinations of S^J and S^L lying on and below the line "J can attack" (in areas 4J, 5J, and 6) are combinations where J can effectively attack. None of these combinations give L deterrence capability. Those combinations of S^J and S^L lying on and to the left of line "L can attack" (in areas 4L, 5L and 6) are combinations where L can effectively attack. We have also indicated in Figure 1.6 a dotted area (3) comprising those combinations where neither J nor L attacks or deters -- where possible casualties that the surviving missiles of an opponent can inflict prevents a nation from attacking. Finally in region 5L, nation L cannot avoid preemption because L has enough weapons to attack J with impunity, but, at the same time, neither has enough weapons to deter the other. L will be forced to attack or J will be forced to preempt, in either case leading to war (Intriligator and Brito, 1989:19).

Region 5J is the obverse case. In region 6 each side can attack the other, neither can avoid preemption, and neither can deter the other.

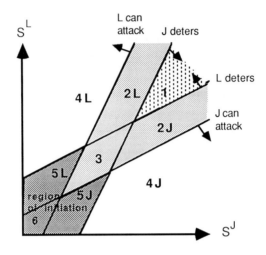

Figure 1.6: The Intriligator-Brito Model

Intriligator and Brito then argue that (a) a small arms race escalation from the origin (0,0), or other low weapons level on both sides, to some other combination represented by a point in area 6 leads to a highly unstable situation with a high probability of war, (b) a large escalation that ends up in area 1 (whether it goes through areas 4L, 3, or 4J leads to a stable situation of mutual deterrence with very low probability of war, (c) a deescalation from a high level in area 3 to a relatively high level that remains in area (3) retains stability, and (d) a major deescalation (disarmament) from area (1) to area (6) leads to instability and high probability of war.

There has been extensive criticism (and support) of this analysis and the implied position that large nuclear weaponry is justifiable. The linearity assumption of the model is considered unjustifiable for policy purposes (Kupperman and Smith, 1976) and is recognized as simply a device to obtain a mathematically tractable model. Even allowing for linearity, Boulding (1978) has pointed out that a very low probability of war with high catastrophic potential (that would be associated with military stocks corresponding to a position in the zone of mutual deterrence) is still not acceptable; earthquakes and volcanic eruptions with very low probabilities do occur. If there is some positive probability that nuclear weapons will go off, and there must be if they are to have a deterrent effect, then eventually they will go off.

Further Anderton (1991) has noted that it is important to distinguish between the traditional I-B (Intriligator-Brito) model and the I-B *methodology*. The I-B methodology gives rise to a whole family of I-B models (the traditional I-B model is a special case), many of which lead to analytical findings quite different from those of the traditional I-B model. For example, implicit in the traditional I-B analysis and model is a specific attitude -- one in which both parties are willing to accept casualties in return for the fruits of victory whatever they may be. However, they may be inclined toward more risk averse behavior. They may contemplate attack only if they can destroy entirely the adversary's forces -- in which case the traditional linear I-B model at the extreme right of Figure 1.7 becomes the linear model at the middle with the region of mutual attack (region 6) eliminated. Or they may be still more cautious and pursue "sure thing" behavior, and contemplate attack only if they can eliminate all the adversary's forces and still have a minimum surviving force (a basic premise around which Radner, 1989 develops his model of "defense-protected build-down"), in which case the linear model at the extreme left of Figure 1.7 becomes relevant. An even more fundamental criticism of the original I-B model is that even if J and L are risk-loving, the mutual attack region is problematic. For example, at point q in Figure 1.7, L has 10 weapons and J has two, yet J is depicted as being able to attack. If f^J and f^L are less than one, however, there is no rational basis whereby J would attack L in the context of the original I-B model. Anderton interprets the original I-B model as pessimistic, and considers the other two as neutral and optimistic, respectively.

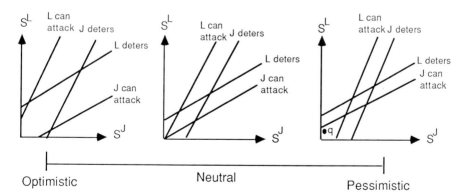

Figure 1.7: Spectrum of Intriligator-Brito Models

The f and υ terms of the Intriligator-Brito model may not be constant; they may be a function of weapons levels. This can give rise to nonlinear relations from which a great variety of analytical results are possible (Mayer, 1986; Anderton and

Fogarty, 1990). In addition, the f and υ terms embody various weapons technologies. The dramatic changes in military technologies throughout history have dramatically affected war, arms rivalry and arms control.

In conducting deterrence and deescalation analysis Fischer (1984) points up the desirability of considering different types of military technology. He maintains that a highly nonthreatening defense system (one comprising purely relatiatory second-strike weapons and lines of antitank, antiaircraft missiles backed up by reservists that could defend their own territory) by itself does not reduce the security of (impose a negative externality on) a rival; it can deescalate an arms race. Schelling (1966a) also stresses the importance of military technology when he argues that in a relationship between armed adversaries there is "something that we might call the 'inherent propensity toward peace or war' embodied in the weaponry, the geography, and the military organization of the time" (p. 234). Schelling's inherent propensity idea is a recognition that there are characteristics embodied in the weapons themselves that push adversaries toward peace or war, independent of the personalities and goals of the decision-makers, the extent of political disagreement between the adversaries, and misperceptions about mutual resolve and hostility. Other studies have employed I-B type models to study various aspects of military technology and its relation to peace and war issues (see Intriligator and Brito, 1986; Wolfson, 1987; Anderton, 1990b, 1992)

The Intriligator-Brito model has been extended in another direction by Wolfson (1985) to point up the basis for economic warfare, using a loose comparative statics framework. Let Figure 1.6 be the fourth quadrant of Figure 1.8 with J's military production (primarily missiles) measured from the origin down the vertical, and L's military production along the horizontal, and retain only the "L can deter" line. Let the production possibility frontier of Figure 1.1 be the PZP' curve in quadrant 1, with civilian goods production measured along the vertical. Let L's current allocation of resources to civilian production C_1^L and military M_1^L be given by point Z. The second quadrant depicts a relationship between gross investment (measured along the horizontal to the left of the origin) and civilian production where, for simplicity's sake only, gross investment is taken to equal savings and savings is taken to be a constant fraction s^L of civilian production. As a consequence, gross investment $I^L = s^L C^L$. Corresponding to allocation Z, OU is the resulting level of gross investment. If OH is the required replacement investment, then UH is net investment which is measured vertically along the I_N^L axis in the fourth quadrant.

Assume L's military concern is with deterrence. As an optimal social welfare response, it has chosen allocation Z to produce military goods M_1^L, adequate for increasing its stock of missiles to match for deterrence purposes the increase in J's stock resulting from J's military production M_1^J. Thus the net investment UH (and the associated expansion of L's production possibility frontier (the non bold curve in quadrant 1) corresponds to M_1^J as indicated in the 4th quadrant.

If J's military production had been M_2^J, L's optimal response would have been a resource allocation to realize M_2^L military production, resulting in zero net investment and no change in its production possibility frontier. If J's military production had been M_3^J, L's optimal responses would have had to be (for deterrence purposes) M_3^L, resulting in *negative* net investment (inadequate replacement of used-up and obsolete plant and equipment) and a contraction of the production possibility frontier. High enough levels of M^J, as might be associated with arms escalation, implies economic collapse (bankruptcy) of L.

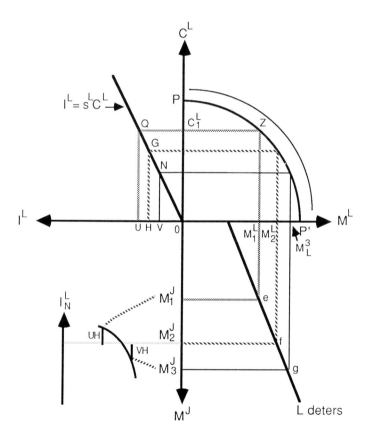

Figure 1.8: Economic Warfare

Return to the arms race dynamics of reality. This simple exercise in comparative statics shows how the escalation of military expenditures by J can in time force another country with a significantly smaller resource base into a situation where it is unable to maintain its productive capacity when opting to continue to deter as J's military production and stock mount. It will choose to attack, Wolfson suggests, before it is economically forced into submission (defeat). Lambelet's chapter in this volume suggests that a nation defeated by economic warfare in the Wolfson sense, may instead withdraw from participating in an arms rivalry. Wolfson's analysis provides a link between the conflict and arms rivalry literature and the literature on the economic effects of arms production and disarmament. Weapons production has important macro- and micro-economic effects and it is to these topics that we now turn.

1.5 Macroeconomic Stability Analysis

Consider the Keynesian literature and the more modern versions of macroeconomics. Consistent with Arrow's observation in the next chapter, we examine Keynesian theory for use for short-run policy analysis, recognizing the controversial nature of Keynesian theory today. One of the earliest analyses was conducted by Suits (1963). His purely schematic model which he used for illustrative purposes is:

$$C = 20 + .7\ (Y\text{-}T) \tag{1.10}$$

$$I = 2 + .1Y_{-1} \tag{1.11}$$

$$T = .2Y \tag{1.12}$$

$$Y = C + I + G \tag{1.13}$$

where consumption C depends on current disposable income (Y-T), investment I depends on income Y_{-1} lagged one period, taxes T depend on income Y, and income Y is consumption C plus investment I plus government expenditure G.[6] Using a 32 equation model (derived from disaggregation of each of the four types of equations noted above) developed from the earlier Klein-Goldberger model, Suits projects the effects on GNP, consumption, government expenditure, tax receipts, government deficit, and employment of the disarmament program of January 1962 proposed by the U.S. Arms Control and Disarmament Agency, for each of several tax reduction offset programs.

A decade later Klein and Mori (1973) used the more extensive Wharton-Econometric Forecasting Unit Model to project the effects of different Vietnam and offset program scenarios upon GNP, unemployment rate, price index (inflation rate) and bond yield (interest rate).

Recently, Klein, following up on his earlier studies and with his associate Kosaka, has scored a major advance through embodying an arms race model, albeit highly simplified, into his 79 nation LINK model. Their procedure, as recorded in Isard (1990), involves four steps:

(i) Obtain military expenditures at year t for nation J as a function of current and past military expenditures by allies and adversaries, that is:

$$ME^J(t) = f^J[ME^A(t),...,ME^K(t),...,ME^U(t); ME^A(t-1),...,ME^K(t-1),...,ME^U(t-\emptyset)] \qquad (1.14)$$

for K=A,B,...,U; K≠ J.

(ii) Relate the level of military expenditures of a nation to the size of its economy (resource base or productive capacity as measured by its GDP). Hence, estimate the fraction of GDP absorbed by military expenditures as follows:

$$\frac{ME^J}{GDP^J}(t) = f^J[\frac{ME^A}{GDP^A}(t),...,\frac{ME^K}{GDP^K}(t),...,\frac{ME^U}{GDP^U}(t);$$
$$\frac{ME^A}{GDP^A}(t-1),...,\frac{ME^K}{GDP^K}(t-1),...,\frac{ME^U}{GDP^U}(t-\emptyset)] \qquad (1.15)$$

for K = A,B,...,U; K≠J. To account for strains or slack in an economy and associated nonlinear effects, a price index, P^J, can be introduced into Equation (1.15) when to do so would be statistically significant.

(iii) With the initial forecasts of GDP^J and P^J of Project LINK over the 1980s and the subsequently derived projections of military expenditures throughout the 1980s, capture the feedback from the military to the civilian economy. To accomplish this, estimate public (government) spending $G^J(t)$ as a function (in a marginal sense) of current and past military expenditures as follows:

$$G^J(t) = g^J[ME^J(t), ..., ME^J(t-\gamma)] \qquad (1.16)$$

This reflects the impact upon present public spending of the military system's obligations, procurement, expenditure and delivery as it is in fact spread over several years.

(iv) Use values of $G^J(t)$ derived from Equation (1.16) to re-solve the LINK system for new values of $GDP^J(t)$ and $P^J(t)$. When completed, the procedure requires a return to step (1) and subsequent iterations.

Klein and his associates have carried out the above operations for Western countries. Some typical findings are recorded in Table 1.1. These findings result

from an assumed shock to the world system that involves an absolute increase in
defense spending equivalent to 10 percent of military expenditures in 1986 and the
same absolute increase in subsequent years in both the U.S. and the Soviet Union.
The table shows percentage deviations for year 1989 from the LINK projections
previously made when the arms race was not incorporated into the model. As a
consequence, for West Germany and the U.S. for year 1989 the projections of real
GDP are, respectively, 1.5 and 2.1 percent higher when the arms race is embodied
in the model and when the system is subjected to the above shock. For these two
countries, the increase in the level of the consumer price index for year 1989 is 0.4
and 0.2 percent, respectively; and the decrease in the unemployment rate is 0.3 and
0.2 percent, respectively.

TABLE 1.1

Deviation from LINK Baseline Projections with Endogenous Defense
Spending: Feedback from Shocked Arms-Race Model
(Estimates in Percent Deviation for Year 1989)

	Real GDP	Consumer Price Index (level)	Interest Rate	Unemployment Rate	Nominal Government Spending
France	1.6	-0.3	nil	-0.6	10.3
W. Germany	1.5	0.4	0.04	-0.3	1.4
Japan	1.4	0.7	0.03	-0.06	7.9
U.K.	1.3	1.1	0.21	-1.7	6.2
U.S.A.	2.1	0.2	0.35	-0.2	12.8

Klein and Kosaka (1988) consider these findings preliminary. The significance
of the data is not in their magnitude, but rather in the fact that they represent
outcomes of a world model in which the arms race is endogenized. Considerable
improvement of the equations interrelating one nation's expenditures to those of
others and to relevant political variables can be effected through linkage with other
multi-national world models that quantitative political scientists have been
developing. (Bremer, 1987; Gigengack, de Haan and Jepma, 1987; Faber, 1987a,
1987b). For one suggested direction, see Isard (1990).

Since then with Gronicki (1990 and in chapter 3 below), Klein has explored the
implications of military cutbacks on Eastern European economies. They employ for
consumers a traditional maximizing utility assumption subject to a budget constraint,
but adopt an hypothesis of "overall-excess-demand" for goods traded on *official*
markets, that is one where effective consumption demands are constrained by the
available output, which in turn serves as a constraint on the amount of labor that is
offered. They, therefore, use techniques of disequilibrium econometrics involving

the specification of an excess-demand adjustment equation. For different scenarios, they carry through diverse simulations. See chapter 3. While recognizing the shortcomings of their model, the simulations do suggest that reduction in military expenditures is likely to have a strong contractionary effect on the economies, *ceteris paribus.*.

Impacts of changes in defense spending have also been examined by scholars using the relatively new CGE (computable general equilibrium) models, which may have both macro-and microeconomic relationships. Liew (1985) employing the ORANI CGE model for Australia studied the impact of an increase in defence expenditures on Balance of Trade, Exports, Imports, Consumer Price Index, GNP and Employment (aggregate and by occupation). Roland-Holst, Robinson and Tyson (1988) have conducted the same type of study for a 1986 arms reduction for the United States. In contrast, and like Klein, Haveman, Deardorff and Stern (1991) have constructed a multi-nation model (covering 18 industrialized and 16 developing nations plus a rest-of-the-world aggregate). However, unlike Klein and his emphasis on macro magnitudes, they focus on microeconomic interconnections among industries and countries and in particular 22 tradable and 7 non-tradable commodities. They nonetheless obtain findings of a macroeconomic nature. Under their "multilateral 25% reduction in military expenditures" scenario, they find, for example, that: (1) there is a larger appreciation of the U.S. dollar than in the scenario of a unilateral 25% reduction in military expenditures by the United States; (2) exports decline more and imports increase more; (3) aggregate employment dislocations are not much different, while there is a greater shift of labor from traded to nontraded industries.

There are, of course, other multi-nation (multi-world region) models, in particular the input-output type, with macroeconomic implications, but they typically focus on sectoral effects, and will be discussed below.

Studies using econometric, CGE, input-output and other operational models have the virtue of being able to treat at one time many of the interdependencies within economies and sets of economies. Equally significant are analyses which are simpler, more partial or both and which point up strategic factors and relationships.

1.5.1 Inflation

While econometric, CGE and other models yield analyses and projections of inflation (e.g. the consumer price index projection in Table 1.1), a number of other kinds of inflation studies have been conducted.

In the United States, inflation has been positively associated with increases in M (military expenditures) during the War of 1812, the Civil War, the Spanish-American War, World Wars I and II, the Korean War and the Vietnam War.[7] However, in the 1980's there was a negative association (Adams and Gold 1987:270 Weidenbaum 1990:239). The evidence seems consistent with Boulding's (1985:618) argument that before 1970 it is probably safe to say that inflation was primarily a war-related phenomenon, but that after 1970 inflation became a "normal characteristic" of society and was hardly related at all to the size of the war industry.

Weidenbaum (1974) argues that the "causes of inflation are complex, and it is rarely strictly true that an increase in spending by the military or in business investment or any other category is the sole cause of inflation." In principle, "the government can adjust its monetary and fiscal policies to economic conditions to keep the price level reasonably stable." (p.28). In time of war, however, "it becomes very difficult to adjust tax, credit, and expenditure policies on the scale needed..." (Burns 1968:64 cited in Weidenbaum 1974:28). These statements seem to be borne out when comparing the strong inflationary pressures associated with the Vietnam War build-up and the declining inflation associated with the Reagan build-up. Weidenbaum (1990) argues that one of the key differences between the two periods was in monetary policy. The Federal Reserve in 1965 began to accommodate the expansion of federal deficit spending while in 1981 it slowed the growth of the money supply.

But there are other factors in any situation studied: the state of the economy (depression, recession, recovery, prosperity), competitive government programs, methods of government deficit financing, subsidization policy, and so forth; and effects are both direct and indirect, and in ways not visible by traditional testing methods. For example, Dumas (1982, 1981, 1979) develops a link between M and inflation based on supply side considerations and the institutional nature of the defense sector. He argues that during the last few decades a significant proportion of the U.S.'s technological resources has been diverted away from the civilian sector by M, leading to lower productivity in the civilian sector than would otherwise be the case. Lower productivity can stimulate inflation and stagflation. Dumas argues that the low productivity/inflationary effect of resource diversion is reinforced by the "cost pass along" or "cost indifferent" behavior of the defense industry, an institutional characteristic of the government/defense sector relationship.

1.5.2 Employment/Unemployment at the National Level

At least four major views can be distinguished regarding the relationship between M (military expenditures) and unemployment. A first view is that M leads to net reductions in unemployment. Klein (1971:510) presents data on U.S. unemployment rates prior to and after World Wars I and II, the Korean War and the Vietnam War. In each case, unemployment rates fell during the war effort and rose after the end of the war. The dramatic fall in the unemployment rate during World War II serves as the strongest example of a seeming negative relationship between M and unemployment. U.S. wartime experience has led many analysts to conclude that increases in M lower the unemployment rate and reductions in M increase it.

A second view is that while M leads to net increases in employment, alternative civilian expenditure patterns would create more employment (Anderson et. al., 1986). Bezdek (1975) uses an 86-industry input-output model of the economy that shows beneficial effects on employment when resources are shifted from military to civilian use (see also Mosley 1985:90).[8]

Another version of the "high M-less employment" or "high M-greater unemployment" thesis rests on the Dumas (1979) argument that the military sector, by lowering national productivity via resource diversion and bureaucratic inefficiency, undermines international competitiveness and economic growth, and thus leads to unemployment rates higher than would otherwise be the case. A similar argument has been put forth and empirically supported by Smith (1977) for fifteen advanced capitalist nations.[9]

A third view is that properly designed offsets or long-term automatic adjustments (or both) imply little or no relationships between M and unemployment. Such a view is supported by the studies of Leontief and Duchin (1983) and Leontief and Hoffenberg (1963) using the input-output method. A recent input-output analysis performed by the Congressional Budget Office (1983:43) suggests that M could be replaced by non-defense private and public sector spending of roughly the same magnitude with little net aggregate impact on employment levels (Adams and Gold 1987:279). More recent analyses by Data Resources Inc. yield similar conclusions concerning Secretary of Defense Cheney's potential reduction in the defense budget over the next five years (Data Resources Inc., 1989:3; cited in Weidenbaum 1990:239). It is recognized, however, that offset policies may not be properly implemented, or properly evaluated by existing macro and nonmacro models, partly because structural change may be taking place and in part induced by offset policies.

A fourth, Marxist type view, suggests that M has a necessary, though perhaps contradictory role, in the maintenance of employment in capitalist systems (Smith 1977:1). M, unlike most civilian government expenditure, is thought by many Marxists to ensure most effectively the viability of the capitalist order because: (1) armaments quickly become obsolete, ensuring a never-ceasing demand for weapons, (2) ideological rationales centering around the Cold War of the 1940s and 1950s exist to reinforce a high level of M, (3) U.S. military power is used to maintain American political and economic hegemony in the capitalist world system, and (4) massive social service expenditure is not a desired alternative because such a policy might compete with private enterprise, redistribute income in favor of labor, or strengthen the working class (Griffin et. al. 1982:4).

Boulding (1973:234-37) calls the idea that M is necessary to give the U.S. full employment and prosperity, the "Great American Myth". He cites the 1964 tax cut as an effective offset to the military cutback of 1963 to 1965; when national defense fell from 8.2 to 7.0 percent of Gross Capacity Product (what GNP would be if there was no involuntary unemployment), unemployment also fell quite sharply, from 5.7 to 4.5%. Similarly, Weidenbaum (1967:173) argues that the U.S. reduced M by 80 percent between 1945 and 1946 and suffered no significant increase in unemployment. A sizeable tax cut, an increase in veterans' benefits and a loan program all helped to offset the reductions in M. Dunne and Smith (1990) develop simple dynamic reduced-form regression equations to test whether military expenditure and unemployment are Granger independent in 11 industrialized countries. Their results seem consistent with the Boulding/Weidenbaum positions: the "evidence suggests that military expenditures and unemployment are Granger independent...Thus as a general conclusion we can accept our null hypothesis that in analyzing unemployment no special account needs to be taken of military expenditures" (p. 70).

1.5.3 Budget Deficits and Defense/Welfare Tradeoffs

Weidenbaum (1989) argues that in the U.S. "the rapid run-up in defense outlays in the early 1980's was a factor in the federal government's incurring triple-digit budget deficits." (p. 2) As defense spending has leveled off, however, the U.S. budget deficit has remained well in the triple-digit range. Obviously, defense spending contributes to budget deficits, but so does federal spending on roads, schools, buildings and Savings and Loan bailouts.

When the share of resources allocated to defense expands or contracts, it necessarily follows as indicated by Figure 1.1 that the share of resources allocated to the nondefense sector (private and government-nonmilitary) will be altered. A number of analyses question whether there is a tradeoff between defense spending and the component of civilian production that is government welfare spending. Domke et. al (1983) argue that in much of the post World War II era, governments have been able to avoid decreases in social spending in the face of increases in defense spending because of government's ability to raise taxes or run larger budget deficits. Thus, there has been no clear tradeoff between defense and social spending for the U.S. and other advanced industrial democracies.

Higgs (1988) reaches similar conclusions for the U.S. stating that the demands of a growing defense sector are likely to draw upon the private sector, not the government non-military sector -- "during the cold war period, the private sector alone has borne the full cost of military buildups" (p. 10). Higgs' result leads to the question, what part of the private sector, investment or consumption, bears the brunt of military buildups? In a comparison of the years 1929 and 1969 for the U.S., Boulding (1973) argues that there is no significant falloff in the investment share of the economy; rather, private consumption bears the brunt of military buildups.

1.5.4 Balance of Payments and Trade

Military expenditures and defense-related transactions have direct impacts on a nation's international balance of payments through (a) imports of military goods or items required in defense procurement, (b) exports of such goods and items, (c) the diversion of potentially exportable resources into defense procurement of a given nation, or of other nations which might restrict imports to the given nation, (d) the receipt of funds from (or outflow of funds to) other nations to support military bases, or provide economic or military assistance, or both. To the direct impacts must be added the many indirect economy-wide impacts.

In 1973, Benoit argued that efforts to estimate the balance of payments and trade impacts of defense spending "is one of the most difficult and unrewarding of enterprises...because of the variety of policy decisions that can significantly affect individual balance of payments items, and the highly interdependent nature of these links." (p. 211) To complicate matters further, the U.S. and many other industrialized economies moved from pegged to floating exchange rates in the early 1970's, thereby introducing the exchange rate as a variable and reducing the significance of the overall balance of payments. Some have argued that the defense-related payments to foreign countries was a major cause of the 1971 balance of payments crisis in the U.S. and the shift from a pegged exchange rate system to a managed float, and that in the past they have been a major devaluating force on the dollar (Dumas, 1982; Huisken, 1983).

More recently, economists have studied the impact of military expenditures in the U.S. on its merchandise trade and international competitiveness. Among others, three hypotheses have been put forth:

1) Large budget deficit hypothesis - In the 1980s U.S. military outlays contributed to large budget deficits. Large budget deficits raised real interest rates, which led to international capital inflows, a strong dollar, reduced international

competitiveness, and a trade deficit. (Reppy, 1985 and Wolfson, 1985 mention this hypothesis; Niskanen, 1988; Stern, 1988; Williamson, 1988; and Meigs, 1988 in general consider the chain from budget deficits to trade deficits).

2) Political risk hypothesis - In the 1970s and 80s, the Soviet military threat to the West created a significant population of foreign investors for whom United States security was a major determinant of the proportion of their wealth kept in the U.S. A rise in the U.S. defense budget share of GNP increased such capital inflows and the real value of the dollar. The strong dollar led to reduced international competitiveness and a trade deficit (Ayanian, 1987).

3) Civilian innovation and productivity hypothesis - Military spending and military R&D competed with and drew resources away from the civilian sector, including civilian R&D. The rate of innovation and productivity was lower in the civilian sector than would otherwise have been the case, lowering the competitiveness and trade position of the U.S. See Dumas, 1982; DeGrasse, 1983; Reppy, 1988. They are concerned with military expenditure impacts on economic growth, investment and technological change, to be discussed further below.

In his paper in this volume Bergstrand uses a gravity model and empirical materials to study the impact of arms reductions on world trade, distinguishing between that in military and non-military products. As expected, general decreases in arms production do reduce trade in military products, but there is an ambiguous a priori effect on trade in non-military products. The 1975 data suggest that decreases in arms production tended to reduce non-military trade; the 1985 data suggest that decreases in arms production increases non-military trade by enhancing non-military export supply.

Huisken (1983) argues that military competition between nations precludes what could have been a high degree of mutually beneficial exchange. Underlying "these lost opportunities for exchange lies the huge waste of resources in terms of the duplication of effort and the inefficient allocation of resources from the global standpoint" (p. 12).

1.6 Disaggregate (Micro-) Analysis of Defense Spending Impacts

In identifying sectoral impacts of defense spending, the familiar Leontief input-output framework, a linear specification of general equilibrium theory, has been most extensively used.

1.6.1 Regional Effects

Federal spending, including defense spending, is not distributed evenly across the regions of the U.S. and other countries, suggesting differential regional economic impacts of changes in defense spending. Such is evident in the data on military prime contracts in total or per capita terms. Subcontracting leads to even greater overall concentration of defense spending within U.S. regions (Anderton and Isard, 1985). Moreover, in the U.S. the regional economic impact of defense spending has changed over time reflecting the dramatic shift in the regional distribution of military contracts away from the Mid-Atlantic and East North Central regions toward the Pacific and West South Central regions (Adams and Gold, 1987:282; Clayton, 1970:51-52; Udis and Weidenbaum, 1973:21). Cumberland (1973:83) identifies three types of structural change in regional economies resulting from defense spending: capital growth in existing firms, the addition of new kinds of industry that had not previously been represented in the regional economy, and technological change in the production functions of industries within the region.

Benoit (1963) provided an early study of the regional employment impacts of complete and general disarmament in the U.S.[10] Although much of Benoit's study is incomplete, he nevertheless concludes that "a considerable regional concentration of defense-dependent economic activity is unmistakable, and this fact will unquestionably create a major set of readjustment problems in the event of disarmament" (p. 49). Benoit also points out that counties which have the highest per capita concentration of prime contracts are not invariably in states with the largest relative dependence on defense manufacturing, suggesting that readjustment policies aimed at state or regional levels may be too blunt to address properly county or city-wide defense spending impact discrepancies.

Isard and Schooler (1964) use input-output analysis to study the local[11] impacts of a 10 percent across-the-board reduction in military spending in the United States, arguing that the problem of offsetting the impact upon local economies of changes in the level and composition of military expenditures can be effectively attacked. Daicoff (1973), after reviewing a large literature on the economic impact of military installations concludes that:

> ...the presence of a defense facility in a community does not necessarily impart a permanent influence on the community with which it is associated. While the installation is active, it contributes people, dollars and activity to the community, but this in itself does not change the community's potential to carry on a high level of activity without the defense installation (p. 162).

Daicoff cautions, however, that many of the base closure studies that he draws from occurred during a full employment and growing national economy.

Weidenbaum (1990:239) argues that after "an initial adjustment period - with its attendant pain and uncertainty - most localities tend to wind up with a stronger economy after the defence cut." He cites a Department of Defense (1986) study of 100 former military bases showing employment gains and a restructuring of bases to industrial and office parks, colleges, and vocational schools.

Dyckman (1965) in his study of regional development impacts of defense spending argued that the pattern of U.S. defense spending reinforced certain industrial and urban development shifts in the nation; for example the concentration of defense spending in California changed the industry mix in the state, produced new industrial location patterns within the state, and concentrated a disproportionately high number of scientists and technicians in California. Reminiscent of Benoit (1964), Dyckman argued that sizable reductions in defense spending accompanied by national offset programs would not adequately offset state and local impacts in California. Markusen et. al. (1991) point out that over the past half century, military spending has created a new economic map of the United States and has played an important role in the decay and prosperity of regions --- the relative decline of the old industrial heartland, the resurgence of New England and the rise of new industrial regions on the nation's southern and western perimeter. Each weapons system has its own unique geography: ships and the coastal areas; aircraft and missiles, the Pacific, Mountain and New England regions; tanks and other military vehicles, the Midwest; and electronics and communications, the Pacific, Mid-Atlantic and East North Central regions.

1.6.2 Industrial and Occupational Effects

Military design and production activities are concentrated in a relatively few industries, companies and occupations (Udis and Weidenbaum, 1973; DeGrasse, 1983:9-10). Changes in defense spending can have immediate and sizable impacts on these sectors as input-output studies have shown (Leontief and Hoffenberg, 1963; Oliver, 1970; Rutzick, 1970; Blond, 1981).

The Almon Interindustry Forecasting Model (see Almon, 1966), was used by Cumberland (1973) to study the industrial and occupational impacts of decreases in defense spending. Cumberland assumes defense expenditure changes compensated by changes in civilian consumption to keep the unemployment rate at 3.7 percent. He also undertakes uncompensated runs where unemployment is permitted to seek its own level. Cumberland's projections of the impacts of lower defense budgets on the employment levels in various industries show the following general patterns: (1) sharp decreases in Ordnance, Communication Equipment, and Aircraft and Parts, (2) moderate decreases in mining of natural resources, basic chemicals, metals productions, and some types of machines, engines and turbines, and (3) moderate increases in agricultural products, construction, clothes and related products, furniture, wholesale and retail trade, and consumer services.

Cumberland also studies the impact of defense spending cutbacks on employment in states and Standard Metropolitan Statistical Areas (SMSAs). The variation in the range of estimated unemployment impacts in SMSAs is wider than among states. "Even with individual states, the rates of unemployment would vary widely between metropolitan areas of the state." (p. 115).

Adams and Gold (1987) caution, however, that when all occupational subsets with the highest proportions in defense work are combined, they still do not constitute a large bulk of the total U.S. job market - only 1.6 percent in 1981. "The vast bulk of the US labour market is far less dependent on defence-related employment" (p.284).

Weidenbaum (1973) studies diversification of defense firms into nonmilitary markets. He cites five major methods of diversification: (1) mergers with a variety of companies in defense and industrial markets, (2) licensing of by-products of the military product line to established commercial companies, (3) joint ventures with foreign companies, (4) creation of a by-products exploration group based on internal inventions, and (5) development by military divisions of nonmilitary products during slack periods of defense business.[12] Weidenbaum concludes that defense firm diversification within military and related high technology government markets has been quite successful. The defense industry's failures at commercial diversification, however, are quite numerous.

1.6.3 The Conversion Problem

The conversion problem must be viewed at three levels at least. One is *macroeconomic*. It is generally accepted by economists that macroeconomic adjustments to cuts in military spending can be developed to maintain aggregate demand (Mosley, 1985:163). The heart of the conversion problem, however, lies not at the macro level but at the *micro level*, that is the microeconomic adjustments of workers, firms, localities and regions impacted by military cutbacks. Macroeconomic policies tend, in rough terms, to be averaged over the economy; their stimulating effects cannot reach deeply into specific areas, sectors, firms and occupations. Nor do they reach down into the *military sector level* where adjustments to reintegrate military personnel and the military bureaucracy to civilian uses are needed (Melman, 1974; Dumas, 1989).

The United States and other countries have had significant experience with the conversion problem. The U.S. successfully underwent a large-scale transition from military to civilian production after World War II (Mosley 1985:167-173; Dumas 1989:7-8). This successful experience could be cited as evidence that large-scale conversion in the U.S. is feasible without extraordinary disruption. Dumas argues, however, that the U.S. experience after World War II must be interpreted with great care if it is to guide present day policy:

> For the US in that period underwent what is most accurately called 'reconversion', and this is quite different from the problem of 'conversion' that faces most highly military-oriented economies today...When the War ended, these firms went back to doing what they were used to doing. They 'reconverted'. For them, military production was a temporary aberration from the norm of the civilian commercial marketplace....
>
> The situation is quite different today...Many contemporary military industrial firms have never operated in civilian markets. (pp. 7-8).

They have had, in practice, only one customer (the government); now they need to compete in highly competitive markets, a number of which have been penetrated by Japanese, German and other firms from outside the U.S. Further, during World War II both the technologies and specific production factors involved in designing and producing military goods were still fairly similar to those in the civilian sector. Now, with the emergence over the last forty years of completely new operations for military goods production, there is no return to something familiar.[13]

Weidenbaum (1990) argues that "any consideration of the economic policy responses to further reductions in defence spending should take account of the fact that the ability of the economy to adjust to shifts in economic forces is greater in the long run than in the short run." The short term effects of military cutbacks can be quite severe, but "the adjustments required by defense cutbacks are not basically different from the responses that occur regularly from shifts in consumer demand or from technological changes which yield new products that eliminate markets for older products, or from changes in the pattern of trade" (pp. 240-41).

1.7 Investment, Research and Development, Productivity and Economic Growth

The impact of military outlays on new investment and capital formation, technological progress, and economic organization and ultimately on economic growth has been a hotly debated issue. One of the difficulties in sorting out the impacts of military outlays on economic growth is that economic growth has many ingredients. Growth may be spurred by an increase in the stock of capital goods or other resources, an increase in technology, the employment of previously idle resources, a change in economic organization, a change in social or cultural factors and so on. Another difficulty is that results can vary depending on the time period of the study. A result that appears for an entire time period may not hold within various subperiods.

Three broad classes of studies of this issue can be distinguished: country-specific time series studies comparing trends in military expenditure and economic growth in developed countries; cross-national studies of the impact of military spending on economic growth of a developed country (usually the U.S.) in comparison with other developed ones, and developing country studies.

1.7.1 Developed Country Analysis: Specific Studies

A first question is whether defense spending crowds out investment in the economy of a developed country, an assertion that has frequently been made. Such an assertion easily finds a basis in the general resource allocation problem discussed in connection with Figure 1.1, section 1.3, or with the economic warfare analysis put forth by Wolfson. Current resources expropriated by the military leaves less for the civilian, and presumably less for both investment and consumption purposes. However, there are divergent views on where the burden of defense mostly falls. Boulding (1973) studies this question. He focusses on the long-term relationship rather than yearly movements over shorter time periods. To measure the aggregate size of the economy, he uses the concept of Gross Capacity Product (GCP) -- what GNP would have been if there had been no involuntary unemployment. Boulding then chooses two years, 1929 and 1969, which have a good deal of comparability (low unemployment, peak of a business cycle boom). In the U.S. a major difference between 1929 and 1969 is the percent of GCP allocated to national defense --- 0.6 percent in 1929 and 8.2 percent in 1969. "What went down when the defense share went up?" Boulding finds no significant falloff in the Gross Private Domestic Investment share of GCP; rather, it was the private consumption share that fell. Weidenbaum (1990) extends Boulding's analysis (and the earlier analysis by Russett, 1970 whose findings are similar to Boulding's) to cover the years through 1988. He concludes that Boulding's results continue to hold.

A second debated issue is the impact of defense expenditures on economic productivity as a whole. Nardinelli and Ackerman (1976), distinguishing between GNP and net GNP, i.e., GNP minus defense expenditures, run a simple regression analysis of the relationship between military expenditures and civilian economic growth for the U.S. for the 1905-1973 period. A weak relationship between the two variables is found, but a strong negative relationship between military expenditure and civilian economic growth is found for the 1946-73 subperiod.

Dumas (1986b) argues that "The military production system, unaffected by the constraints that face market-oriented producers, operates as a command sector that asserts and enforces its claim to the productive resources of the society through the special political priority it has been accorded." (p. 350). It is a distractive activity in that it takes large quantities of physical, financial, and human capital away from contributive activity (activity which increases the stock of consumer and producer goods). A distractive activity produces products that do not enhance the material standard of living. He states that productive competence (the result of an appropriately skilled and motivated work force, a sufficient quantity and quality of capital, and up-to-date process and product technology) is of central importance to the long-term health of a nation. He argues that channeling productive resources, technology and capital into noncontributive (i.e., neutral and distractive) activities can erode society's productive competence. To Dumas military-oriented activity is the preeminent (but not the only) example of noncontributive activity. Stressing that classifying military goods as noncontributive does not imply that they have no value, Dumas maintains that military activity erodes productive competence, perhaps not all at once, but slowly and persistently over time, in a magnitude that is greater than its size as a fraction of GNP would indicate.

Some authors (e.g., Gold and Adams, 1990; Weidenbaum, 1989) reject the view that defense spending in the U.S. can compellingly explain the peaks and the valleys of U.S. economic performance or the change in U.S. economic position relative to other countries. Other determinants and more significant causes of the ups and downs of U.S. economic preformance may exist. Moreover, some analysts argue that the direction of causality runs the other way. For example, Nincic and Cusack (1979) find a positive relationship between real military expenditure and growth in real GNP between 1946 and 1978, leading them to conclude that military spending has been used to stimulate economic growth in the U.S. See also Cypher (1981) and Griffin et. al. (1982).

The military sector can also affect economic growth and productivity via its impact on technology. This raises another controversial question: does large-scale R&D (research and development) spending and technological progress in the military sector occur at the expense of R&D and technology development in the civilian sector?

Weidenbaum (1974:134-140) cites positive contributions of military research and development programs to civilian products and technology: eradication of yellow fever, chlorination of water, blood plasma substitutes, modern aircraft, new high-temperature alloys, electronics and the modern automobile transmission system. Lesser-known military contributions to civilian society include nitrogen mustard treatment of leukemia, flameproof fabrics, fire-retarding paints, helicopters, communications satellites and the like (see also Striner et. al. 1958:16-17). Lederman (1971:3), Rosenberg (1976), Trebilcock (1969) also conclude that military spending on R&D has had a positive contribution to economic growth, productivity and consumer living standards.

More recently, Weidenbaum (1990) has presented a scatter diagram plotting the relationship between annual percentage changes in military and civilian R&D expenditures for the 1955-1988 period. He concludes that changes in military and civilian R&D "are just as likely to be in the same direction as in opposite directions."[14]

On the other hand, Solo (1970), Etzioni (1971), DeGrasse (1983), and others argue that the overall impact of military research and development in one way or another is a decline in the rate of commercial R&D and innovation, of course not denying that there are examples of successful transference of military technology to civilian uses.

Reppy (1989) argues that there are technological and institutional features of the defense market that promote and limit opportunities for transference of military R&D; and we must turn to empirical evidence to evaluate the relative importance of these opposing tendencies. She states that aggregate productivity studies and patent studies suggest little or no benefit to the civilian economy from military R&D. Preliminary data from international trade competiveness studies, however, show a stronger U.S. performance in military-related high technology product groups than in product groups based on civilian technology. Reppy suggests that general conclusions about military R&D and innovation are hard to make because each technology and industry is potentially a special case. Nevertheless, Reppy suggests that military R&D can benefit the civilian economy to the extent that: "it is aimed at developing generic technologies with wide applicability; ...institutional barriers such as secrecy and specialized accounting requirements are minimized; and...the military customer values low cost and producibility as well as high performance." However the "record for reform of military R&D and procurement is not good, and we are entitled to be skeptical as to whether the current interest in using military R&D as the vehicle for improved commercial competitiveness is likely to succeed" (pp. 7-8).

1.7.2 Developed Countries Analysis: Cross-national Studies

It is often argued that Japan's and West Germany's superior economic performances in recent decades can be attributed to their low level of military spending, while countries with higher military burdens, such as the USA and UK, have been unable to find the path to sustained economic growth. And many statistical studies suggest that countries that devote a small proportion of their output to military goods tend to have higher investment or economic growth than countries with high proportions of military spending to GNP (Smith, 1977; Smith, 1980; DeGrasse, 1983; Szymanski, 1973; Bezdek, 1975; Leontief and Duchin, 1983; Rothschild, 1973). However, see Gold and Adams (1990) for criticisms of the analyses suggesting a negative relationship between defense spending and investment.

On the subject of patterns of military/civilian R&D spending and relative performance in international markets, Reppy (1991) has studied the case for the U.S. and four other OECD countries. In comparing the U.S. and Japan, she finds, as already noted, that the U.S. does better in products that are identified as having a military-based technology and relatively worse in the civilian-based product groups. "From these observations one could infer either that the U.S. investment in military R&D...has paid off, or that its civilian industries have suffered from lower levels of R&D spending, or both" (p. 109). Adding other countries (France, UK, W. Germany) to the analysis does not alter Reppy's argument that general conclusions from the data about how military R&D affects economic performance in international markets cannot now be drawn.

1.7.3 Developing Country Analysis

In the study of the impact of defense spending there has been a clear distinction between effects in developed countries (covered in the previous sections) and developing ones. The impacts upon developed countries have been studied almost exclusively by scholars from these countries and trained in the use of methods and techniques designed for such study. The impacts upon developing countries have been studied by scholars from both developed and developing countries, but still using methods and techniques designed for study of impacts in developed countries. Thus the findings for developing countries must be regarded with still more caution and skepticism than those for developed countries, especially since, as Chatterji points out in chapter 11, there are: (1) major problems in any attempt at defining developing countries and in setting up a classification; (2) major data deficiencies; and (3) major difficulties in measuring security expenditures.

Benoit's 1973 path breaking study stimulated a tremendous amount of research. His findings are reported in some detail in Chatterji's chapter in this book. In brief, the strong version of the Benoit thesis is that defense and economic growth are positively correlated in developing countries; the weak version is that they are not negatively correlated.

Chatterji reports upon a number of studies critical of Benoit's findings: Ball (1983), Lim (1983), Deger and Smith (1983), Nabe (1983), Biswas and Ram (1986), and Adams, Behrman and Bolden (1991). To these might be added others such as: Boulding (1974) who concludes that there is no relationship at all between defense burden and economic growth in the high growth countries, and a negative relationship in the low growth countries; Faini et. al. (1984) who find a strong positive relationship between the investment share of GDP and the defense burden for India, but also find that the increased capital accumulation does not lead to faster growth; and Frederiksen and Looney (1983) who find a positive relationship between defense and growth for some LDCs and a negative correlation for others. Chatterji reports on other studies that are, in one way or another, supportive of Benoit's thesis: Whynes (1979) and Weidenbaum (1974) who in turn refers to a Rand Corporation study. To these might be added others such as: Mariana (1990) who undertakes a macrosimulation analysis of defense expenditures and economic growth in the Philippines and finds that all "the simulations show higher growth in GDP as a consequence of increased military expenditure", but "negative consequences of defense spending are not adequately captured in the model as well as their simulations" (p. 6); and Kupchan (1989) who cites the experiences of Taiwan and South Korea as "prime examples of states that have coupled relatively high defense spending (roughly 6% of GNP) with impressive rates of economic growth (over 10%)" (p. 44).

In digesting these and other studies, one is not able to reach any firm conclusions. A recent review of the literature by Grobar and Porter (1989) recognizes this outcome and the authors call for more sophisticated structural models, desirably ones which incorporate explicitly motivation for government spending on the military, and even optimizing behavior with respect to security and growth. The Adams, Behrman and Bolden study (1991) adds sophistication with finer distinctions among variables made possible by the use of Feder-type analysis. But one wonders whether more sophisticated structural models, with or without motivation and optimizing behavior, will enable analysts to get any closer to understanding the direct and indirect relationships between defense expenditures of LDCs and their growth. Would not there result further imbalance between the types of factors developed country models can handle and those noneconomic factors (social, political, ecological, etc.) that should but cannot be incorporated into these models, given existing data and methods of analysis. Is not the situation one where, as stated by Ball (1983), understanding "will only be reached if case studies founded on the socioeconomic, political and ecological realities of individual countries are undertaken" (p. 522). Or perhaps more appropriate methods of analysis will evolve.

1.8 Political Economy, Organizational and Other Non-Economic Factors

In formulating and analyzing scenarios for arms reduction and studying defense expenditure impacts, one cannot ignore the influence of the socio-political system and the behavior of its institutions. Economists have paid attention to some of the issues in this realm, in particular, defense budgeting, weapons procurement and the military industrial complex.

Defense budgeting is the process of governmental decision making that determines the defense budget. The process typically involves an initial DOD (Department of Defense) budget proposal to the President who submits a revised one in his January budget proposal to Congress. Congress then critically examines the proposal, requiring of DOD constant justification of items, and approves a final version. However, supplementary appropriations may be subsequently required. Such a process has been modelled by political scientists (e.g. Majeski, 1983) using a disequilibrium partial adjustment mechanism (see Benassy, 1987) and an adaptive expectations model (Parkin, 1987). Economists and other social scientists have highlighted inefficiencies in this process (Niskanen, 1967; Grosse and Proschan, 1967; McKean, 1967; Alchian, 1967; Rogerson, 1990; Gansler, 1989).

Weapons procurement is the process of acquiring quantities and qualities of weapons once budget allocations have been made. On this process and related defense economics much has been written since the seminal work of Hitch and McKean (1960). Major differences exist between the operation of the free market and that of the defense market. Peck and Scherer (1962) forcefully state: "A market system in its entirety can never exist for the acquisition of weapons" (p. 57) because (1) the very large expenditures required by individual weapons projects almost invariably preclude private financing, (2) the unique uncertainties of weapons acquisition stemming from technological change and complexity, defense policy changes, change in enemy plans and numerous other factors raise extreme difficulties in predicting cost, development time, and performance quality of output, (3) the seller confronts a single buyer (the government) which has the bargaining power of a monopsonist who does not clearly specify desired characteristics of a weapons program. A recent publication (Gansler, 1989) reinforces the non-market characteristics of weapons procurement, as partly summarized in Table 1.2.

TABLE 1.2

Selected Differences Between Free-market Theory and Defense Market Practice

Free-market Theory	Defense-market Practice
Many small buyers	One buyer (DOD)
Many small suppliers	Very few, large suppliers of a given item
All items are small, and bought in large quantities	Each item is extremely expensive, and bought in very small quantities
Market sets prices	Monopoly or oligopoly pricing - or "buy in" to "available" budget dollars
Free movement in and out of market	Extensive barriers to entry and exit
Prices fall with reduced demand to encourage buying more	Prices rise with reduced demand, owing to cost-based pricing
Market shifts rapidly with changes in supply and demand	7-10 years to develop new system, then at least 3-5 years to produce it
Profits are equalized across economy	Wide profit variations between sectors; even wider between firms
No government involvement	Government is regulator, specifier, banker, judge of claims, etc.
Selection is based on price	Selection is based primarily on promised performance
Size of market is established by buyers and sellers	Size of market is established by "third party" (Congress) through annual budget
Buyer has the choice of spending now or saving for a later time	DOD must spend its congressional appropriation or lose it

Source: Gansler (1989, pp. 159-60).

Beyond the area of defense economics, the writings on political economy and related subjects by economists are meager. A number of both general and specific non-economic factors which fall within the scope of political economy are discussed in Isard (1988) and summarized in the final chapter of this book. One of these, however, to which economists have pointed extensively is the operation of the military industrial complex. The ways it places pressures upon Congresspersons to support general increases and specific items in the defense budget, to oppose cuts, is clearly discussed in Adams (1968), Rosen (1973), and most recently in the writings of Ullman (1985), Markusen (1986), Markusen et. al. (1991) and Higgs (1990).

In addition to pressures on Congresspersons from the military industrial complex, there are always pressures from a Congressperson's local groups and constituents. As Weidenbaum (1990) puts it:

> I can cite from personal experience the frustration of dealing with members of Congress who, in public, advocate large reductions in military spending and the next day come to the White House in a frantic but private effort to "save" the weapon system being produced in their districts...
>
> Part of the problem is that what passes as benefit/cost analysis in the political sphere is usually done from a local rather than a national perspective. Try closing any unneeded defence base - or reducing the numbers of aircraft or missiles being purchased. The overwhelmingly negative public reaction will quickly demonstrate the point that the political process gives the benefits to the locality far greater weight than the costs borne by the rest of the nation. (p. 238).

Moreover, as implied by Arrow in the next chapter, future gains from alternative uses of a population's assets (resources) do not get equal weight as immediate losses.

1.9 Conflict Management Analyses and Procedures

It is difficult when to date the start by economists of significant work on conflict management. One could go back to Cournot and Edgeworth and even to Adam Smith, or just to Zeuthen (1930) whose seminal contribution concerned conflict between labor and management. Using a cardinal utility measure, Zeuthen suggested a procedure involving a series of rounds whereby at any round the party who has the least to lose should make a small concession -- a principle which Harsanyi (1956) later demonstrated requires only lineal utility and formally yields the Nash principle (maximization of the product of utilities). Implicit in Schelling (1960) and in Boulding (1962) who discussses a broad range of conflicts in detail and remarks generally on conflict management are various procedures for coping with conflict. Of significance, too, is Tinbergen (1990) who develops quantitative world welfare models (scenarios).

A specific, veto-incremax procedure was developed by Isard and T. Smith (1966, formalized later in 1969) utilizing Cournot and Edgeworth concepts. They had in mind: (1) the problem of moving participants from the Nash equilibrium point e depicted in Figure 1.5 to a point within the improvement set (the dashed-football shaped area), let alone to the core CD; (2) the desirability, should one or both participants be conservative, of having many rounds, where on each round only a limited commitment to change in proposed action (policy) is permitted; (3) the need to guarantee improvement on each round for each participant; (4) the need to have a procedure which requires participants to be able only to rank joint outcomes in terms of desirability; (5) the need for the outcome to be preindeterminate in order to avoid conflict over which procedure to use since each participant would desire that procedure which yields a joint action closest (indifference curve-wise) to its optimal point; and (6) the need to give each participant the veto power for a predetermined number of times to encourage him/her to engage in (overcome psychological barriers to) seeking a compromise joint action. The rules to be followed by participants using the veto-incremax procedure require that: (1) on each round each participant specify his maximum commitment to change of action, the lesser of the two being used to define the commitment set; (2) each participant next propose (state his most desired) joint action in the intersection of the commitment and improvement sets; and (3) if the desired joint actions are not identical, the participants should propose as a compromise that joint action defined by the midpoint of the line segment connecting the two proposed joint actions. This midpoint then serves as the reference point for the next move. Were the participants to follow these rules, one possible sequence of compromise joint actions is indicated in Figure 1.9, which is a rough enlargement of the eCD part of the football of Figure 1.5 (p.11). See Isard et. al. (1969) for a rigorous statement of this procedure, and variants of it, which might be said to provide a theoretical basis for the Single Negotiations Text procedure used today in international conflicts. See Raiffa (1982, pp. 211-17) for a more realistic statement.

In Isard and C. Smith (1982), more than one hundred conflict management procedures are discussed. Among those by economists are:

1.) the concordance - discordance (Electre) method of Delft and Nijkamp (1977).

2.) demand revealing (no bluffing) method of Vickrey (1978).

3.) min discrepancy from the ideal (using rank correlation) in Nijkamp et al. (1979).

4.) permutation method (max correspondence to outcomes weighted by relative importance) of Paelinck (1976).

Raiffa (1982) has presented and designed a number of practical procedures applicable to business conflicts, which have considerable value for attacking conflicts among nations. Kuenne (1988, and chapter 9 of this volume) advances oligopoly theory for mature rivals and examines the potential use of his rigorous analysis involving a mix of competitive and cooperative factors in the goal seeking of key political leaders in the international arena.

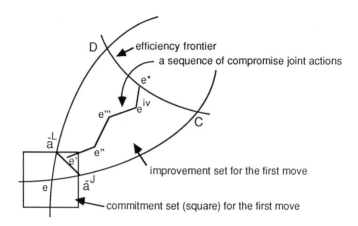

Figure 1.9: A Sequence of Split-the-Difference Compromises in a
Veto Incremax Procedure

Finally, there have been a number of studies of special diverse topics which we cannot review in detail in this compact survey. For example there is the study of Lundborg (1991) who in a careful econometric analysis of U.N. voting during the Cold War period, finds support for the "gift exchange" hypothesis, namely that the relative political support for the US is positively affected by US aid and negatively affected by Soviet aid. This "implies that US aid rises as a result of increased political support for the US and that Soviet aid falls." (p. 24). Another careful econometric study is by van Bergeijk (1988) on the success and failure of economic sanctions; he finds that the "probability that an economic sanction succeeds is higher the larger the pre-sanction trade linkage, the more unstable the target's political situation and the shorter the sanction period." (p. 28), with the tendency for the efficacy of a sanction to decrease as the duration is prolonged. There is also a significant literature on terrorism (e.g., Cauley and Sandler, 1988; Sandler and Lapan, 1988; Lee and Sandler, 1989), insurrection (Grossman, 1991), and a general treatment of political violence (Gupta, 1990).

1.10 Some Final Comments

At this point we could attempt a summary of the state of the peace economics literature and point out gaps, areas insufficiently developed, and key directions for research. However, in the chapters to follow, there will be coverage of still more of the literature and, more important, seminal contributions to the literature. Therefore, we postpone evaluation of the literature and the identification of key directions for further research to the final chapters of this book.

Footnotes

[1]In the order stated these functions are:

$$\phi(F_i, G_i) = R_i \qquad\qquad i=1,2 \qquad\qquad\qquad\qquad (1.1n)$$

where in a conflict each side i divides its endowed resources R_i between contestable productive effort F_i and appropriative effort (weaponry, etc.) G_i;

$$I = \eta(F_1, F_2) \qquad\qquad\qquad\qquad\qquad\qquad (1.2n)$$

where the social aggregate of contestable income I is a function of the parties' productive commitments F_i;

$$p_i = Q_i(G_1, G_2) \qquad\qquad\qquad\qquad\qquad\qquad (1.3n)$$

which determines the proportion p_i of social aggregate income i receives (through coercion or actual battle); and

$$I_i = I\{\alpha_i + p_i(1-a_1 -a_2)\} \qquad\qquad\qquad\qquad (1.4n)$$

where α_1 and α_2 represent "protected" fractions of social aggregate income available to the respective parties, and a_1 and a_2 are productivity coefficients. Working with specific forms of these four equations, Hirshleifer obtains interesting results for Cournot, Stackelberg and Threat and Promise type situations.

[2]See Isard et. al. (1969) for a discussion of such commodities.

[3]In Chicken, the payoff table of ranking of actions may take the form:

B's actions

		cooperate	noncoop.
A's actions	cooperate	5, 5	4, 10
	noncoop.	10, 4	2, 2

Here, two stable equilibrium outcomes (10,4) and (4,10) exist. If the players are initially at (5,5) because both have chosen the cooperative action, A could change his action, choosing to be non-cooperative thereby increasing the ranking of his indifference curve to 10. B could do the same, that is change to a non-cooperative action thereby increasing her ranking to 10. However, if both were to make these changes simultaneously they would both receive their worst outcome, namely utility represented by an indifference curve with ranking 2. Whoever is the more aggressive, and changes his/her action first obtains his/her most preferred outcome. The other must then accept the utility represented by an indifference curve with a lower rank. For once the outcome set (10,4) or (4,10) is reached, neither A nor B has any incentive to change his/her action. For if A were the less aggressive, and were to change from a cooperative to a noncooperative action when B had already chosen to be noncooperative, his utility would fall being given by his indifference curve with ranking 2 because the new set of outcomes (2,2) would result. A in effect is the "chicken." Although at the start he could have increased his payoff by changing his action from coop to noncoop provided he did so before B, he hesitated to do this for fear B would simultaneously change her action from coop to noncoop and that as a result they would end up in a situation with outcomes (2,2).

[4]Where 0 to θ^L is the time interval during which L attacks and θ^L to $\theta^L + \psi^J$ is the time interval during which J retaliates, Eq. (1.7) is more appropriately stated as:

$$S^J \geq f^L[1 - \exp(-\bar{\beta}\theta^L)]S^L + \bar{C}^L/\upsilon^J[1 - \exp(-\bar{\alpha}\psi^J)] \tag{1.5n}$$

where $\bar{\beta}$ is the rate at which L fires its missiles in the first-strike strategy and $\bar{\alpha}$ is J's rate of retaliation. There have been other refinements; for example, in Brito and Intriligator (1973, 1974), account is taken of the response lag and uncertainty about whether a missile site is empty.

[5]The equation is more appropriately stated as:

$$S^J \geq \frac{1}{f^J[1 - \exp(-\bar{\alpha}\theta^J)]} S^L - \frac{\hat{C}^J}{f^J[1 - \exp(-\bar{\alpha}\theta^J)]\upsilon^L[1 - \exp(-\bar{\beta}\psi^L)]} \tag{1.6n}$$

[6]Supposing next year's government expenditure is 20, and the preliminary estimate of this year's income is 100, then Suits solves the above equations to yield next year's consumption, investment, taxes and income to be 86.2, 12, 23.7 and 118.2, respectively.

[7]For the War of 1812, the Spanish-American War, World War II and the Korean War see Klein (1971:511). For the Civil War see Robertson and Walton (1979:245-246), Lerner (1955), Engerman (1966), and Klein (1971:511). For World War I see Clark (1931), Gilbert (1970), and Klein (1971:511). For the Vietnam War see McCarthy (1972), Klein (1971:511) and Weidenbaum (1990:239).

[8]Similar results have been put forth by Gold et. al. (1981) and DeGrasse (1983:10,28-30).

[9]Smith's views have been critiqued by Hartley and McLean (1978), Chester (1978), and Griffin et. al. (1982).

[10]See Zimmerman and Klingemann (1966:75-76) for data on uneven defense contracts by region for West Germany.

[11]Six areas are considered: Los Angeles-Long Beach; San Francisco-Oakland; California; St. Louis; Kalamazoo County; and Philadelphia.

[12]Udis (1978) cites ten motives for diversification by defense firms: avoid layoffs, avoid government red tape, assure survival of the firm, depend less on government support, change image, depend less on the military, smooth out operations, keep abreast of new technology, increase profits, keep research and design teams together. He also discusses in detail the obstacles to diversification.

[13]For discussions of conversion in other nations see Thee (1989:59-62) and Udis (1978) for Western Europe; Thorsson (1989) for Sweden; Gleditsch et. al. (1989), Bjerkholt et al. (1980) and Cappelen et al. (1982) for Norway; and Filip-Kohn et al. (1980) for W. Germany.

[14]Weidenbaum (1990:237) lists three possible reasons for these results: (1) trends in both military and civilian R&D may be influenced by a common set of factors; (2) nondefense and defense engineers and scientists are not perfect substitutes; and (3) the supply of scientists and engineers is not fixed; it responds to variations in job opportunities, migration and pay.

References

Adams, G.F., Behrman, J.R. and Boldin, M. (1991). Government expenditures, defense and economic growth in LDCs: a revised perspective, *Conflict Management and Peace Science*, 11, 19-35.

Adams, G.F. and Gold, D.A. (1987). The economics of military spending: is the military dollar really different? in C. Schmidt and F. Blackaby (eds.) *Peace,Defense and Economic Analysis.* New York: St. Martin's Press., pp. 266-300.

Adams, W. (1968). The military-industrial complex and the new industrial state. *American Economic Review* 58, 652-665.

Alchian, A.A. (1967). Cost effectiveness of cost effectiveness. in E. Benoit and K. Boulding (eds.) *Disarmament and the Economy.* New York: Harper and Row, Publishers, pp. 74-86.

Almon, C., Jr. (1966). *The American economy to 1975: an interindustry forecast.* New York: Harper and Row.

Anderson, M., Frisch, M. and Oden, M. (1986). *The empty pork barrel: the employment cost of the military build-up 1981-1985.* Lansing, MI: Employment Research Associates.

Anderton, C.H. (1990a). Teaching arms-race concepts in intermediate microeconomics. *Journal of Economic Education*, 21, 148-166.

Anderton, C.H. (1990b). The inherent propensity toward peace or war embodied in weaponry. *Defence Economics*, 1, 197-219.

Anderton, C.H. (1991). A new look at the relationship between arms races, disarmament and the probability of war. in M. Chatterji and L. Forcey (eds.) *Disarmament, Economic Conversion and Management of Peace.* Praeger, forthcoming.

Anderton, C.H. (1992). Toward a mathematical theory of the offensive/defensive balance. *International Studies Quarterly,* forthcoming.

Anderton, C.H. and Fogarty, T. (1990). Consequential damage and nuclear deterrence. *Conflict Management and Peace Science*, 11, 1-15.

Anderton, C.H. and Isard, W. (1985). The geography of arms manufacture. in A. Jenkins and D. Pepper (eds.) *The Geography of Peace and War.* Oxford: Basil Blackwell, pp. 90-104.

Axelrod, R. (1984). *The evolution of cooperation.* New York: Basic Books, Inc.

Ayanian, R. (1987). Political risk, national defense and the dollar. mimeo

Ball, N. (1983). Defense and development: a critique of the Benoit study. *Economic Development and Cultural Change*, 31, 507-524.

Benassy, J. (1987). Disequilibrium analysis. in *The New Palgrave: A Dictionary of Economics,* Vol. I, London: Macmillan, pp. 858-63.

Benoit, E. (1963). The disarmament model in the war economy of the United States. in E. Benoit and K.E. Boulding (eds.) *Disarmament and the Economy.* New York: Harper and Row, Publishers, pp. 28-49.

Benoit, E. (1964). Comments on Isard and Schooler and on North, Brody and Holsti. *Papers, Peace Science Society,* 1, 48-56.

Benoit, E. (1973). *Defense and economic growth in developing countries.* Lexington: Lexington Books.

Benoit, E. and Boulding, K.E. (eds.) (1963). *Disarmament and the economy.* New York: Harper and Row, Publishers.

Bergeijk van, P.A.G. (1988). *Expected utility and economic sanctions.* Research Memorandum 247, Institute of Economic Research, University of Groningen.

Bezdek, R. (1975). The 1980 economic impact - regional and occupational - of compensated shifts in defense spending. *Journal of Regional Science,* 15, 183-197.

Bishop, R.L. (1960). Duopoly: collusion or warfare. *The American Economic Review,* 50.

Bishop, R.L. (1963). Game theoretic analyses of bargaining. *Quarterly Journal of Economics,* 77, 559-602.

Bishop, R.L. (1964). A Zeuthen-Hicks theory of bargaining. *Econometrica* 32, 410-417.

Biswas, B. and Ram, R. (1986). Military expenditures and economic growth in less developed countries: an augmented model and further evidence. *Economic Development and Cultural Change,* 34, 361-372.

Bjerkholt, O., Cappelen, A., Gleditsch, N.P. and Moum, K. (1980). *Disarmament and development: a study of conversion in Norway.* Oslo: International Peace Research Institute.

Blackaby, F. and Ohlson, T. (1982). Military expenditure and arms trade: problems of data. *Bulletin of Peace Proposals,* 13, 291-308.

Blond, D.L. (1981). *Impact of the Reagan defense program on the United States economy, 1981-1987.* Office of the Secretary of Defense (December).

Boulding, K.E. (1962). *Conflict and defense.* New York: Harper & Row.

Boulding, K.E. (1973). The impact of the defense industry on the structure of the American economy. in B. Udis (ed.) *The Economic Consequences of Reduced Military Spending.* Lexington, MA: Lexington Books.

Boulding, K.E. (1974). Defense spending: burden or boon. *War/Peace Report,* 13.

Boulding, K.E. (1978). *Stable peace.* Austin: University of Texas Press.

Boulding, K.E. (1985). The war industry. Reprinted in L.D. Singell (ed.) *Kenneth Boulding/Collected Papers.* Vol. VI. Boulder: Colorado Associated University Press, 613-624.

Boulding, K.E. (1986). The economics and the noneconomics of the world war industry. *Contemporary Policy Issues* 4, 12-21.

Brams, S.J. (1985). *Superpower games.* New Haven, CT: Yale University Press.

Brams, S.J. and Kilgour, D.M. (1988). *Game theory and national security.* New York: Basil Blackwell.

Bremer, S.A. (ed.) (1987) *The GLOBUS model.* Boulder: Westview.

Brito, D. L. (1972). A dynamic model of an armaments race. *International Economic Review,* 13, 359-75.

Brito, D.L., and Intriligator, M.D. (1973). Some applications of the maximum principle to the problem of an armaments race. *Modeling and Simulation*, 4, 140-4.

Brito, D.L., and Intriligator, M.D. (1974). Uncertainty and the stability of the armaments race. *Annals of Economic and Social Measurement,* 3, 279-92.

Bueno de Mesqita, B. (1981). *The war trap.* New Haven, CT.: Yale University Press.

Burns, A.F. (1968). The defense sector: an evaluation of its economic and social impact. in Jacob K. Javits et. al. (eds.) *The Defense Sector and the American Economy.* New York: New York University Press.

Cappelen, A., Bjerkholt, O. and Gleditsch, N.P. (1982). *Global conversion from arms to development Aid: macroeconomic effects on Norway.* Oslo: International Peace Research Institute.

Cauley, J. and Sandler, T. (1988). Fighting world war III: a suggested strategy. *Terrorism: An International Journal*, 11, 181-195.

Chester, E. (1978). Military spending and capitalist stability. *Cambridge Journal of Economics*, 2, 293-298.

Clark, J.M. (1931). *The costs of the world war to the American people.* New Haven: Yale University Press.

Clayton, J.L. (ed.) (1970). *The economic impact of the cold war: sources and readings.* New York: Harcourt, Brace & World, Inc.

Congressional Budget Office (1983). *Defense spending and the economy.* Washington, D.C.

Cumberland, J.H. (1973). Dimensions of the impact of reduced military expenditures on industries, regions, and comunities. in Bernard Udis (ed.) *The Economic Consequences of Reduced Military Spending.* Lexington, MA: Lexington Books, pp. 79-147.

Cypher, J. (1981). The basic economics of rearming America. *Monthly Review* November 1981.

Daicoff, D.W. (1973). The community impact of military installations. in Bernard Udis (ed.) *The Economic Consequences of Reduced Military Spending.* Lexington, MA: Lexington Books, pp. 149-166.

Data Resources Inc. (1989). *U.S. forecast summary, December.* Washington, D.C.: Data Resources, Inc.

Deger, S. and Sen, S. (1985). Technology transfer and arms production in developing countries. *Industry and Development*, 15, 1-18.

Deger, S. and Smith, R. (1983). Military expenditure and growth in less developed countries. *Journal of Conflict Resolution*, 27, 335-353.

DeGrasse, R.W., Jr. (1983). *Military expansion, economic decline: the impact of military spending on U.S. economic performance.* New York: Council on Economic Priorities/Sharpe.

Delft, A. van, and Nijkamp, P. (1977). *Multi-criteria analysis and regional decision-making.* The Hague: Martinus Nijhoff.

Department of Defense (1986). *Summary of complete military base economic adjustment projects.* Office of the Assistant Secretary of Defense, Force Management and Personnel. Washington, D.C.: U.S. Department of Defense.

Dixit, A. and Nalebuff, B. (1991). *Thinking strategically.* New York: W.W. Norton and Company.

Domke, W.K., Eichenberg, R.C. and Kelleher, C.M. (1983). The illusion of choice: defense and welfare in advanced industrial democracies. *The American Political Science Review*, 77, 19-35.

Downs, G.W. and Rocke, D.M. (1990). *Tacit bargaining, arms races, and arms control.* Ann Arbor: The University of Michigan Press.

Dumas, L.J. (1972). Armament, disarmament and national security: a theoretical duopoly model of the arms race. *Journal of Economic Studies,* 6, 1-38.

Dumas, L.J. (1979). Parametric costing and institutionalized inefficiency. *AIIE Transactions,* June 1979: 147-154.

Dumas, L.J. (1981). Disarmament and economy in advanced industrialized countries - the U.S. and the U.S.S.R. *Bulletin of Peace Proposals*, 12, 1-10.

Dumas, L.J. (1982). Military spending and economic decay. in Lloyd J. Dumas (ed.) *The Political Economy of Arms Reduction.* Boulder: Westview Press. pp.1-26.

Dumas, L.J. (1986a). *The overburdened economy.* Berkeley: University of California Press.

Dumas, L.J. (1986b). Commanding resources: the military sector and capital formation. in Dwight R. Lee (ed.) *Taxation and the Deficit Economy: Fiscal Policy and Captial Formation in the United States.* San Francisco: Pacific Institute for Public Policy Research, pp. 323-356.

Dumas, L.J. (1989). Economic conversion: the critical link. in L.J. Dumas and M. Thee (eds.) *Making Peace Possible: The Promise of Economic Conversion.* New York: Pergamon Press, pp. 3-15.

Dunne, P. and Smith, R. (1990). Military expenditures and unemployment in the OECD. *Defense Economics*, 1, 57-73.

Dyckman, J.W. (1965). Some regional development issues in defense program shifts. *Papers, Peace Science Society,* 2, 191-203.

Edelstein, M. (1990). What price cold war? Military expenditures, the accumulation of physical capital and economic growth: the United States, 1890-1980. *Cambridge Journal of Economics*

Engerman, S.L. (1966). The economic impact of the Civil War. *Explorations in Economic History*, 3, 176-99.

Etzioni, A. (1971). Federal science as economic drag, not propellent. in S. Melman (ed.) *The War Economy of the United States.* New York: St. Martin's Press, pp. 132-137.

Faber, J. (1987a). The Theoretical Foundation of the Project Sire, unpublished, Europa Instituut, University of Amsterdam.

Faber, J. (1987b). Measuring Cooperation, Conflict, and the Social Network of Nations, *Journal of Conflict Resolution,* 31, 438-464.

Faini, R., Annez, P. and Taylor, L. (1984). Defense spending, economic structure, and growth: evidence among countries and over time. *Economic Development and Cultural Change,* 32, 487-98.

Filip-Kohn, R., Krengel, R. and Schumacher, D. (1980). Macroeconomic effects of disarmament policies on sectoral production and employment in the Federal Republic of Germany, with special emphasis on development policy issues. Report, May. Berlin: German Institute for Economic Research.

Fischer, D. (1984). *Preventing war in the nuclear age.* Totowa, New Jersey: Rowman Allanheld.

Fraser, N.M. and Hipel, K.W. (1984). *Conflict analysis: models and resolutions.* New York: North-Holland.

Fredriksen, P.C. and Looney, R.E. (1983). Defense expenditures and economic growth in developing countries. *Armed Forces and Society*, 9, 633-645.

Friedman, J.W. (1990). *Game theory.* New York: Oxford University Press, 2nd edition.

Gansler, J.S. (1989). *Affording defense.* Cambridge, MA: The MIT Press.

Gigengack, A.R., DeHaan, H., Japma, C.J. (1987). Military expenditure dynamics and a world model. in C. Schmidt and F. Blackaby (eds.) *Peace, Defense and Economic Analysis.* New York: St. Martin's Press.

Gilbert, C. (1970). *American financing of world war I.* Westport, CT: Greenwood.

Gleditsch, N.P., Bjerkholt, O. and Cappelen, A. (1989). Conversion: global national and local effects. A case study of Norway. in Lloyd J. Dumas and Marek Thee (eds.) *Making Peace Possible: The Promise of Economic Conversion.* New York: Pergamon Press, pp. 3-15.

Gold, D. and Adams, G. (1990). Defence spending and the American economy. *Defence Economics* 1, 275-293.

Gold, D.A., Paine, C. and Sheilds, G. (1981). *Misguided expenditure: an analysis of the proposed MX missile sytem.* New York: Council on Economic Priorities.

Griffin, L.J., Wallace, M. and Devine, J. (1982). The political economy of military spending and evidence from the United States. *Cambridge J. of Economics*, 6, 1-14.

Grobar, L.M. and Porter, R.C. (1989). Benoit revisited: defense spending and economic growth in LDCs. *Journal of Conflict Resolution,* 33, 318-345.

Gronicki, M. and Klein, L.R. (1989a). Impact of military cuts on the Soviet economy. mimeo

Gronicki, M. and Klein, L.R. (1989b). Trade-offs between military and civilian programs in the Warsaw Pact. mimeo (preliminary version).

Grosse, R.N. and Proschan, A. (1967). The annual cycle: planning-programming-budgeting. in E. Benoit and K. Boulding (eds.) *Disarmament and the Economy.* New York: Harper and Row, Publishers, pp. 99-111.

Grossman, H.L. (1991). A general equilibrium model of insurrections. *American Economic Review*, 81, 912-921.

Gupta, D.K. (1990). *The economics of political violence.* New York: Praeger.

Harsanyi, J.C. (1956). Approaches to the bargaining problem before and after the theory of games: a critical discussion of Zeuthern's, Hick's, and Nash's Theories. *Econometrica,* 24, 144-157.

Hartley, K. and McLean, P. (1978). Military expenditure and capitalism: a comment. *Cambridge Journal of Economics*, 2, 287-292.

Haveman, J.D., Deardorff, A.V. and Stern, R.M. (1991). The economic effects of unilateral and multilateral reductions in military expenditures in the major industrialized and developing countries. *Conflict Management and Peace Science,* 12.

Higgs, R. (1988). U.S. military spending in the cold war era: opportunity costs, foreign crises, and domestic constraints. Cato Policy Analysis, no. 114. Washington, D.C.: Cato Institute.

Higgs, R. (ed.) (1990). *Arms, politics, and the economy: historical and contemporary perspectives.* New York: Holmes and Meier.

Hirshleifer, J. (1987). *Economic behavior in adversity.* Chicago: The University of Chicago Press.

Hirshleifer, J. (1988). The analytics of continuing conflict. *Synthese*, 76, 201-233.

Hitch, C.J. and McKean, R.N. (1960). *The economics of defense in the nuclear age.* Cambridge, MA: Harvard University Press.

Hollenhorst, J. and Ault, G. (1971). An atlernative answer to: who pays for defense? *American Political Science Review*, 65, 760-63.

Huisken, R. (1983). Armaments and development. in H. Tuomi and R. Vayrynen (eds.) *Militarization and Arms Production*. New York: St. Martin's Press., pp. 3-25.

Intriligator, M. C. and Brito, D.L. (1976). Formal models of arms races. *Journal of Peace Science*, 2, 77-88.

Intriligator, M. C. and Brito, D.L. (1986). Arms races and instability. *Journal of Strategic Studies*, 9, 113-131.

Intriligator, M. C. and Brito, D.L. (1989). Arms race modeling: a reconsideration. mimeo. (published in N.P. Gleditsch and O. Njolstad (eds.) *Arms Races: Technological and Political Dynamics*. London: Sage, 1990).

Isard, W. (1988). *Arms races, arms control and conflict analysis.* New York: Cambridge University Press.

Isard, W. (1990). Progress in global modeling for world policy on arms control and environmental management. *Conflict Management and Peace Science*, 11, 57-94.

Isard, W. and Schooler, E.W. (1964). An economic analysis of local and regional impacts of reduction of military expenditures. *Papers, Peace Science Society*, 1, 15-44.

Isard, W., and Smith, C. (1982). *Conflict analysis and practical conflict management procedures.* Cambridge, MA: Ballinger Publishing.

Isard, W. and Smith, T.E. (1966). A practical application of game theoretical approaches to arms reduction. *Peace Research Society Papers*, 4, 85-98.

Isard, W., Smith, T.E., Isard, P., Tung, T.H. and Dacey, M. (1969). *General theory: social, political, economic, and regional with particular reference to decision-making analysis.* Cambridge, MA: MIT Press.

Klein, L.R. (1971). The role of war in the maintenance of American economic prosperity. *Proceedings of the American Philosophical Society*, 115, 507-516.

Klein, L.R. and Gronicki, M. (1990). Conversion: the trade-off between military and civilian production in Warsaw Pact countries. *Conflict Management and Peace Science*, 11, 5-6.

Klein, L.R. and Kosaka, H. (1988). The Arms Race and the Economy. Vortrage des Festkolloquiums aus Analass des 70 Geburtstages von Wilhelm Krelle, Bonn: Bouvier Verlag Herbert Grundmann.

Klein, L.R. and Mori, K. (1973). The impact of disarmament on aggregate economic activity: an econometric analysis. in B. Udis (ed.) *The Economic Consequences of Reduced Military Spending.* Lexington, MA: Lexington Books.

Kupchan, C. (1989). Defence spending and economic performance. *Survival*, 31, 447-461.

Kupperman, R.H., and Smith, H.A. (1976). Formal models of arms races: discussion. *Journal of Peace Science*, 2, 89-96.

Kuenne, R.E. (1988). Conflict management and the theory of mature oligopoly. *Conflict Management and Peace Science*, 10, 37-57.

Lederman, L.L. (1971). Introduction and general summary. in *A Review of the Relationship Between Research and Development and Economic Growth/Productivity*. Washington: National Science Foundation.

Lee, D. and Sandler, T. (1989). On the optimal retaliation against terrorists: the paid-rider option. *PUblic Choice*, 61, 141-52.

Leontief, W. (1964). Disarmament, foreign aid and economic growth. *Journal of Peace Research,* No. 3-4, 155-169.

Leontief, W.W. and Duchin, F. (1983). *Military spending: facts and figures*. New York: Oxford University Press.

Leontief, W.W. and Hoffenberg, M. (1963). Input-output analysis of disarmament impacts. in E. Benoit and K. Boulding (eds.) *Disarmament and the Economy*. New York: Harper and Row, Publishers.

Lerner, E.M. (1955). Money, prices and wages in the Confederacy, 1861-1865. *Journal of Politaical Economy*, 63.

Liew, L.H. (1985). The impact of defense spending on the Australian economy. *Australian Economic Papers,* December, 326-336.

Lim, D. (1983). Another look at growth and defense in less developed countries. *Economic Development and Cultural Change*, 31, 377-384.

Lundborg, P. (1991). Foreign Aid and International Support as a Gift Exchange, Industrial Institute for Economic and Social Research, Stockholm, Sweden, mimeo.

Majeski, S.J. (1983). Dynamic properties of the U.S. military expenditure decision-making process. *Conflict Management and Peace Science*, 7, 65-86.

Mariano, R.S. (1990). Defense expenditures and economic growth in the Philippines: a macrosimulation analysis. mimeo.

Markusen, A. (1986). Defence spending: a successful industrial policy? *International Journal of Urban and Regional Research* ,10, 105-122.

Markusen, A., Hall, P., Campbell, S., Deitrick, S. (1991). *The rise of the gunbelt*. New York: Oxford University Press.

Mayer, T. F. (1986). Arms races and war initiation: some alternatives to the Intriligator-Brito model. *Journal of Conflict Resolution,* 30, 3-28.

McCarthy, T. (1972). "What the Vietnam war has cost. in S. Melman (ed.) *The War Economy of the United States*. New York: St. Martin's Press.

McGuire, M. C. (1965) *Secrecy and the arms race*. Cambridge, MA: Harvard University Press.

McKean, R.N. (1967). Remaining difficulties in program budgeting. in E. Benoit and K. Boulding (eds.) *Disarmament and the Economy*. New York: Harper and Row, Publishers, pp. 60-73.

Meigs, J.A. (1988). Dollars and deficits: substituting false for real problems. *The Cato Journal,* 8, 533-553.

Melman, S. (1974). *The permanent war economy*. New York: Simon and Schuster.

Mosley, H.G. (1985). *The arms race: economic and social consequences*. Lexington, MA: D.C. Heath and Company.

Nabe, O. (1983). Military expenditures and industrialization in Africa. *Journal of Economic Issues,* 17, 575-587.

Nardinelli, C. and Ackerman, G. (1976). Defense expenditures and the survival of American capitalism." Armed Forces and Society 13 (1): 13-16.

Nijkamp, P., Rietveld, P., Spronk, J., van Veenendaal, W., and Voogd,H. (1979). *Multi-dimensional spatial data and decision analysis*. New York: Wiley.

Nincic, M. and Cusack, T. (1979). The political economy of U.S. military spending. *Journal of Peace Research*, 16, 101-115.

Niskanen, W.A. (1967). The defense resource allocation process. in E. Benoit and K. Boulding (eds.) *Disarmament and the Economy*. New York: Harper and Row, Publishers, pp. 3-22.

Niskanen, W.A. (1988). The uneasy relation between budget and trade deficits. *The Cato Journal*, 8, 507-518.

Oliver, R.P. (1970). Increase in defense-related employment during Vietnam build-up. *Monthly Labor Review*, 93, 3-10.

Paelinck, J.H.P. (1976). Qualitative multiple-criteria analysis, environmental protection, and multiregional development. *Papers of the Regional Science Association,* 36, 59-74.

Parkin, M. (1987). Adaptive expectations. in *The New Palgrave: A Dictionary of Economics,* Vol. I, London: Macmillan, pp. 20-21.

Peck, M.J. and Scherer, F.M. (1962). *The weapons acquisition process: an economic analysis*. Boston: Harvard University Graduate School of Business Administration.

Perroff, K. (1977). The warfare-welfare tradeoff: health, public aid and housing. *Journal of Sociology and Social Welfare*, 4, 366-81.

Pursell, C.W. (1972). *The military industrial complex*. New York: Harper and Row.

Radner, R. (1989). A model of defense-protected build-down. in J.N. Barkenbus and A.M. Weinberg (eds.) *Stability and Strategic Defenses*. Washington, D.C.: The Washington Inst. Press., pp. 266-96.

Raiffa, H. (1982). *The art and science of negotiation*. Cambridge, MA: Harvard University Press.

Reppy, J. (1985). Military R&D and the civilian economy. *Bulletin of the Atomic Scientists*, October,10-14.

Reppy, J. (1988). Military research and development and international trade performance. in Andrew L. Ross (ed.) *The Political Economy of Defense: Issues and Implications*.

Reppy, J. (1989). Technology flows between the military and civilian sectors; theory and evidence. Prepared for the Panel, "Defense Spending as Technology Policy for the U.S." American Association for the Advancement of Science, January 19, 1989.

Reppy, J. (1991). Military research and development and international trade performance. in A.L. Ross (ed.) *The Political Economy of Defense*. New York: Greenwood, 91-112.

Robertson, R.M. and Walton, G.M. (1979). *History of the American economy*. New York: Harcourt, Brace, Jovanovich, Inc. 4th edition.

Rogerson, W.P. (1990). Quality versus quantity in military procurement. *American Economic Review*, 80, 83-92.

Roland-Holst, D., Robinson, S., Tyson, L. (1988). Impact of Military Expenditures on the U.S. Economy, Paper presented at the 1987 meetings of the American Economic Association.

Rosen, S. (1973). *Testing the theory of the military-industrial complex*. Lexington, MA: Lexington Books.

Rosenberg, N. (1976). *Perspectives on technology*. New York: Cambridge University Press.

Rosthchild, K.W. (1973). Military expenditure, exports and growth. *Kyklos*, 26, 804-813.

Russett, B.M. (1970). *What price vigilance? The burdens of national defense*. New Haven, CT: Yale University Press.

Rutzick, M.A. (1970). Skills and location of defense-related workers. *Monthly Labor Review*, 93, 11-16.

Sandler, T. and Lapan, H. (1988). The calculus of dissent: an analysis of terrorists' choice of targets. *Synthese*, 76, 245-61.

Schelling, T.C. (1960). *The strategy of conflict*. London: Oxford University Press.

Schelling, T.C. (1966a). *Arms and influence.* New Haven, CT: Yale University Press.

Schelling, T.C. (1966b). The strategy of inflicting costs. in R.N. McKean (ed.) *Issues in Defense Economics.* New York: Columbia University Press., pp. 105-27.

Shubik, M. (1968). On the study of disarmament and escalation. *Journal of Conflict Resolution*, 12, 83-101.

Shubik, M. (1982). *Game theory in the social science, v. 1.* Cambridge, MA: The MIT Press.

Shubik, M. (1984). *Game theory in the social science, v. 2.* Cambridge, MA: The MIT Press.

Shubik, M. (1987). The uses, value and limitations of game theoretic methods in defence analysis. in C. Schmidt and F. Blackaby (eds.) *Peace, Defense and Economic Analysis.* New York: St. Martin's Press., pp. 53-84.

Smith, R.P. (1977). Military expenditure and capitalism. *Cambridge Journal of Economics*, 1, 61-76.

Smith, R.P. (1980). Military expenditure and investment in OECD countries, 1954-1973. *Journal of Comparative Economics*, 4, 19-32.

Solo, R.A. (1970). Military R&D: a drag on the economy. in James L. Clayton (ed.) *The Economic Impact of the Cold War: Sources and Readings.* New York: Harcourt, Brace & World, Inc., pp.157-164.

Stern, G.H. (1988). Budget policy and the economy. *The Cato Journal*, 8, 521-527.

Striner, H.E. et al. (1958). *Defense spending and the U.S. economy v. 4.* Baltimore: Johns Hopkins University, Operations Research Office.

Suits, D.B. (1963). Econometric analysis of disarmament impacts. in E. Benoit and K. Boulding (eds.) *Disarmament and the Economy.* New York: Harper and Row, Publishers, pp. 99-111.

Szymanski, A. (1973). Military spending and economic stagnation. *American Journal of Sociology*, 79, 1-14.

Thee, M. (1989). Swords into ploughshares: the quest for peace and human development. in Lloyd J. Dumas and Marek Thee (eds.) *Making Peace Possible: The Promise of Economic Conversion.* New York: Pergamon Press, pp. 3-15.

Thorsson, I. (1989). Conversion from military to civil production in Sweden. in Lloyd J. Dumas and Marek Thee (eds.) *Making Peace Possible: The Promise of Economic Conversion.* New York: Pergamon Press, pp. 3-15.

Tinbergen, J. (1990). *World security and equity.* Brookfield, Vt.: Edward Elgar.

Trebilcock, C. (1969). Spin-off in British economic history: armaments and industry, 1760-1914. *Economic History Review*, 22

Tullock, G. (1974). *The social dilemma: the economics of war and revolution.* Blacksburg, VA: University Publications.

Udis, B. (1978). *From guns to butter: technology organizations and reduced military spending in western Europe.* Cambridge, MA: Ballinger.

Udis, B. and Weidenbaum, M.L. (1973). The many dimensions of the military effort. in Bernard Udis (ed.) *The Economic Consequences of Reduced Military Spending.* Lexington, MA: Lexington Books.

Ullman, J.E. (1985) *The prospects of Amercian industrial recovery.* Westport, CT: Quorum Books.

Vickery, W. (1978). Demand revealing procedures and international disputes, *Peace Science Society Papers,* 28, 97-104.

Weidenbaum, M.L. (1967). Defense expenditure and the domestic economy. in S. Enke (ed.) *Defense Management.* Englewood Cliffs, N.J.: Prentice-Hall.

Weidenbaum, M.L. (1974). *The economics of peacetime defense.* New York: Praeger.

Weidenbaum, M.L. (1989). *Military spending and the myth of global overstretch.* Washington, D.C.: The Center for Strategic and International Studies.

Weidenbaum, M.L. (1990). Defense spending and the American economy: how much change is in the offing? *Defense Economics,* 1, 233-242.

Whynes, D.K. (1979). *The economics of third world military expenditure.* London.

Williamson, J. (1988). Conflicting views of the twin deficits. *The Cato Journal,* 8, 529-532.

Wittman, D. (1979). How a war ends: a rational model approach. *Journal of Conflict Resolution,* 23, 743-63.

Wolfson, M. (1985). Notes on economic warfare. *Conflict Mangagement and Peace Science,* 8:1-20.

Wolfson, M. (1987). A theorem on the existence of zones of initiation and deterence in Intriligator-Brito arms race models. *Public Choice,* 54, 291-297.

Wolfson, M. (1991). *Essays on the Cold War.* London: Macmillan.

Zeuthen, F. (1930). *Problems of monopoly and economic welfare.* London: G. Routledge and Sons.

Zimmerman, H. and Klingemann, H.D. (1966). The regional impact of defense purchases in the Federal Republic of Germany. *Papers, Peace Science Society,* 6, 71-86.

Economics of Arms Reduction and the Peace Process
W. Isard and C.H. Anderton (Editors)

Chapter 2

THE BASIC ECONOMICS OF ARMS REDUCTION

Kenneth J. Arrow

Stanford University[*]

[In this paper, Kenneth Arrow provides a general framework for analysis by economists of the forces lying behind the deescalation and escalation of military expenditures. On the basis of his long experience and leadership in the development of economic theory, he addresses the question: what are the ways suggested by such theory for estimating the economic effects of a major reduction of current arms expenditure, particularly with reference to the United States? (eds.)]

2.1 Introduction

In this paper, I want to set forth different ways suggested by economic theory for estimating the economic effect of a major reduction of the current arms expenditures in the United States. These approaches will help illuminate the possible directions of research to come to better grips with the economic gains possible by arms reduction. Some popular discussion has suggested very large gains, drawn by simple comparisons with Japan, which, among its many other differences with the United States, does use a much lower proportion of its national income in military expenditures. The discussion may also help in the reorientation of economic theory to accommodate better many strongly positive feedback features, which are beginning to find emphasis in the theory of economic growth.

I will in fact consider, though very unevenly, four possible approaches suggested by economic reasoning. The first is neoclassical welfare theory, in which the standard assumptions of competition, absence of externalities, and constant or diminishing returns of scale are made. This is the best developed theory, and I will have the most to say about its implications. The second is Keynesian and more modern versions of macroeconomics. The third is modern growth theory, a revival and more rigorous version of development economics of the immediate post-war periods, which tend to emphasize externalities and increasing returns, but with some notions of equilibirium and market-clearing to provide structural parallels to competitive equilibrium. Finally, the fourth economic paradigm is that of political choice theory, where we consider the political system as attached to the economic and feeding back into it.

2.2 Standard Resource Allocation Theory

If prices truly reflected scarcity, as they do under ideal conditions, then the resources used for defense can be measured at their market values. Thus, we may easily measure the gain in other uses of national income corresponding to a reduction in defense expenditures. In this paper, although by no means a full-blown empirical analysis, I will refer to some quantitative statements about the United States economy, which are collected for easy reference in the following Table.

TABLE 2.1

Defense in the United States Economy

Year	Defense/GNP	Defense/Fed. Budget	Defense/R&D
1960	9.3%	52.2%	48%
1980	4.9%	22.7%	22%
1988	6.0%	27.3%	33%

Estimated Marginal Excess Burden of Taxation: 30%

Standard Deviation of Log Defense Expenditures: .112

Standard Deviation of Log Federal Budget: .060

Sources: U.S. Department of Commerce, Bureau of the Census, *Statistical Abstract of the United States*, 1989 and earlier issues. Washington D.C.: Government Printing Office, Tables 685, 446, 489,.526, 970, 971.

If we refer to the first column, we see the fraction of national income devoted to defense. For the purposes of this paper, we will take as cononical a reduction of 50% in military expenditures. It has been responsibly argued (e.g., Kaufman 1989) that such a reduction is feasible without infringing on national security; indeed, such arguments were advanced before the remarkable changes in Eastern Europe in 1989 and 1990 and the corresponding perception that the cold war is at an end.

The simplest calculation, then, using the figures for 1988, is that a 50% cut in defense expenditures increases the availability of resources for other purposes by 3% of national income (50% of 6%). The resources can be used in many different ways, of course. They can be used for private consumption or investment, as individuals choose, by leaving all other government expenditures unchanged.

Alternatively, the resources can be used for other forms of collective consumption. One possibility is an increase of expenditures on health, particularly public health. If one is concerned about the increase in crime, additional expenditures on prisons or police or on programs to reduce drug dependency are possible. To take an issue on which there is widespread agreement, highways, bridges, mass transit and other forms of infrastructure are regarded as deficient, i.e., having a high marginal return. Or finally, to take another form of infrastructure, improvements in education to create better citizens and increase productivity would form a suitable use. Which of these directions, public or private, would give an optimal use of the released resources is a matter of individual judgment and political process. If indeed resources are currently allocated optimally, then, to a first approximation it will make little difference in which direction the expenditure is to go. But under this condition, one cannot expect an increase of more than 3% in national income available for non-military uses.

But in fact the allocation of resources between the public and private sectors is not fully governed by optimality criteria. There are several aspects of this departure from optimality. One, to be discussed briefly later, is that the level and direction of government spending is determined by a political process which does not necessarily share the Pareto efficiency properties of the price system. A second is that goods used for public purposes are financed primarily by taxation. As is well known, all taxes create deadweight losses or excess burdens. All practical taxes fall on some economic activity, whether it be purchase and sale of goods, working, or saving. Given such a set of taxes, there is an alternative set of lump-sum taxes yielding the same revenue (and therefore the ability to buy the same goods and supply the same public services) which would make everyone better off. Hence, the social cost of a dollar of tax-financed government expenditures is greater than one dollar by the amount of the excess burden.

In discussing excess burdens, it is important, as elsewhere in economics, to distinguish among marginal, average, and total magnitudes. The total excess burden of taxation is, roughly, proportional to the *square* of the tax rate. Hence, the marginal excess burden is proportional to the tax rate, and the average excess burden of taxes is about half the marginal tax rate. A reduction of 50% in defense expenditures is, from the second column of Table 2.1, a reduction of 13% in government expenditures. If we assume all expenditures are tax-financed, this is a considerable change, so that the marginal excess burden changes significantly, being reduced in the same proportion.

There are by now a number of estimates of the excess burden of Federal taxation in the literature. They start with a partial equilibrium approach due to

Browning (1976). Among the more recent and more richly detailed general equilibrium approaches, the best seem to be those of Ballard, Shoven, and Whalley (1985) and Jorgenson and Yun (1990). The estimates of the latter two are considerably higher than earlier estimates. The magnitude of the excess burden depends on the elasticities of supply of basic factors, especially of savings and of labor supply. Neither elasticity is known well. Ballard, Shoven and Whalley make two alternative assumptions about each elasticity, giving four estimates altogether; the estimates of total gain from replacing the taxes by lump-sum taxes range from 13% to 24% of the revenues, which imply that the marginal excess burden per dollar of taxation from a small reduction in taxes is between 26% and 48% of the reduction (Table 3, p. 133). The estimate of marginal excess burden made by Jorgenson and Kun is even higher, 46% (see Table 1, entry for 5% reduction of, "All Tax Bases"). However, they assume that savers maximize a sum of discounted utilities, an assumption which, in my judgment, leads to an unacceptably high estimate of the elasticity of saving with respect to after-tax rate of return, and therefore to high excess tax burdens. I have therefore estimated the marginal excess burden of taxes to be 30%, though a slightly higher figure could be defended.

Under that assumption, a cut of 50% in military expenditures and a corresponding cut in taxes will increase private real purchasing power, not by 3% but by 3X1.3%, since the excess burden on the amount cut will also be eliminated. Thus, we could have raised total private consumption and investment by 4%. This would be about $200 billion dollars a year. To achieve this gain, however, it would be necessary to cut all taxes more or less proportionately. Since the major effect is to increase the incentives to save and to work, the efficiency gain is greater for those who save more or whose work is more highly valued in the market. If the "peace dividend" were used to improve income distribution, by cutting taxes or increasing transfer payments disproportionately to the lower income groups, the efficiency gain would be reduced, though not eliminated; there are important efficiency gains to be obtained by increasing work incentives at the lower end of the income scale. How the tax reduction is allocated among the income classes is a matter for social value judgment; efficiency can be traded off against equity if desired.

Alternataively, the resources released by arms reduction could be allocated to other parts of the federal budget or to state or local expenditures. In principle, this reallocation should take place only if a dollar of government expenditures in the direction chosen is worth more than the marginal cost of taxes (one dollar plus marginal excess burden). Since marginal excess benefit is approximately linear in taxes, a cut of half the defense budget or 14% of the total budget should reduce the marginal excess burden from 30% to about 25%. Therefore the cut somewhat increases the range of government expenditures than can be justified on efficiency grounds.

In all the above analysis, I have assumed that a reduction in military expenditures would be accompanied by an equal reduction in taxes. It might and probably would be accompanied by some reduction in the deficit, that is, in the rate of increase in the government debt. It is not my purpose here to present an analysis of the effects of deficit reduction; a deficit has some of the same characteristics as a tax in creating an excess burden.

2.3 Macroeconomic Stability

The analysis of fluctuations in the general economic level of activity is still in a state of great dispute. For a long part of the postwar period, a dominating paradigm was the Keynesian theory. Briefly summarized, prices, especially wages, did not move to equate supply and demand, or at least did not move quickly enough to prevent periodic conditions in which there was an excess of supply on labor markets (unemployment) [Tobin, 1975]. In at least some versions, it was also possible to have an excess of supply on product markets, in the sense that firms would be willing to supply more products at the going wages and prices than they can in fact sell. Under these conditions, an increase in demand for any cause could increase total national income by causing idle resources to be used. In fact, the usual view was that there was a "multiplier" effect in which those employed as a result of the initial increase in demand would themselves increase demand still further and therefore employ still more resources.

In this model, an increase in government spending for any purpose would increase national income, except at those times when the economy was already fully employed. In this context, military expenditures were not at all costly, and reducing them would per se reduce national income, perhaps by more than the reduction in military expenditures. During the 1960's there was a widespread joke that the Cold War aided both sides; it shored up the Soviet political system and the United States economic system.

Of course, military expenditures had no special role in stimulating demand in the Keynesian framework. Any other form of expenditure would do as well and of course might be preferred on other grounds. Some Marxist critics, particularly Paul Baran (1969:290), did argue that it was not politically possible to substitute other government expenditures in sufficiently large amounts, because they would begin to serve functions which were competitive with private enterprise. But most

Keynesian theorists found it perfectly possible to argue for more government spending in general and less military spending in particular.

Subsequent research and experience has undermined some of the confidence in the Keynesian theory. Some still argue for variations of the original theory, others, the so-called real business cycles theorists such as Kydland and Prescott (1980), have arrived at a theoretical structure in which markets always clear. Variations in employment, for example, are regarded as variations in the willingness to supply labor, so that all unemployment is voluntary, that is, unwillingness to work at the current wage levels. Clearly, if markets always clear, then any change in government expenditures can only redirect resources, not create new ones.

In view of the uncertainty in macroeconomic analysis, one cannot use any particular model with any confidence. Simple Keynesian stories make little sense to me for long-run analysis, otherwise one can get the absurd conclusion of Joan Robinson that fixed real wages would be compatible with indefinitely increasing unemployment. Stagnationist views are incompatible with both history and any economic logic which ascribes some element of rationality to economic agents. But that is not to say that disequilibria in the labor and product markets cannot exist for some periods of time, even of the order of magnitude of observed business cycles.

I confine the analysis here to one element common to most, perhaps all versions of macroeconomic analysis. Variabaility in government or other exogenous expendiutures will in general increase the variability of broad economic magnitudes, such as national income and employment. In general, one would expect this variability to lower the average level of performance along each of these dimensions, for two reasons. One is that upward movements will sometimes reach the full employment ceiling, so that they do not offset the downward movements; the second is that the unpredictability of future movements will decrease the willingness to invest and especially the ability to invest efficiently.

In this paper, I simply compare the variability of military expenditures with that of the total Federal budget. To measure variability in relative rather than absolute terms, I have used the standard deviation of the logarithms for each of the two kinds of expenditures. As can be seen in Table 2.1, the variability of defense expenditures, so measured, has been almost twice that of the Federal budget as a whole. It is reasonable to conclude that military expenditures have added to the instability of the American economy.

2.4 Modern Growth Theory

There is a new tradition, which is in fact a revival of an old one, which concentrates on explanations for growth rates of an economic system. Instead of the static analysis of section 2.2, it gives emphasis to factors which influence growth rates rather than levels of national income and the like. There has been a rich neo-classical theory of optimal growth. However, in the absence of technological progress, growth of per capita income is attributed to increase of capital per worker and therefore must diminish over time. This effect would be even stronger if limited natural resources were included as a separate factor. But, it appears, rates of per capita income growth in advanced countries have not shown diminution over a century.

Tinbergern (1942), Solow (1957), and other pioneers simply postulated exogeneous factors which gave rise to growth; these were understood to be increases in knowledge, which in effect multiplies the productivity due to capital and labor. However, innovations which increase productivity arise to a large extent from deliberate resource allocations to achieve them. Hence, one might attempt to construct a model in which investment in research and development increase total factor productivity (the ratio of output to an index number which combines labor and capital inputs).

This would lead to a model with increasing returns to scale, at least in a dynamic sense; a proportional increase in capital and labor alone will increase output proportionally, but a simultaneous proportional increase in labor, capital, and research and development devoted to innovations should increase output more than proportionately. Naturally, such a model cannot be one of perfect competition, and some form of monopolistic competition must be introduced. Ideas like this were already present in Allyn Young's presidential address to the Royal Economic Society (1928). Examples of subsequent development are to be found in Rosenstein-Rodan (1943) and Nurkse (1953); for a survey of this literature and its relation to general economic theory, see Arrow (1988). The current revival of interest in this area stems from the work of Romer (1986), who in particular pointed to the lack of tendency to convergence among the per capita incomes of different countries as evidence for increasing returns models.

Look then at the last column in Table 2.1. Research and development has been a roughly constant share of gross national product, about 2.6%. However, the military share of research and development has fallen below its earlier levels in line with the general reduction in the share of military expenditures, although not as much. Therefore, the share of R&D in military expenditures has, if anything, risen.

What would be the effect of a cut in military expenditures with a corresponding cut in military R&D? I can offer only speculation. One question is whether the private sector will in fact absorb all the R&D resources released. If the supply were elastic, then since the decrease in military demand would reduce the overall demand and therefore the price, one would expect some diversion of R&D resources now used by the military to other purposes. The constancy of the R&D fraction in the entire economy does suggest an inelastic supply of R&D resources, so that in fact they would all flow to the private sector.

This suggests a model for analyzing the effect of a budget cut. Preliminary calculations by Junjie Li and myself along these lines do not lead to any great departure from the results predicted in Section 2.2, that is, roughly an increase in private use equal to the defense budget cut (apart from the effect of the excess burden of taxation). However, the methods are so schematic that not much confidence should be placed in them.

There is one more point that should be mentioned. Another strand of the new growth economics and of the earlier literature which it echoes is the role of externalities. In some versions of the theory, it is assumed that there are considerable externalities, particularly with regard to the creation of knowledge; thus, knowledge created by the use of R&D resources in one firm or sector increases productivity in other sectors, even though the latter do not pay for these resources. It has sometimes been argued that military R&D has created externalities ("spillover effects") on the civilian economy. This would be particularly true of electrronics. Unquestionably, the demand for radar stations with minimal maintenance for detection of incoming ballistic missiles in the 1950's was a great stimulus to the development of transistors. There is a general impression that the military demands in the last twenty years are so remote from civilian requirements that very little spillover has occurrred. If this is true, the view that defense R&D enhances civilian productivity would not hold.

2.5 Political Economy

In analyzing the effect of a cut in defense expenditures on the economy, we cannot forget the influence of the political system on the choice, direction, and magnitude of the reductions. I simply lay out the directions in which the analysis has to go, and much of it is hardly surprising. The questions do raise some issues about the analysis of public choice in a dynamic context and about increasing returns to scale in the political field.

A reduction in military expenditures typically has a negative economic effect on some subset of the population. Clearly, there is a direct economic gain to part of the population, namely the taxpayers and those to whom public expenditures will be redirected. Indeed, apart from the public goods value of the military expenditures, any reduction in defense expenditures is trivially a social gain. Yet holders of specialized assets, including human skills, may well lose by a redirection of demand. A classical example, again in the newspapers as this is being written, is the possible closing of bases. The Defense Department has long made clear its preference for closing many of the bases now being used and has always found public opposition represented politically by congressmen from the affected districts. Some of this perceived loss may be illusory, by individuals who do not realize the value of their assets in the alternative uses created by the released demand. But immobility of resources between places and between sectors is real enough, particularly over periods of time which are long enough to matter to individuals, even though they are short on some longer national time scale.

Of course, shifts in demand are occurring all the time for reasons other than changes in the level of military expenditures: innovation, foreign competition, poplulation movements. Many of these are alleviated, if not totally offset, by the forces of the market. Labor and capital made idle by demand shifts will be used in other sectors, if at a reduced level of compensation; land rents will fall; and of course in the United States economy migration of labor is always present.

The logic of political economy does have some interesting problems of asymmetry between gainers and losers. Reductions in defense expenditures, as I have remarked, are a net private gain. The losses to some workers and asset-holders are more than offset by the gains to others. If one takes a naive model, where rent-seeking effort is proportional to the gains at stake, then the political pressure from the potential gainers should outweigh the opposition of the losers. There are of course a number of objections which could be made to this simple argument. One is a question of returns to scale. The cost of mobilizing political support may be proportional to the number of individuals involved; hence, for a given total stake, it is easier to exert pressure if the number of gainers is small. Many military expenditures are highly concentrated by firm and by geographical area, while the benefits to taxpayers and to the sectors to whom the reduced expenditures will flow are widely spread. A second problem, which is frequently adduced in the determination of tariffs and other restrictions on foreign trade, is that the losing industries exist while the gains will accrue only in the future. In economic theory, gains and losses would be equally effective; but it is sometimes argued that in a democratic society the future industries do not get equal weight.

Finally, it should be noted that there are policies which might help to convert potential to actual Pareto improvements. I refer to adjustment aid for retraining laborers and assisting in the redirection of management, especially in small firms. Such policies exist today for meeting adjustments to import-induced shifts and have been very successful in Sweden. Adjustment policies are provided in connection with current defense cuts, but I do not know how effective they are.

2.6 Final Remark

It is probably true that the misallocation due to the arms race is not much more than the direct expenditures. This is still a fairly large sum, 3% or 4% of national income. It may be recalled that Robert Fogel (1964) attracted much critical attention for arguing that the net gain due to the existence of railroads was approximately 5% of national income in 1890. This was held to be too low a figure for what appeared to be the obviously large role of railroads in 19th century economic development. Yet a little calculation showed that it constituted perhaps 20% of the gain in total factor productivity over the relevant period, by no means a trivial proportion. Similarly a cut of 50% in defense expenditures will constitute a major addition to growth in disposable national income in a five-year period.

Needless to say, the major economic case for defense expenditure cuts is the reduction in the probability and cost of war, the economic consequences of which are only too easy to predict.

Footnotes

*This work was aided by the Center for Economic Policy Research at Stanford University. I am greatly indebted to my research assistant, Junjie Lie. The Paper was originally presented to the Conference on the Economics of Disarmament at Notre Dame University, under the sponsorship of Economists Against the Arms Race and the Institute of International Relations of Notre Dame University, November, 1990.

References

Arrow, K.J. (1988). General economic theory and the emergence of theories of economic development. In K.J. Arrow (ed.), *The Balance Between Industry and Agriculture in Economic Development*, Volume 1 (Basic Issues). Basingstoke and London: Macmillan in association with the International Economic Association. pp. 22-32.

Ballard, C.L., Shoven, J.B. and Whalley, J. (1985). The total welfare cost of the United States tax system: a general equilibrium approach. *National Tax Journal*, 38, 125-140.

Baran, P. (1969). Economic progress and economic surplus. In P. Baran, *The Longer View*, New York and London: Monthly Review Press. pp. 271-307. Reprinted from *Science and Society*, 1953.

Browning, E.K. (1976). The marginal cost of public funds. *Journal of Political Economy*, 84, 283-298.

Fogel, R. (1964). *Railroads and American economic growth.* Baltimore: Johns Hopkins University Press.

Jorgenson, D., and Yun, K.-Y. (1990). The excess burden of taxation in the U.S. Unpublished.

Kaufman, W.W. (1990). *Glasnost, perestroika, and U.S. defense spending.* Washington, D.C.: Brookings.

Kydland, F., and Prescott, E. (1980). A competitive theory of fluctuations and the feasibility and desirability of stabilization policy. In S. Fischer (ed.) *Rational Expectations and Economic Policy.* Chicago and London: University of Chicago Press.

Nurkse, R. (1953). *Problems of capital formation in underdeveloped countries.* Oxford: Oxford University Press.

Romer, P. (1986). Increasing returns and long run growth. *Journal of Political Economy*, 94, 1002-10037.

Rosenstein-Rodan, P.N. (1943). Problems of industrialization of eastern and southeastern Europe. *Economic Journal*, 53, 202-211.

Solow, R.M. (1957). Technical change and the aggregate production function. *Review of Economics and Statistics*, 39, 312-320.

Tinbergen, J. (1942). Zur Theorie de langfristigen Wirtschaftsentwicklung. *Weltwirtschaftliches Archiv.*

Tobin, J. (1975). Keynesian models of recession and depression. *American Economic Review, Papers and Proceedings*, 65, 195-202.

Young, A.A. (1928). Increasing returns and economic progress. *Economic Journal*, 38, 527-542.

Economics of Arms Reduction and the Peace Process
W. Isard and C.H. Anderton (Editors)
1992 Elsevier Science Publishers B.V.

Chapter 3

IMPACT OF MILITARY CUTS ON THE
SOVIET AND EASTERN EUROPEAN ECONOMIES:
MODELS AND SIMULATIONS

Lawrence R. Klein, Miroslaw Gronicki and Hiroyuki Kosaka
University of Pennsylvania
edited by
Walter Isard
Cornell University

[The survey of chapter 1 lays out past and current contributions of economists to the peace economics literature, and the Arrow paper provides a broad look at the contributions of four different approaches in economic analysis. We now wish to probe deeply into critical theoretical and actual problems. There are many ways in which we can organize the different contributions of the scholars that follow. However, at the time of writing, an extremely critical problem of world-wide interest was the impact of the revolutionary political changes taking place in Eastern Europe and Soviet Asia upon the nations and regions involved as well as those in Western Europe and elsewhere. We therefore begin with the contributions of Klein, Gronicki and Kosaka. Their focus is on the *Impact of Military Cuts on the Soviet and Eastern European Economies*, a contribution which falls within Arrow's category: Macroeconomic Stability Analysis. With the information now available the authors are able to dig more deeply than ever before into the past and evolving economic structures in Eastern Europe. They add to our knowledge of the effects of military expenditures upon the development of totalitarian economies with a set of scenarios realistic for the turn of the decade. (eds.)]

3.1 Preface

Because of visa and other problems caused by the recent political upheavals in Eastern Europe, it was not possible for Lawrence R. Klein and Miroslaw Gronicki to complete the work for the paper to be presented in this chapter. However, because of the importance of their work for the development of peace economics and for the analysis of problems currently confronting the Eastern European countries and the republics emerging from the partial (or full?) dissolution of the Soviet Union, the senior editor of this book undertakes in what follows a pulling together, hopefully effective, of several of their past and currently unpublished contributions plus some of his own appraisal of the work of Klein, Gronicki and Kosaka.

Section 3.2 is an edited version of an introductory statement written by Miroslaw Gronicki alone in the Spring, 1991. Section 3.3 is a concise restatement by the editor of the Klein-Kosaka arms race submodel, an ingredient of both the model of section 3.4 and the model used to generate the simulations of section 3.5. Section 3.4 is a model of a Centrally Planned economy developed by Miroslaw Gronicki alone; it represents a further development of the Klein-Gronicki model behind the simulations of section 3.5. Section 3.5 presents some unpublished simulations from the 1990 Klein and Gronicki model, important for the insights they yield on the functioning of centrally planned economies and useful for comparative analysis. Section 6 contains concluding remarks by the senior editor.

3.2. Introductory Remarks (By Miroslaw Gronicki)

It is possible that economic and strategic relations between East and West are now changing toward a mode of coexistence. The leaders of Warsaw Pact countries have acknowledged former difficulties and the late 80s became a period of serious economic and political reform. Now, military cuts have been announced in all countries of the Pact. In December 1988, Soviet leader Gorbachev proposed unilateral cuts of 10% in military spending and a reduction of 500,000 in army forces. After the huge budget deficit (which according to some estimates reached 9% of the Soviet GNP) was revealed, further cuts were proposed, which amount to a total reduction of 14.2% in military spending. Similar cuts have been proposed by leaders of other Warsaw Pact countries: for example, Poland plans to reduce its military budget by about 40% and to dissolve several army units, decreasing military personnel by 50%. Moreover, the GDR army disappeared after unification. At the same time, Gorbachev implemented withdrawal of some Soviet conventional forces from Eastern Europe and proposed further reductions in strategic and conventional forces during disarmament talks.

In 1989, after revolutionary change in Eastern Europe, the Warsaw Pact practically disappeared. In 1990 communist regimes were ousted in each country of the region and new governments demanded a complete withdrawal of the Soviet forces and formal dissolution of the Warsaw Pact. These demands and unification of Germany in October 1990 led in April 1991 to the dissolution of all formal institutions of the Warsaw Pact.

This new political situation will not only influence the internal politics in the region. It may also affect the world's security, because first Eastern Europe will create a buffer between the West and the Soviet Union, and second there will be a need for new political and military alliances.

Political changes and bold economic reforms in Eastern Europe will have significant impact on the military sector in the economy. It is highly probable that the share of military related expenditure in GNP will be cut significantly but the question is: what will be the influence of military cuts on the economy as a whole. Will they improve economic performance or will they further exacerbate existing economic difficulties?

A properly formulated economic analysis of former and current regimes will be useful for an ex post examination of the transition process, as well for guiding and analyzing economic reform and its impact on the military in the short term.

There are significant relationships between military spending and economic performance; their effects on the economy depend on the economic system and the phase of business cycle. In market economies, increases in military outlays during times of economic slack may be beneficial in providing jobs, but in periods of full capacity utilization they may cause inflation. In Centrally Planned Economies (CPEs), increases in military expenditures may increase the hidden inflation and reduce the supply of civilian goods. In the reforming economy cuts in military expenditure may have the same negative effect as in the market economy depending, however, on the significance of the military sector in the economy and on the level of imbalances. It is thus interesting to ask whether cuts in military expenditures might improve the economic performance of these countries. In other words, how much can military cuts help the reforming East European countries?

Over the years, there has been a debate about the impact of defense spending on the Soviet type economies. [Earlier results are given, for example, in Pryor (1968); more recent ones can be found in Becker (1985) and Rosenfielde 1987)]. According to a series of UN reports [United Nations (1972), (1977), (1981), (1982)] military spending is mainly unproductive and an appropriate reallocation of resources may improve the overall performance of the economy. Other researchers, for example, Benoit (1973), Smith (1977), and Adams et al (1988), (1989), claim that military spending, especially in the developing economies, has positive effects on economic growth. Gronicki and Klein (1988, 1989) suggest that the military sector in a Centrally Planned Economy (CPE) is separated to such an extent that any attempts to accelerate growth and increase efficiency of the economy may fail due to the inefficient civilian sector. The civilian sector of a CPE has always been treated as of lesser importance and, unlike the situation in Western economies, spin-off of R&D from the military to civilian sector has usually been delayed and weak.

3.3   The Klein-Kosaka Arms Race Submodel (by Walter Isard)

In Klein and Kosaka (1988), as summarized in Isard (1988), and in chapter 1 of this book, an initial attempt is made to capture the dynamics of the arms race within a multi-nation econometric model. Recognizing that arms spending ME^J of a nation J is potentially affected by the spending of other nations K $(K = A,..,U; K \neq J)$; that lags are involved in this relationship and that J's spending is in a major way directly related to its GDP^J, Klein and Kosaka specify:

$$\frac{ME^J}{GDP^J}(t) = f_1[\frac{ME^A}{GDP^A}(t),...,\frac{ME^K}{GDP^K}(t),...,\frac{ME^J}{GDP^J}(t\text{-}1), \frac{ME^A}{GDP^A}(t\text{-}1),...,\frac{ME^U}{GDP^U}(t\text{-}\theta)] \qquad (3.1)$$

Using forecasts of GDP^K $(K = A,...,J,...,U)$ over a relevant time period from the basic LINK Model, they then determine ME^K $(K = A,...,J,...,U)$. Also, since military expenditures may be judged to strain the resources of an economy and thus affect its price level P^K, the relationship (3.1) may be modified to incorporate the P^K variables. However, ME^J is part of J's government spending G^J. Hence, there is feedback captured by the relationship

$$G^J(t) = f_2(ME^J(t),...,) \qquad (3.2)$$

which leads to new projected values of GDP^J and P^J. Iterations of this procedure are then required. Klein and Kosaka thus extended the basic LINK model to incorporate these relationships for 19 countries (including US and USSR) and the NATO bloc whose variables were taken to be sums of member country variables. Table 1.1 in Chapter 1 records some of the model's outcomes. In Klein and Gronicki (1990), the arms race submodel is extended to cover Eastern European countries.

3.4 A Model of the Centrally Planned Economy (CPE)
(by Miroslaw Gronicki)

The econometric models of the Soviet Union and East European countries assume that the "official economy" (socialized sector) in the unreformed economy is in a state of permanent disequilibrium (that is, in almost all periods demand is greater than supply). In modeling such an economy, methods of disequilibrium econometrics must be applied (for a review see Quandt, 1987). Such models have been formulated according to propositions of recently developed economic theory, for example Balicki (1983), and Benassy (1984). Typical models of CPEs are comprised of the following sectors: the state sector (including, *inter alia*, state owned enterprises, the military sector, and state and local budgets); the household sector; the private sector; and the foreign trade sector.

The "official economy" consists of the state and foreign trade sectors, and of the household supply of labor to, and demand for consumer goods from, the official economy. As is well known, CPEs differ in important respects from market economies. Accordingly, econometric models of these economies differ in their approach and formulation. Probably the most important difference between models of CPEs and market economies (for example, see Charemza and Gronicki,1988) is an explicit examination of the state sector and the treatment of the supply side of the economy. Because of the assumption of macroeconomic disequilibrium, financial flows are of limited use in explaining historical data. Although it might be argued that some economies were somewhat more monetized than a typical CPE, enterprises still operated according to the dictates of the plan.

In CPEs and also in the reformed economies, the private sector is substantially smaller than in a typical market economy and therefore it is not analyzed in detail. A more precise formulation of consumer and enterprise behavior would explicitly include interactions between the official and unofficial sectors, but there is a lack of sufficient data for a proper analysis. The only readily observable indicator of second economy activity is the black-market exchange-rate (with the exception of Poland since 1990). Accordingly, the black-market exchange-rate is used as an indicator of the spillovers from the official to unofficial markets.[1]

The proposed model is developed along the lines of Charemza and Gronicki (1988). Consumers are assumed to maximize a traditional utility function of the form:

$$U = U(C, L, M/p) \qquad\qquad (3.3)$$

subject to the budget constraint:

$$M_0 + wL = pC + M \qquad\qquad (3.4)$$

where C is consumption, L is labor supplied by the consumer, M_0 is initial wealth (cash plus savings), M is final wealth, p are prices, and w are wages.[2] In an economy without quantity constraints, maximization of the utility function yields a Walrasian consumption demand:

$$\bar{C}^d = \bar{C}^d(w, p, M_0) \qquad\qquad (3.5)$$

Walrasian labor supply:

$$\bar{L}^s = \bar{L}^s(w, p, M_0) \tag{3.6}$$

and Walrasian demand for money:

$$\bar{M}^d = \bar{M}^d(w, p, M_0) \tag{3.7}$$

However, in the present analysis, the hypothesis of "overall-excess-demand" for goods traded on official markets is assumed.[3]   Therefore, the Walrasian demand, $\bar{C}^d$, and Walrasian labor supply, $\bar{L}^s$, are not applicable. Instead, agents choose effective consumption demands, C^d, and effective labor supplies, L^s, based on applicable constraints.

The amount of the consumption good available, C^s, is assumed to be less than the effective amount demand, C^d. Hence the amount transacted, C^q, is equal to the amount provided, C^s. Thus:

$$C^s = C^q < C^d \tag{3.8}$$

In turn, this implies that the amount of labor supplied to the economy will be effected by the quantity of the consumption good available. That is, the existence of constraints on the consumption market feed back into labor supply. Therefore, the earlier equation for labor supply (measured in "efficiency units") must be modified to reflect the availability of consumption goods:

$$L^s = L^s(w, p, M_0, C^q) \tag{3.9}$$

Again, assuming excess demand for labor, the amount of labor transacted equals the supply. That is:

$$L^d > L^q = L^s \tag{3.10}$$

In determining consumption demand, agents adjust their labor supply. Nonetheless, it is assumed that consumption demand exceeds consumption supply. Thus:

$$C^d = C^d(w, p, M_0, L^q) \tag{3.11}$$

Standard econometric models of CPEs generally assume that planners treat the supply of consumption goods as a residual in the planning process. That is investment and defense receive priority in the non-monetized allocation system, and consumption markets are supplied "last." In Czechoslovakia, however, consumption supply was the product of deliberate planning which attempted to maintain the standard of living. Thus, consumption supply can be assumed to be a function of planned output:[4]

$$C^s = C^s(Q^p) \tag{3.12}$$

where Q^p is planned output.

The assumption that consumption demand exceeds consumption supply implies that C^d is not directly observable, and hence techniques of disequilibrium econometrics should be applied. One possible methodology to answer questions regarding the unobservability of demand is the specification of an excess-demand adjustment equation. The economic "center" is assumed to adjust plan variables to "some extent" endogenously, taking into account current output as well as current disequilibrium.

Planned consumption output in the next period, C^p_{+1}, is assumed to be a fraction of planned total output in the next period, Q^p_{+1}. Moreover, the change in planned consumption output over current consumption output is assumed to be a fraction of the change in planned total output over current total output. Thus, the adjustment of planned consumption may be represented as:

$$C^p_{+1} - C^q = \alpha(Q^p_{+1} - Q^q) \tag{3.13}$$

Planned output is based, *inter alia*, on current disequilibrium on the consumption market:

$$Q^p_{+1} - Q^q = g_1(C^d - C^q) \tag{3.14}$$

Then, given appropriate restrictions, this equation may be inverted in order to derive an operational expression for adjustment to disequilibrium on the consumption market:

$$C^d - C^q = f_1(Q^p_{+1} - Q^q) \tag{3.15}$$

Planners are also able to adjust wages and prices in order to move the economy towards what the planners consider to be equilibrium.[5,6] Thus, an alternative adjustment equation for excess demand on some markets for consumer goods:

$$C^d - C^q = f_2(\Delta w, \Delta p) \tag{3.15'}$$

where Δ is the first difference operator. *Ceteris Paribus*, increasing wages will increase excess-demand and increasing prices will decrease excess-demand.[7]

Maximizing behavior of enterprises, in the neoclassical sense, is not well-defined in CPEs because the maximization function of enterprises is unknown. In some sense, the quantitative output plan can be assumed set simultaneously with the demand for inputs, generally as a result of a bargaining process between the enterprises and the planning authorities.

Nonetheless, labor demand is assumed to be a function of the future output plans:

$$L^d = L^d(QP_{+1}) \tag{3.16}$$

Again, given the fact that a typical CPE economy exhibited strong indications of "repressed inflation," it is assumed that demand for labor exceeds supply. Thus, by arguments similar to those described above for the consumption market, the excess demand for labor may be represented as:[8]

$$L^d - L^q = f_3(QP_{+1} - Q^q) \tag{3.17}$$

In a typical CPE, it is officially proclaimed that the state (central planners) seeks to maximize the long-run fulfillment of social needs, generally through the maximization of investment in the short-run. Early in the experience with planning, however, economists realized and debated the danger of this approach to economic growth, and the resulting investment cycles.[9] This realization, coupled with a "social compact" to provide a "high" standard of living, creates a contrast with what is considered to be typical CPE behavior. Nonetheless, it is assumed that investment supply is a function of plans:

$$INV^s = INV^s(QP) \tag{3.18}$$

Investment demand is a function of plans, of the capital stock available from the previous period, K_{-1}, and of the backlog of unfinished investment, BI:

$$INV^d = INV^d(QP_{+1}, K_{-1}, BI) \tag{3.19}$$

Again, it is assumed that demand for investment exceeds supply:

$$INV^d > INV^q = INV^s \tag{3.20}$$

Investment plans may be thought of as the reaction of planners to current disequilibrium in investment:

$$INVP_{+1} - INV^q = h_1(INV^d - INV^s) \tag{3.21}$$

and adjustment of investment may be found from a transformation, yielding the adjustment equation:

$$INV^d - INV^s = h_1^{-1}(INVP_{+1} - INV^q) \tag{3.22}$$

Military expenditures, ME, may reflect tradeoffs between current investment and military expenditures. Thus, an alternative adjustment equation would be:

$$INV^d - INV^s = h_2(\Delta ME) \tag{3.22'}$$

The stock of fixed assets equals the amount of fixed assets available in the previous period, less depreciation, d, plus the gross increment of fixed assets, R, less liquidation, IK:

$$K = (1 - d) \cdot K_{-1} + R - IK \tag{3.23}$$

where the gross increment of fixed assets is a function of lagged $L(\cdot)$, investments:

$$R = R[L(I_{-\tau})] \tag{3.24}$$

The backlog of unfinished investments is defined as the sum of the differences between investment and the gross increment of fixed assets:

$$BI = \sum_i (INV_{-i} - R_{-i}) \tag{3.25}$$

Typically foreign trade has been monopolized by state agencies which considered trade a source of goods and technologies which could not be produced in the state sector, and planners treat foreign trade as a "last refuge" for dealing with domestic disequilibrium. Thus, imports in the current period reflect the real side of the economy (for example, fuel imports depend on demand by the manufacturing sector), but imports are also adjusted according to previous disequilibrium. Previous exports act as a financial constraint.[10]

Exports are determined by the real side of the economy, but affected by current disequilibrium, which may encourage planners to limit exports. Lagged exports reflect constraints on the world market as well as (especially CMEA) trade norms.[11]

The equations for the foreign trade block can be specified along the lines of Gronicki and Klein (1989), where imports (supply) are a function of the appropriate variables on the real side of the economy, R, and/or, of current plans, previous disequilibrium, $(Q^p - Q^q_{-1})$, previous period exports, EXP_{-1}, and world market prices, P^w.[12]

$$IMP^s = IMP^s[R, Q^p, (Q^p - Q^q_{-1}), EXP_{-1}, P^w] \qquad (3.26)$$

Exports (transacted) are a function of the real side of the economy, and/or, of plans, of current disequilibrium, and of previous period exports:

$$EXP^q = EXP^q[R, Q^p, (Q^p_{+1} - Q^q), EXP_{-1}, P^w) \qquad (3.27)$$

Output[13] by sector of origin can be obtained from technical production functions. As stated above, maximizing behavior of enterprises, in the neoclassical sense, is not well-defined in CPEs, because the maximization function of enterprises is unknown. Therefore, Cobb-Douglas production functions are used, constrained to be homogeneous of degree one:

$$Log(Q^s_i/L^q_i) = \alpha_0 + \alpha_1 Log(K_i/L^q_i) + \varepsilon \qquad (3.28)$$

where K_i are fixed capital assets, and L^q_i is labor utilized in the respective sectors.
    The supply of Q is defined to be the sum of the consumption of material goods and services, CM; military, ME, and non-military, GC, government consumption; investment less total depreciation, DEPR; the change in inventory stock, ΔST; the balance of trade, BT; and losses, LOSS:[14]

$$Q^s = \sum_i Q^s_i \equiv CM^s + (GC + ME) + (INV^q - DEPR) + \Delta ST + BT + LOSS \qquad (3.29)$$

In order to capture the implications of subsidy reduction, some budgetary flows are included in the simulation exercises. The state budget deficit is defined to be the difference between expenditure and revenue:

$$BuD = EXP_{tot} - REV_{tot} \qquad (3.30)$$

where revenue is the total of excise taxes, TAX_2; income taxes, TAX; and other revenue REV_{oth}:

$$REV_{tot} = TAX_2 + TAX + REV_{oth} \qquad (3.31)$$

and expenditure is the total of subsidies SUB; military expenditure; the nominal interest rate, i, times the previous period savings deposits, SAV_{-1}; and other expenditure EXP_{oth}:

$$EXP_{tot} = SUB + ME + i \cdot SAV_{-1} + EXP_{oth} \qquad (3.32)$$

The budget deficit is financed either by debt or by money creation. Thus, the change in money, ΔM, equals the budget deficit less changes in savings and changes in external indebtedness, where $\Delta DEBT$ is measured in dollars and EXCHK is the official exchange rate. Thus:

$$\Delta M = BuD - \Delta DEBT \cdot EXCHK - \Delta SAV \qquad (3.33)$$

Equations (3.8) through (3.33) represent the complete economic model.

3.5 Simulation Exercises (by Lawrence R. Klein and Miroslaw Gronicki)[15,16]

In this paper, we present results of simulation experiments in which military spending during the period 1989-1993 would be cut annually by: 15%, 13%, 11%, 9%, 7%, 5%, 4%, 3%, 2%, 1% (in the first experiment, it means that military expenditures could be halved during the next five years). For the comparison, we have provided another series of experiments, in which we assumed zero growth in military expenditures and 1%, 2%, 3%, 4%, and 5% annual growth. Other assumptions for these experiments are the same as used for the latest LINK forecast.

We have analyzed an impact of military expenditures (denoted by ME) on personal consumption (CONS), non-military government spending (GOV), investment in "material sectors" (INMAT), investment in "non-material sectors" (INNMAT), and on Gross National Product (GNP). The summary of simulation experiments is given in the attached graphs. Assuming that there will not be any significant structural changes in the Warsaw Pact economies and that current economic trends will be preserved the following conclusions can be drawn:

1) The trade-off between civilian spending (excluding investment in the military-oriented material sectors INMAT) and military spending is expected to be weak; Poland and Hungary could be the only exceptions (see the full set of charts). The former has still unutilized capacity in industry and has recently improved macroeconomic efficiency. The latter has the economic structure which is closest to

that of the market economy and could accommodate the military cuts. In the other countries graphs show limited trade-offs (the curves are relatively flat, which means that response to the military cuts is weak).

2) The highest growth rates of consumption (see chart 3.2 and the consumption curve of chart 3.1) are for Poland and Hungary (7.2% and 4.5% respectively for the experiment with the largest, 15%, cuts). The growth rates of consumption for Romania are distinctly lower than in the rest of the Warsaw Pact. It can be explained by the economic policy of Causescu aimed at repayment of all debts. The costs of this policy are: small investment in "non-material" sectors, and undercapitalized light industry. In order to overcome this policy a period longer than 5 years would be required.

Chart 3.1:   Soviet Union. Military Expenditures versus Consumption, Investment in Nonmaterial Sectors, Nonmilitary Government Expenditures, Investment in Material Sectors, and GNP

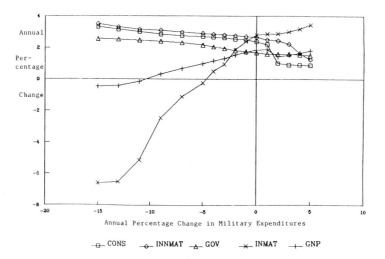

Chart 3.2: Personal Consumption versus Military Expenditure

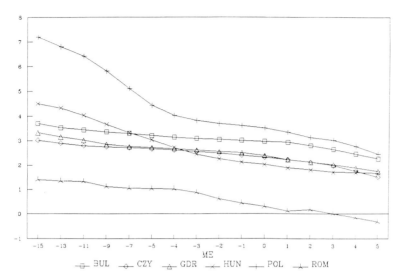

3) The pattern of responses of non-military government consumption and "non-material" investment (see Charts 3.3 and 3.4 and the corresponding curves of Chart 3.1) is the same as in the consumption case. In the most optimistic experiment (15% cuts in military spending) for all the countries of the region, the growth rates for the government spending are lower than for "non-material" investment.

Chart 3.3: Government Expenditures versus Military Expenditures

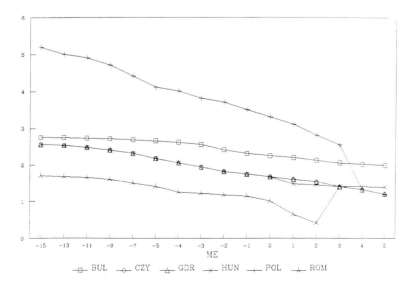

Chart 3.4:   Investment in Non-material Sectors (INNMAT) versus Military Expenditures

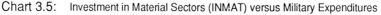

4) The growth rates for "material" investment (see Chart 3.5 and the INMAT curve of Chart 3.1) behave in a different way, as they are, in most cases complements for military spending. In three countries we observe negative growth rates. For Hungary they start from the experiment with 3% annual increase of military spending. A similar pattern is observed for Poland and the Soviet Union. The negative rates start, however, in more optimistic experiments. In the other countries growth rates go down but are still positive.

Chart 3.5:   Investment in Material Sectors (INMAT) versus Military Expenditures

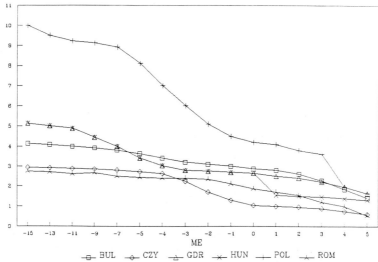

5) Growth rates of GNP (see Chart 3.6 and GNP curve in Chart 3.1) in Bulgaria, GDR, and the Soviet Union go down following cuts in military spending. In the Soviet case they could be negative mainly because they have the largest ratio of military spending to GNP. For Czechoslovakia and Romainia growth rates are quite stable. In the Polish case, growth rates are stable and grow starting from (-7%) experiment, whereas for Hungary the response of GNP may be characterized by a flat U-shaped curve.

Chart 3.6:   Gross National Product (GNP) versus Military Expenditures

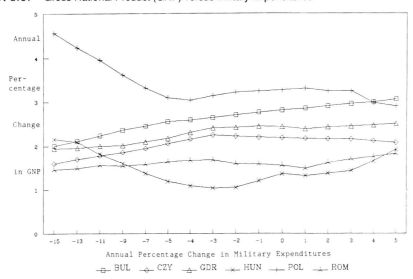

3.6   **Evaluative and Summary Remarks (by W. Isard)**

Apart from the construction of an arms race submodel, a major step forward by Klein and his associates is the effective inclusion of the submodel coupled with feedback effects within a first-rate econometric model. Undoubtedly this submodel will be greatly improved by scholars to follow, as Klein and Kosaka clearly expect. A second contribution lies in the fact that the inclusion of this submodel within LINK opens up the door for the effective incorporation into LINK (and other multi-nation economic models) of important political variables that are closely associated with arms races, and that have been included in a number of arms race models by others. See comments in Chapter 13.

The Klein/Gronicki work is significant on several accounts. Although the unification of Germany, the republic independence movements in the Soviet Union and other major events make obsolete the simulations reported upon in this chapter, nonetheless they represent important findings. Regardless of what structures emerge in the Eastern European and Soviet republic economies, the problem of transition to these structures are going to be exacerbated by the past heavy dependence of investment in material sectors (INMAT) on the military sector, as revealed by Chart 3.5 and the corresponding curve on Chart 3.1. Clearly, this problem is much more severe than any conversion problem in the United States.

A second important insight gained from the simulations relates to hypotheses and theories regarding the impact of military expenditures on developed and developing economies. Many studies of this impact have been made for both types of economies. As noted in chapter 1, the findings on developing countries are clearly inconclusive, and those for developed countries quite controversial. Now with the Klein/Gronicki simulations we have another set of findings, however rough and incomplete they may be, useful for analysis on what the impact can be on the functioning of totalitarian economies and for comparative purposes --- a set of findings that can help in firming up general hypotheses on impacts.

Footnotes

[1]Any increase in disequilibria on official markets affects the actual level of equilibria elsewhere, resulting in a depreciation of the domestic currency on the black market. This means that the black-market exchange-rate may be used as an indicator of spillovers, under the assumption that this market is always in equilibrium.

[2]The labor/leisure trade-off is implicit in this formulation.

[3]The existence of an "overall-excess-demand" regime has been established, for example, by Gronicki and Klein (1989, 1990). The existence of "shortage" is generally accepted in the literature of CPEs although the *definition* of shortage may vary. For a discussion, see Portes (1986), with his comments on Kornai.

[4]Consumption supply is taken to be a fraction of total output, since no detailed information exists about consumption plans.

[5]A more detailed description of this type of formulation can be found in Charemza and Gronicki (1988).

[6]It can be assumed that the planning process itself can increase excess demand by imposing "taut" plans which defer output away from current consumption markets;

on the other hand, by increasing output, plans may drive the market towards equilibrium.

[7]In the empirical results, both types of adjustment were observed.

[8]$L^d = L^d(QP_{+1})$ implies that $L^d = L^d(Q^q, C^d - C^s)$. Thus (3.17) follows from (3.9) and (3.15).

[9]Some confusion may arise from the practice of using the terms "supply" and "demand" with respect to state sector investment, since prices and financial constraints are determined by mechanisms which are different from their counterparts in market economies.

[10]An example of exports acting as a financial constraint would be that an increase in the world market price of oil would have no impact on imports in the current period. In subsequent periods, all imports would contract, not only oil because of the financial constraint imposed by export earnings. This specification assumes that there is not a strong response to changes in world market prices.

[11]This stylization of behavior prevailed for most CMEA countries (except Hungary).

[12]As stated above, it is assumed that world market prices have a smaller effect on imports and exports than in market economies.

[13]Net Material Product (NMP) is the official measure of output in CPEs. In this paper $Q \equiv NMP$; thus non-material services are excluded from the definition of Q.

[14]Accordingly, this definition *does not include* non-material services.

[15]These simulations are generated by the model reported in Klein and Gronicki (1990), written before the unification of Germany, and not by the Gronicki model presented in the previous section which draws heavily upon the former. (Ed.).

[16]Charts 3.2, 3.3, 3.4, and 3.5 of this section represent unpublished materials which together with Charts 3.1 and 3.6 (from Klein and Gronicki, 1990) provide basic insights for understanding the problems currently confronting the Eastern European and Soviet economies. They also provide significant insights on the impact of military expenditures which will be discussed in the next section. The comments of this section are edited versions of statements in Klein and Gronicki on a set of complementary charts in their 1990 article. (Ed.).

References

Adams, F. G. et al. (1988). Defense expenditures and economic growth in the LCDs: a preview of ongoing research. Paper prepared for the Meeting of the Peace Science Society. College Park, Maryland.

Adams, F. G. et al. (1989). Defense expenditures and economic growth in the LCDs. Paper prepared for the Meeting of the Peace Science Society. SUNY, Binghamton.

Balicki, W. (1983). Theory of disequilibrium in centrally planned economies. *Jarhbuch der Wirtschaft Osteuropas*, 10, 9-39.

Becker, A.S. (1985). *Sitting on bayonets.* RAND/UCLA.

Benassy, J.-P. (1984). *Macroeconomie et theorie du desequilibre*, Paris: Dunod.

Benoit, E. (1973). *Defense and economic growth in developing countries.* Lexington, MA: Lexington Books.

Charemza, W. and Gronicki, M. (1988). *Plans and disequilibria in centrally planned economies (Empirical investigation for Poland).* Amsterdam: North Holland.

Gronicki, M. and Klein, L.R. (1988). Impact of military cuts on the Soviet economy. Paper presented to the AEA Conference in New York.

Gronicki, M. and Klein, L.R. (1989). Trade-offs between military and civilian programs in the Warsaw Pact. Paper presented for the Peace Science Conference at SUNY, Binghamton.

Klein, L.R. and Gronicki, M. (1988). Defense spending among Warsaw Pact countries: implications for LINK simulations of the arms race. Paper presented for the Peace Science Society Conference at the University of Maryland.

Klein, L.R. and Gronicki, M. (1990). Conversion: the trade-off between military and civilian production in Warsaw Pact countries. *Conflict Management and Peace Science,* 11, 45-56.

Klein, L.R. and Kosaka, H. (1988). *The Arms Race and the Economy*, in Vortrage des Freskolloqiums aus Anlass des 70 Geburstages von Wilhelm Krelle, Bonn: Bouvier Verlag Herbert Grundmann.

Portes, R. (1986). *The theory and measurement of macroeconomic disequilibrium in centrally planned economies.* Discussion Paper Series No. 91, Center for Economic Policy Research, London.

Pryor, F. (1968). *Public expenditures in communist and capitalist nations.* Homewood.

Rosefielde. (1987). *False science: underestimating the Soviet arms buildup.* New Brunswick, NJ: Transaction Books.

Quandt, R.E. (1988). *The econometrics of disequilibrium.* New York: Basil Blackwell.

Smith, R.P. (1977). Military expenditure and capitalism. *Cambridge Journal of Economics*, 1, 61-76.

United Nations. (1972). *Economic and social consequences of the armament race and military expenditure.* New York: United Nations.

United Nations. (1977). *Economic and social consequences of the armament race and its extremely harmful effects on world peace and security.* Report of the Secretary-General. New York: United Nations.

United Nations. (1981). *Review of the implementations of the recommendations and decisions adopted by the General Assembly at its tenth special session on development and international economic cooperation. Study on the relationship between disarmament and development.* New York: United Nations.

United Nations. (1982). *Economic and social consequences of the armament race and its extremely harmful effects on world peace and security.* Report of the Secretary-General. New York: United Nations.

Economics of Arms Reduction and the Peace Process
W. Isard and C.H. Anderton (Editors)

Chapter 4

CONFLICT AND TRADE: AN ECONOMICS APPROACH TO POLITICAL INTERNATIONAL INTERACTIONS

Solomon William Polachek

State University of New York, Binghamton[*]

[The Klein/Gronicki/Kosaka contributions dig deeply into the impact of revolutionary political change in Eastern European countries upon their economies and indirectly through trade upon Western European economies, focussing particularly on the repercussions of anticipated arms cutbacks. However, when we examine trade, a critical issue to most national and regional economies, and a phenomena that is directly and indirectly tied in a major way to a country's military expenditures (Polachek provides empirical support for this assertion), it then becomes absolutely essential to inquire in general how political conflict affects trade and vice versa. In his contribution Polachek concentrates on political conflict as affected by trade. Can one argue that the greater the trade between an actor country and a target, the smaller the amount of actor to target conflict (or the greater the amount of cooperation)? Since the greater the inelasticity of the demand for imports and the supply of exports, the greater with increased trade the respective consumer surplus and producer surplus (measures of welfare gains), can we state: the greater the inelasticity of import demand and export supply of an actor country to a target, the smaller the amount of actor to target conflict. Polachek also looks at the reverse question, though not as extensively: does political conflict affect the level of trade? The author ingeniously exploits the several sets of data developed by political scientists, each inadequate in certain ways, and several analytical techniques (each also deficient in one way or another), to obtain relatively robust findings on the first of these two critical questions. (eds.)]

4.1 Background

Currently over 12 billion dollars of the U.S. government budget is devoted directly to international relations. When defense expenditures and foreign aid are added, this figure soars to over 275 billion dollars, roughly 30 cents of every government dollar spent.[1] Despite the importance of international relations, modern economists tend to concentrate only on narrow aspects such as the costs of war or more mathematically oriented depictions of arms races. International economists deal with economic trade concentrating on tariffs, embargoes, quotas, and even trade wars, but neglect the more subtle and perhaps more important aspects of trade, namely how trade relations and political interactions are related.[2]

Why the benign neglect is not apparent, but there are at least two reasons. First, from the theoretical perspective, it is conceptually difficult to embed such notions as war and peace or conflict and cooperation into the cost-benefit type analysis so innately part of the economic methodology. Second, from the empirical perspective there are simply very few readily available data sets quantifying international relations. Nevertheless, despite this, there is some precedence for economists to study international relations.

David Hume believed "that commercial restrictions deprive the nations of the earth of that free communication and exchange, which the author of the world had intended by giving them soils, climates, and geniuses, so different from each other."[3] In short, "free trade is the vital principle by which the nations of the earth are to become united in one harmonious whole."[4] Baron de Montesquieu[5] was more direct: "Peace is the natural effect of trade. Two nations who traffic with each other become reciprocally dependent; for if one has an interest in buying, the other has interest in selling; and thus their union is founded on their mutual necessities." In short, trade between two countries results in mutual economic benefits, and hence peace.

This paper entails and extends my earlier research[6] to study the principle that economic trade affects political conflict and cooperation.[7] Section 4.2 shows how a model can be derived using classic economic theory.   Section 4.3 provides empirical tests, and extensions are provided in Section 4.4. Section 4.5 concludes.

4.2 Theoretical Basis

The motivation of this paper is that one country can be both cooperative and hostile at the same time. For example, just as the US and Iraq exhibit hostility, these *same* countries, for example, the US as it relates to Canada or Iraq as it relates to Syria, cooperate in their political relations. If there are reasons to explain why the US has good relations with Canada but poor relations with Iraq, then these insights could be applied to understanding how cooperation evolves between countries.

This paper takes the perspective of a given country, called an actor. It assumes that each actor has a given factor endowment not easily changed at least in the short-run. Given factor endowments, trade patterns emerge and given these trade patterns, a country is assumed to behave rationally in its foreign relations decisions. Specifically, if conflict leads to a diminution of trade, then one implicit cost of conflict is the lost welfare gains associated with trade. In short, trade enhances cooperation and deters conflict.

Begin with the standard assumptions used by international trade theorists to describe an actor country. Let the convex set (q) containing possible output vectors q_i such that $\{q\} = U q_i$ for, $i=1, \ldots, n$ be the actor's production possibility frontier. In a two commodity world $\{q\}$ can be represented by the set $\{q_1, q_2\}$ where output levels of each commodity q_1 and q_2 can be defined by the implicit function $f(q_1, q_2) \leq K$. Graphically this is merely the region on or below the production possibility frontier (AB) defined in Figure 4.1.

Next, to obtain rational behavior, define a welfare function $W(C,Z)$ for the decision maker in the country, assumed to be derived from the preference sets of the entire population.[8] This function depicts welfare levels associated with each possible consumption basket $C \equiv (c_1, c_2, \ldots, c_m)$, but is also dependent on another variable, $Z \equiv (z_1, z_2, \ldots, z_k)$, representing conflict or cooperation toward any of k target countries, but which for now is assumed constant, and thus not part of the optimization process. The welfare function is assumed to be quasi concave such that $w(c,z) > 0$, $w_c > 0$, but that $w_{cc} < 0$. No assumptions are necessary of the effect of z on welfare levels, since z is for now constant. Iso-welfare curves w^i are depicted in Figure 4.1, with optimal consumption at $c_2 = (c_{12}, c_{22})$.

The very simplest bilateral trade model assumes trade to occur at a constant price ratio $m = p_{c_1}/p_{c_2}$. In the short run this yields an equilibrium $c_4 = (c_{14}, c_{24})$, while in the long run because of increased specialization in domestic production, $c_5 = (c_{15}, c_{25})$ is achieved, with trade equalling $c_5 - c_2$. The combined gain from both specialization in production and trade is $W_5 - W_2$.

Suppose, for example through quotas, embargoes, or even blockades, conflict implies the cessation or at least diminution of trade. Then the implicit cost of conflict is the lost gains from trade $(W_5 - W_2)$ associated with decreased trade.[9] Obviously, the greater the welfare loss the greater the costs of conflict, and hence the smaller the incentive for conflict. Even if conflict does not directly diminish trade, but instead leads to trade restrictions that ultimately affect the terms of trade, the same result applies. In this case less desirable terms of trade result (e.g., m' in Figure 4.1) implying a new equilibrium (C_3) and a lower welfare. Again the implicit price of conflict is $(W_5 - W_3)$, the lost welfare associated with diminished trade brought about by conflict.

S.W. Polachek

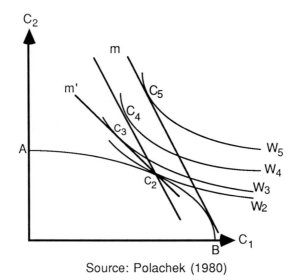

Source: Polachek (1980)

Figure 4.1: Effect of Conflict on Welfare

To see how these potential welfare losses lead to greater cooperation and less conflict, we introduce more structure. Domestic consumption of commodity i equals domestic production of q_i plus imports m_i minus exports x_i. As such

$$C_i \equiv q_i + m_i - x_i \qquad (4.1)$$

$$m_i \equiv \sum_{j=1}^{k} m_{ij} \qquad (4.2)$$

$$x_i \equiv \sum_{j=1}^{k} x_{ij} \qquad (4.3)$$

where j indexes import and export partners, with k being the number of countries. Next define $Z \equiv [z_1, z_2,..., z_s,..., z_k]$ to represent conflict (from the actor) to any target country j. The actor's welfare function as we have defined it is

$$W \equiv w(C, Z) \equiv w([q_i + \sum_j m_{ij} + \sum_j x_{ij}], [z_j]) \qquad (4.4)$$

where the bracketed terms are the commodity and conflict vectors just defined. Including C_i within the welfare function is obvious. Higher levels of consumption yield greater welfare levels. Including Z within the welfare function is unnecessary.

However, including Z merely allows for the possibility of non-economic motivations for conflict or cooperation.

Our purpose is to derive a relationship of the effect of economic trade on political conflict. As such we must identify optimal conflict/cooperation levels *given current* consumption and trade patterns.

Trade can be represented as the value of exports of each commodity (i) to country (j) minus the value of imports. If no balance of payments problems exist then

$$\sum_{i}^{m}\sum_{j}^{k} x_{ij}P_{xij} - \sum_{i}^{m}\sum_{j}^{k} m_{ij}P_{mij} = 0 \tag{4.5}$$

where,

$\quad$ $P_{xij} \equiv$ unit export price charged to country j for commodity i.

$\quad$ $P_{mij} \equiv$ unit import charged by country j for commodity i.

Prices are determined in the international market, but as indicated contain at least a component assumed to be dependent on dyadic conflict. Thus

$$P_{xij} = f(z_j) \tag{4.6}$$

$$P_{mij} = g(z_j) \tag{4.7}$$

such that hostility raises the price that must be paid for imports and lowers the prices at which exports can be sold.

$$\partial P_{mij}/\partial z_j = P'_{mij} = g' > 0 \tag{4.8}$$

$$\partial P_{xij}/\partial z_j = P'_{xij} = f' < 0 \tag{4.9}$$

If conflict such as through embargoes or boycotts leads to the complete cessation of trade then $f' = -\infty$ and $g' = \infty$, though as will be indicated the net welfare loss associated with lost trade need not be great if alternative trade avenues exist.

Given this structure as well as predetermined trade, rational behavior on the part of a country's decision makers implies choosing optimal levels of Z that maximizes welfare level (4.4) subject to (4.1) through (4.3) and (4.5) through (4.9). This implies maximizing the following Lagrangian

$$\text{Max } L = W[(q_i + \sum_i m_{ij} + \sum_j x_{ij}), z_j] + \lambda[\sum_i\sum_j x_{ij}P_{xij}(z_j) - \sum_i\sum_j m_{ij}P_{mij}(z_j)] \tag{4.10}$$

First order optimality conditions for optimal conflict requires

$$\partial w/\partial z_j + \lambda[\sum_i x_{ij} (\partial P_{xij}(z_j)/\partial z_j) - \sum_i m_{ij}(\partial P_{mij}(z_j)/\partial z_j)] = 0 \quad (4.11)$$

$$\partial w/\partial \lambda = \sum_i \sum_j x_{ij} P_{xij}(z_j) - \sum_i \sum_j m_{ij} P_{mij}(z_j) = 0 \quad (4.12)$$

Equation (4.12) is merely the balance of payments constraint. Equation (4.11) describes the mechanism by which a country decides on the amount of belligerence. Since the bracketed term is the implicit price of receiving less money for exports while at the same time having to pay more for imports, it represents the net cost associated with extra hostility (MC). This term can be represented graphically (Figure 4.2) as an upward sloping curve[10] whose position depends on m and x levels. In equilibrium, the marginal cost of hostility must just balance the

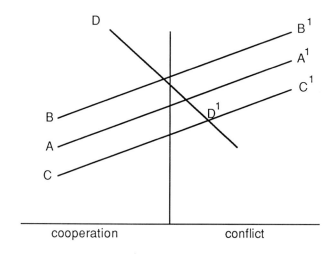

cooperation   conflict

Source: Polachek (1980)

Figure 4.2: Determination of Optimal Conflict/Cooperation

welfare benefit of added hostility (dw/dz_j) so that the intersection of the (dw/dz_j) curve and the MC curve depicts equilibrium conflict/cooperation. Note that the equilibrium conflict/cooperation levels still arise even if hostility or cooperation implies no welfare gain (dw/dz_j=0). In this case, optimal conflict is based purely on economic grounds at the point where the MC curve intersects the horizontal axis. If imports or exports are increased, the MC shifts up, thereby implying lower levels of conflict. Thus,

Proposition <u>One</u>: The greater an actor country's level of trade with a target, the smaller the amount of actor to target conflict.

If increases in foreign debt are not permitted (especially in the long-run), conflict induces a change in optimal imports and exports. The more unfavorable the relative price of trade induced by conflict, the more greatly exports are forced to increase and imports decrease. The exact change in imports and exports can be derived from the maximization of (4.4) with respect to x and m. Eliminating subscripts,

$$(\partial w/\partial c)(\partial c/\partial x) + \lambda P_x(z_j) = 0 \qquad\qquad (4.13)$$

$$(\partial w/\partial c)(\partial c/\partial m) + \lambda P_m(z_j) = 0 \qquad\qquad (4.14)$$

imply demand and supply curves for imports and exports from which the implicit welfare losses associated with changed foreign trade can be computed. From the above one can show that welfare losses are largest, the more inelastic the import and exports demand and supply curves. Hence,

Proposition <u>Two</u>: The more inelastic (elastic) an actor country's import and export demand and supply to a target country, the smaller (larger) the amount of actor to target conflict.

Other propositions follow as well. However, at this point, insufficient data exist for appropriate statistical tests. As such this paper concentrates solely on these two propositions.

The remainder of the paper divides the tests for these hypotheses into two parts: Part 4.3 concentrates purely on the conflict trade relationship. Part 4.4 augments the empirical work to include information on trade elasticities.

4.3 Proposition One: The Trade Conflict Relationship

Multivariate statistical analysis relating conflict and trade holding constant other variables are used. First, cross-sectional data are employed to test the relationship between conflict and trade. Second, in order to corroborate these results, various conflict measures are used. Third, to test whether the conflict/trade relationship holds over time, a case study of U.S./Soviet Union and of U.S./Warsaw Pact relations is examined. Finally, to ascertain causality, both cross-sectional simultaneous equations models and time-series Granger causality tests are performed. Before getting into the statistical analysis, a discussion of the data is in order.

4.3.1 Data

Three data sets are described containing information on (1) dyadic conflict, (2) dyadic trade, and (3) country attributes. Reasons for choosing these data sets are given, but a description of the political data is emphasized since they are more alien to economists.

(1) Political Interactions Data. There are many philosophical problems in measuring political interactions. What hostility and cooperation constitute, as well as how and to whom such activities are vented must be defined in the data.

Current measures, such as defense expenditures, war data with resulting causality estimates, as well as United Nations voting records do not fit the bill. For example, defense expenditures indicate general levels of hostilities of a country, yet defense expenditure need not reflect hostility at all. Such expenditures could be viewed as a warning, therefore serving as a deterrent toward other nations. Alternatively, the defense expenditures can be taken as a measure of the repression of domestic unrest. Even if defense expenditures constituted a measure of conflict, such expenditures need not yield the crucial dyadic information concerning to whom hostilities are vented. In addition, the extent and type of conflict would be camouflaged.

War data are better in that they yield information on a particular conflict as well as establish the involved nation states. The problem, however, is that wars are a particularly intensive and relatively rare form of interaction. The number of dead or wounded varies with technology as well as country size. Similarly war data, as well as the defense expenditure data just eluded to, deal only with hostility and neglect instances of cooperation as well as acts less hostile than war. Further, UN general assembly voting data also are ruled out because such information measures political attitudes, and need not reflect actual conflict between two countries.

Because of these deficiencies, events data, which only recently became available, are adopted. Events data comprise dyadic (bilateral) interactions reported in newspapers.[11] Although there are now several such data sets, we concentrate on the Azar conflict and peace data bank (COBDAB), though comparisons are made with another events data bank compiled by McCleland (the WEISS data). COBDAB is an extensive longitudinal collection of about one million daily events reported from forty-seven newspaper sources between 1948 and 1978.[12] These events are coded on a 15 point scale representing different kinds of conflict and cooperation. The annual frequency of events in each category represents the amount of each type dyadic interaction contributable to an actor/target dyad. Currently over 105 countries and hence about 11 thousand possible dyadic interaction measures are included for each year.

Events data are not free of bias. The problem with events data is that they comprise interactions reported only in newspapers. Many secret treaties and negotiations, as well as multi-country interactions not reported in newspapers are obviously omitted. In addition, newspapers often find certain country pairs more newsworthy so that extreme selectivity biases can exist.

The benefit of events data is that they measure cooperation as well as hostility. In addition, actor and target countries can easily be identified. Precise measures of amounts of different kinds of conflict can be ascertained, just by using the 15 point scale representing different kinds of conflict and cooperation contained in the data. In addition, selectivity issues can be controlled by looking at the *relative* frequency of conflict compared to the total reported frequency of dyadic political interactions. This way, under or over reporting can be avoided by concentrating not on the absolute frequency of reported events, but instead on the relative amount of conflict, the logic being that reporting biases are more related to the specific country than the type of event. It is presumed that any tastes by newspapers for reporting conflict more readily than cooperation would not be nation-specific so that comparisons of - one country pair's relative conflict compared to another would also not be biased. Several such measures were chosen. One is the net frequency of conflict (NETF) defined as the frequency of conflictual events (those in category 9 to 15) minus the frequency of cooperative events (those in category 1 to 7). Here, a negative value of NETF implies that more events fall into categories 1 to 7 than 9 to 15, hence that cooperative interaction exists. A positive value implies that the preponderance of events fall into categories 9 to 15 so that on balance there exists a conflictual relationship.[13]

(2) Economic Trade. Ideally dyadic commodity by commodity trade flows are needed. Unfortunately, such data was not available on an annual basis in each year for which conflict data exist.[14] On the other hand, aggregate import and export data collected on a country by country directional basis are available. These data compiled from the International Monetary of Fund series of annual volumes under the heading "Directions of Trade" were used. The trade data are measured in U.S. dollars.

(3) Attribute Data. Standardizing variables holding constant factors relating to country levels of development that may exogenously affect trade and conflict are included. Several international data sets were merged for this purpose. The

largest, Banks' (1973) Cross-National Time-Series Data Archive,[15] was used to select country attributes for each year. Defense expenditure data (compiled mostly from UN Statistical Yearbook by Gillespie and Zinnes)[16] to standardize for general levels of country militancy were included, as were other data listed in Table 4.1.

TABLE 4.1

Trade - Attribute Data Set Variable List

Variable Name	Source	Units	Definition
ACTOR	COPDAB		COPDAB Actor Code
YEAR		48-77	
XTOT	DOT	$US x 1,000,000	Total Exports
MTOT	DOT	$US x 1,000,000	Total Imports
XYPCT	DOT	%	% of Yearly World Exports
MYPCT	DOT	%	% of Yearly World Imports
CPI	IFS	1975 = 100	Consumer Price Index
GDP	IFS	Billions of Local Currency	Gross Domestic Product
GNP	IFS	Billions of Local Currency	Gross National Product
GDPUSA	IFS	Billions of U.S. Dollars	US GDP
GNPUSA	IFS	Billions of U.S. Dollars	US GNP
POP*	IFS	x 1,000,000	Population
MAR	IFS	$US per Local Currency	End of Year Market Exchange Rate
MILEXP	E/G	$US x 1,000,000	Military Expenditures
ECONS	BANKS/UNS	Tons Coal x 1000	Energy Consumption
EPROD	BANKS/UNS	Tons Coal x 1000	Energy Production
INDPCT*	BANKS/UNY	%	% GDP Originating in Industry
NATINC	BANKS/UNY	$US	National Income Per Capita
PRIM	BANKS/UNS	x 1000	Primary School Enrollment
SEC	BANKS/UNS	x 1000	Secondary School Enrollment
UNIV	BANKS/UNS	x 1000	University Enrollment
NEWS*	BANKS/UNS	x .0001	Newspaper Circulation Per Capita
PHYS	BANKS/UNS	x .000,0001	Physicians Per Capita
FERT	UNS	Births per 1000	Fertility
PQLI*	ODC	0 through 100	Physical Quality of Life Index
IMORT*	UND	Deaths per 1000 births	Infant Mortality Rate
LEXP*	UND	Years	Life Expectancy
PCT 15	UND	%	% of Population Under 15
PCT 64	UND	%	% of Population Over 64
EDEXP	WMSE	Dollars	Educational Expenditure Per Capita
PCTURB	UND/PRB	%	% of Population in Urban Areas
LIT*	BANKS/UND	%	% Literate in the Population
PCTED	UNS	%	% Govt. Expenditures for Education
CPIPCT	IPS	%	% Change in CPI

*interpolated version of this variable also included

Sources: COPDAB: COPDAB actor coding scheme; DOT: Directions of Trade; IFS: International Financial Statistics; Z/G: Zinnes and Gillespie Military Expenditures Data; BANKS/UNS: Banks Data Set and UN Statistical Yearbooks; BANKS/UNY: Banks Data Set and Yearbook of National Account Statistics; UNS: UN Statistical Yearbook; ODC: Index Developed by Overseas Development Council; UND: UN Demographic Yearbook; WMSE: World Military and Social Expenditures.

4.3.2 Cross-Sectional Analysis

(1) Cross-Sectional Regressional Analysis of the Trade-Conflict Relationship.

The general specification is given by equations (4.15) and (4.16) below.

$$CONF_{ij} = \alpha_0 + \alpha_1 x_{ij} + \alpha_2 x_{ij}^2 + \alpha_3 A_i + \alpha_4 A_j + \alpha_5 t + \varepsilon_{ij} \tag{4.15}$$

$$CONF_{ij} = \alpha'_0 + \alpha'_1 m_{ij} + \alpha'_2 m_{ij}^2 + \alpha'_3 A_i + \alpha'_4 A_j + \alpha'_5 t + \varepsilon'_{ij} \tag{4.16}$$

where:
   $CONF_{ij} \equiv$ relative conflict of actor country i toward target country j.
   $x_{ij} \equiv$ exports of actor country i to target country j (the squared X_{ij} term is
         introduced to test for nonlinearity).
   $m_{ij} \equiv$ imports of actor country i to target country j (the squared m_{ij} term is
         introduced to test for nonlinearity).
   $A_i \equiv$ a vector of actor country attributes.
   $A_j \equiv$ a vector of target country attributes.
   $t \equiv$ a time trend.
   $\varepsilon_{ij} \equiv$ a random error term assumed to be normally distributed with zero mean.

   Negative coefficients for α_1 and α'_1 would imply thatcountries with a greater
trade dependence would engage in lessrelative conflict. Coefficients α_3, α_4, α'_3 and
α'_4 reflect theimpact of country attributes on conflict can be thought of as other
aspects of the price vector for conflict. The intercept terms reflect levels of conflict
that would result independently of attributes or trade. For the purposes of this
paper, we present only the coefficients for α_0, α'_0, α_1, α'_1, α_2, α'_2, α_5, α'_5 and treat the
attributes as exogenous identification variables.
   A consistent pattern appears (Table 4.2) for these coefficients. Independent of
the functional form, whether bivariate or multivariate, linear or hyperbolic, in each
year a negative and statistically significant relationship emerges: those dyads
engaged in the most trade have the lease conflict even when adjusting for country
attributes. The results hold on an annual basis, as well as for pooled cross-
sectional regressions.[17]
   The empirical significance of this inverse relationship between conflict and
trade can be assessed by computing the elasticity of conflict with respect to trade.
Based on the pooled cross-sectional regressions (last column), the elasticities
indicate that a one percent increase in trade is associated with a decrease in con-

TABLE 4.2

Impact of Trade on Conflict by Year (t-values in parentheses)[3]

Specification (1)	Adjust for Country Attributes?	Independent Variable[2]	1958	1961	1964	1967	1958-67 Pooled	1948-78 Pooled	Elasticity
(1)	no	intercept	-1.2980 (4.0)	-.3831 (1.1)	-1.5750 (9.0)	-1.6016 (4.7)	-1.3241 (13.7)		
		x	-.0051 (4.7)	-.0074 (7.7)	-0.0019 (4.8)	-.0020 (3.7)	-0.0028 (13.3)		.192[5]
(2)	no	intercept	-1.2946 (4.0)	-.4001 (1.2)	-1.5741 (9.0)	-1.6975 (4.7)	-1.3341 (13.8)		
		M	-0.0052 (4.8)	-.0072 (7.4)	-0.0019 (4.9)	-0.0019 (3.5)	-0.0027 (12.8)		.185[5]
(3)	yes	intercept	10.8405 (1.6)	11.7426 (1.6)	-1.3963 (0.8)	-4.6669 (1.2)	-0.0984 (0.1)	1.6101 (0.3)	
		x	-0.0022 (2.2)	-.0056 (4.3)	-0.0024 (5.2)	-0.0048 (5.6)	-0.0023 (9.8)	-.0359 (22.3)	.152[5] .161[6]
		x^2						1.511×10^{-6} (13.9)	
		time trend						-3.558 (4.8)	
(4)	yes	intercept	10.8327 (1.6)	11.7499 (1.6)	-1.3997 (0.8)	-4.7328 (1.2)	-0.1119 (0.1)	2.1227 (.04)	
		M	-0.0023 (2.3)	-.0056 (4.3)	-0.0025 (5.5)	-0.0046 (5.4)	-0.0023 (9.9)	-0.0316 (21.2)	.152[5] .149[6]
		M^2						1.18×10^{-6} (13.3)	
		time trend						-.3672 (5.0)	
Number of Country Pairs (Dyads) in sample			407	409	457	460	4252	48,340	

[1] The specifications refer to the following regressions:

    (1) $NETF_{ij} = \alpha_0 + \alpha_1 x_{ij} + \varepsilon$

    (2) $NETF_{ij} = \beta_0 + \beta_1 m_{ij} + \varepsilon$

    (3) $NETF_{ij} = \alpha_0 + \alpha_1 x_{ij} + \alpha_2 A_1 + \alpha_3 A_j + \varepsilon$

    (4) $NETF_{ij} = \beta_0 + \beta_1 m_{ij} + \beta_2 A_i + \beta_j A_j + \varepsilon$

[2] Intercepts are the coefficients α_0 and β_0 of the regressions. The trade coefficients correspond to the coefficients in equations (4.15) and (4.16).

[3] A t-value exceeding 1.96 implies statistical significance at the 0.05 level.

[4] The percentage of impact on conflict given a one percent change in trade. Computed as:

        Elasticity= $(\partial NETF/\partial x)(x/NETF)$ and *Elasticity*= $(\partial NETF/\partial m)(m/NETF)$

[5] Based on Pooled 1958-67 data.

[6] Based on Pooled 1948-78 data.

flict (increase in cooperation) by between 0.15 to 0.19 percent. Thus doubling trade between two countries imply that on average there would be a 15 to 19 percent decline in the relative frequency of conflict.

(2) <u>Corroborative Evidence.</u> One can easily be skeptical of inferences drawn from one unique data set. One should not rely on the COPDAB data alone. Other measures of conflict are possible though one must be careful despite inherent definitional problems. For this reason corroborative evidence was obtained using other events data as well as other type conflict measures. I do so not because the other measures are intrinsically better, but rather as alternatives: If the inverse correlation between trade and conflict prevails, then despite potential measurement biases, rejecting the plausibility of the hypothesized relationship would be more difficult. For this reason I turn first to an alternative events data set, and second to defense expenditures, an alternative conflict measure. In addition published work which yield consistent results is examined.

TABLE 4.3

Corroborative Evidence

Conflict Regressions Disaggregated by Type of Interaction
WEIS DATE (1966-1967) (t-values in parentheses)

scale	type	number of events	intercept	coefficients	elasticity
1	yield	22	3.035 (0.9)	-.00006 (-1.5)	-.27
2	comment	120	10.251 (1.4)	-.00002 (-0.3)	-.017
3	consult	528	11.919 (0.8)	.000028 (1.7)	.005
4	approve	86	10.479 (2.0)	.00012 (2.1)	.139
5	promise	46	1.006 (0.3)	.000017 (0.4)	.037
6	grant	79	1.715 (0.4)	-.00014 (-2.6)	-.177
7	reward	80	1.225 (0.2)	.0001 (1.5)	.125
8	agree	247	7.261 (0.6)	-.00006 (-0.4)	-.024
9	request	81	2.144 (0.4)	-.00001 (-0.2)	-.012
10	propose	97	1.526 (0.2)	-.0001 (-1.4)	-.103
11	reject	89	-6.674 (-0.9)	-.00015 (-1.7)	-.168
12	accuse	284	-2.754 (0.1)	-.00070 (-2.2)	-.246
13	protest	31	-0.429 (-0.1)	-.000006 (-0.2)	-.019
14	deny	31	0.610 (0.1)	-.0001 (-2.2)	-.322
15	demand	17	-0.332 (-0.1)	-.00006 (-2.3)	-.352
16	warn	33	1.179 (0.3)	-.0001 (-2.8)	-.302
17	threaten	13	2.648 (1.6)	-.00003 (-1.4)	-.231
18	demonstrate	40	3.293 (1.0)	.000001 (0.0)	.002
19	reduce relations (as negative sanction)	64	-9.056 (-2.0)	-.00003 (-0.6)	-.046
20	expel	17	2.867 (1.3)	-.00004 (-1.4)	-.234
21	seize	30	-0.548 (-0.2)	-.00005 (-1.3)	-.166
22	force	22	-0.270 (-0.1)	-.00001 (-.6)	-.045
NCONW			-62.897 (-1.5)	-.001 (-2.9)	-.136
NETF (AZAR DATA)			-61.342 (-0.8)	-.002 (-2.7)	-.145

The WEISS data is an event data set compiled using only events reported in the *New York Times*. As such it is not as comprehensive as COPDAB, though obviously similarities exist. One test of the validity of COPDAB would be to perform similar type regression analysis with WEISS data to ascertain whether the COPDAB results can be replicated. Since WEISS data for 1966 and 1967 were available to me, I chose then to replicate our previous regressions for those dyads and years in common for both data sets (Table 4.3).

The results are upheld. Again there is a negative correlation that is surprisingly similar for both data sets. Indeed the elasticity for each is approximately -.15 which is the same result obtained for the entire pooled COPDAB data. Again both elasticities are strongly significant according to the usual statistical levels.[18]

In some studies defense expenditures are assumed indicative of potential conflictive behavior. While skeptics question such a measure on various grounds, there is precedence in its use.[19] For this reason I adopt the measure merely to test whether it is consistent with events data.

One obvious problem with defense expenditure measures is the lack of directionality regarding identification of target nations. Actors may have high defense expenditures, but it is impossible to determine an appropriate target. For this reason we are forced to perform statistical analysis devoid of directionality. Thus aggregate defense expenditures are used on a country basis, and correlated with trade measures. The results are reported for 30 countries over a ten year period (Table 4.4).[20] Again there is a strong negative relationship between trade and defense expenditures, the pseudo conflict measure of about -15, yielding an elasticity of -.31, implying that a doubling of trade leads to a 31% decline in defense expenditures, holding GNP and other attributes constant. Here it is interesting to note that the most important predictor of defense expenditure is GNP but that higher levels of education holding constant GNP decreases defense expenditures.

There is other corroborative evidence of the trade-conflict relationship, as well. For example, in his classic study, Lewis Richardson[21] used trade as a measure of cooperation. He presents graphical evidence that in the post-depression era of the 1930's trade dramatically diminished perhaps leading to some of the conflictive events preceding World War II.

UN voting data has also been used as a measure of cooperation between countries. Voting patterns in accord with another country is taken to reflect political compatibility and cooperation. As already mentioned, much criticisms exist on the capability of voting data to reflect conflict or cooperation. Nevertheless in lieu of better data some have looked at UN voting patterns. Neil Richardson, for example[22] looks at the relationship between voting and what he calls "dependence," namely the sum of exports foreign investment as well as foreign aid. He, too, finds a correlation implying that those country pairs with the greatest economic dependence are the ones with the most similar voting records. (see his Figure 8, p. 133).

TABLE 4.4

Dependent Variable Defense Expenditure (N=204)

	(1)	(2)
INTERCEPT	597.86 (1.5)	504.06 (1.27)
EXPORTS	-15.88 (-4.3)	
IMPORTS	-14.51 (-4.4)	
SIZE (square miles)	0.21 (1.3)	0.28 (1.8)
SECONDARY SCHOOL ENROLLMENT	-3.73 (-3.3)	-2.98 (2.4)
GNP	1.03×10^{-4} (30.5)	0.99×10^{-4} (36.3)
R^2	0.947	0.947

(3) <u>Cross-Sectional Causality: The Trade-Conflict Relationship With Trade Treated Endogenously.</u> The coefficients presented thus far do not indicate the direction of causality. Thus from the tables one cannot ascertain whether trade diminishes conflict, or whether the reverse is true: conflict reduces trade. Although this paper argues that both are true, this distinction is important for policy purposes. If trade is only a response to pre-existing conflict levels, then no viable policy implications for the reduction of conflict would result from increased trade. Thus tests for causality are important.

To test for causality one should view the trade-conflict relationship as a simultaneous set of equations. In one equation conflict affects trade, while in the other trade affects conflict. In effect both trade and conflict are treated endogenously while country attribute data are used as exogenous factors for identification. To test this endogeneity, two-stage and three-stage least-squares are used.

S.W. Polachek

TABLE 4.5

The Simultaneous Determination of Trade and Conflict

Two-Stage Least-Squares
(t-values in parentheses)

Specification	Adjustments for Country Attributes	Variable	Intercept	Coefficient	Elasticity
(3)	Yes	X	-1.358 (-5.5)	-.0057 (-6.68)	.363
(4)	Yes	M	-1.310 (-5.4)	-.0049 (-5.8)	.314

Three-Stage Least-Squares
(t values in parentheses)

Dependent Variable:		Net Conflict	Exports	Elasticity
Independent Variables				
Constant		-.77 (-4.3)	-119.02 (-3.4)	
Exports		-.0045 (-5.8)		.29
Conflict		1.83 (0.3)		-.03
Defense Expenditures	Actor	-.00018 (-5.6)		
	Target	-.00025 (-8.0)		
Population Density	Actor	-.0015 (-3.3)		
	Target	-.0016 (-3.5)		
GNP	Actor	1×10^{-8} (3.0)	3.3×10^{-7} (3.7)	
	Target	2×10^{-8} (7.3)	1.2×10^{-7} (1.7)	
GDP/GNP	Actor		0.73 (1.5)	
	Target		0.92 (1.6)	
Highway Vehicles per capita	Actor		1174.5 (7.4)	
	Target		1002.2 (7.1)	
Secondary School Enrollments	Actor		0.048 (1.3)	
	Target		0.076 (2.1)	
Electrical Production per capita	Actor		-6.68 (-.7)	
	Target		0.81 (-.1)	
Annual Population Growth	Actor		-.066 (-1.2)	
	Target		-.138 (-2.6)	

The hypothesized causality is as predicted (Table 4.5). An even stronger, more negative coefficient (-.0057 versus -.0028) is obtained. Thus, even when accounting for simultaneity, the causality from trade to conflict remains. Increases in trade diminish conflict such that a doubling of trade would reduce conflict by over 30%. When the entire two equation system is estimated simultaneously with three stage least- squares, there is no evidence that conflict affects trade.[23] Thus we are confident that trade acts as a barrier to conflict, while at the same time enhancing an actor's incentive for cooperation.

Despite these results, a cross-sectional determination of causality is opened to criticism. Often, the strength of the particular relationships depend crucially on exogenous variables. As is often the case, little theory exists as to which exogenous variables are most appropriate. Often parametric estimates prove not to be robust with changes in these variables. For this reason many have undertaken to analyze causality in a time-series rather than a cross-sectional, framework. We adopt such an approach by looking in detail at time-series data.

4.3.3 Time-Series Analysis

Time-Series data are important for two reasons. First to establish whether or not the cross-sectional results can be generalized from an analysis across many countries at a point in time to the behavior of a single country over time. Whereas in cross-sectional analysis, countries with the most trade exhibited the least conflict, it is also essential to know whether changes of a given country's trade is at all related to changes in political cooperation and hostility. Second, issues of causality can perhaps better be disentangled with time-series data. If changes in trade levels are associated with corresponding changes in political behavior, then causality can be established on the basis of leads and lags in the time series data.

(1) A Case Study: U.S./Warsaw Pact Interactions Because the COPDAB data have been collected over a long time period, time series tests of the hypothesis can be performed by linking the panel aspects of the COPDAB data to corresponding trade variables. To illustrate, the U.S. and Soviet Union between 1967 and 1979 were taken as a case study. These countries during this time period are important because of the volatility in US-Soviet relations during three years. Recall the easing of US-Soviet hostilities in the detente period of the late sixties and early seventies, and the abrupt shift that began to take place in the mid-1970s.

Time series plots of US-Warsaw Pact and US-Soviet Union Trade and Conflict from 1967 through 1978 are to be analyzed in a later manuscript. (These plots are available upon request from the author). The trade measures, consisting of the sum of imports and exports, are given in real quarterly dollars. The conflict measures are intensity-weighted sums of conflictual events, aggregated quarterly from the COPDAB data. (Relative conflict measures are not needed in time series analysis because selectivity issues are reported to occur for differential reporting by nation and not by time.) The trends apparent are in accord with prediction. Conflict declines as trade rises in the 1971-1972 period, the levels off until late 1975 as trade remains fairly constant. Both conflict measures show fairly strong inverse correlations with trade before 1976. This is particularly apparent for Warsaw pact conflict directed at the US, which is substantially higher than US conflict directed at the Pact before mid-1968. There, inverse relationships support the contention that greater levels of trade are associated with lower levels of conflict.

The inverse trade/conflict relationship becomes more apparent when the trade and conflict data are plotted directly with Warsaw Pact conflict directed at the US plotted on one axis and US-Warsaw Pact trade on the other. For the 1967-1975 data the inverse relationship between conflict and trade is clear. In addition, it is evident that the relationship is probably hyperbolic.

(2) Time Series Causality.[25] Time-Series data enable one to compute Granger type causality tests. The logic is straightforward. With time-series data one can ascertain whether trade levels in one period affect future conflict levels, and vice versa. Put simply, increases in explanatory power induced by lagged trade values in a regression of conflict as a function of trade would be indicative of causality running from trade to conflict. With T representing Trade and Z representing conflict, Granger causality exists if past values of T affect present values of Z. The Granger method thus involves a test of the joint hypothesis that $c_{-i} = 0$ for $i = 1$ to j, where c_{-i} is the coefficient of T lagged i periods in the following equation:

$$Z = c_0 + at + bT + (c_{-1}T_{-1} + ... + c_{-j}T_{-j}) + (d_{-1}Z_{-1} + ... + d_{-j}Z_{-j}) \qquad (4.17)$$

where c_0 is the constant term, t is the time trend, T_{-i} and Z_{-i} are the twice lagged values of T and Z, and c_i, and d_i are coefficients.

The null hypothesis that $c_{-i} = 0$ for $i = 1$ to j implies that the past values of trade do not predict (and hence "cause") current conflict. This hypothesis can be tested with Fischer's F-Test. Rejection of this hypothesis implies that some past value of T significantly affects present Z. Thus, the condition for Granger causality to hold is rejection of the null hypothesis.[26] By the same token one can also test the reverse, that is whether past conflict "causes" current trade by re-specifying equation 4.17 as follows:

$$T = T_0 + a' + b'Z + (c'_{-1}T_{-1} + ... + c'_{-j}T_{-j}) + (d'_{-1}Z_{-1} + ... + d'_{-j}Z_{-j}) \qquad (4.18)$$

In this case, rejection of the null hypothesis that $d'_{-i} = 0$ for $i = 1$ to j implies that past conflict affects current trade.

Table 4.6 contains probability values for Granger F-tests of the null hypotheses that trade does not cause conflict (Column 1) and that conflict does not cause trade (Column 2) in the 1967-1978 time period. In Table 4.6 probability values of less than .05 indicate rejection of the null hypothesis, thereby implying the existence of Granger causality. High values indicate no causalities. The "LAGS" column indicates the number of quarters over which Granger causality is tested.

In Column 1, the null hypothesis that lagged values of trade do not significantly affect present conflict as rejected for the first six lag periods. In Column 2, the hypothesis that lagged conflict does not affect present trade is rejected only in lag periods for, 5 and 6. These results are consistent with trade affecting political interactions.

These results can be viewed as strengthening our previous findings based on a contemporaneous trade conflict relationship. Specifically one can improve on the ability of contemporaneous trade to predict conflict by incorporating lagged trade values. In other words, the underlying relationship between trade and conflict is not strictly contemporaneous, but corresponds to distributed lagged framework. Further work on the appropriate lagged structure is obviously necessary.

TABLE 4.6

Probability Values for the Granger Causality Test, 1867-1978 US/WARSAW PACT Data

LAGS	TRADE CONFLICT	CONFLICT TRADE
1	.0009	.1046
2	10018	.3165
3	.0004	.1394
4	.0054	.0110
5	.0071	.0201
6	.0126	.0240
7	.0874	.0661
8	.0515	.0604
9	.1917	.1486
10	.2739	.2300

NOTE: column 1 gives probability values for tests of the hypothesis that trade does not cause conflict (in Granger's sense). Column 2 tests the converse hypothesis that conflict does not cause trade. Low probability values (e.g., less than .05) indicate that the hypothesis is rejected; high values indicate acceptance. Lag periods indicate the number of quarters over which Granger causality is tested (j in equation 4). Examination of Durbin-Watson statistics indicated that autocorrelation was not significant at the .05 level in any of these equations.

Source: M. Gasiorowski and S. Polachek, "East-West Trade and Linkages in the Era of Detents," *J. Conflict Resolution* (1982).

4.4 Proposition Two: The Trade Conflict Relationship Augmented By Trade Elasticities[27]

Thus far the empirical work concentrated on how trading countries exhibit less conflict and more cooperation than dyads with little trade. Yet theory indicates that it is not trade alone, but "gains from trade" that are relevant to the trade-conflict relationship. As was stated, if conflict leads directly to a cessation of trade, then one implicit cost of conflict is the lost gains from trade.[28] The higher the gains from trade, the higher the implicit costs of conflict, and the greater the incentives for cooperation.

So far this paper tested the theory only in its most primitive form by concentrating solely on the relationship between conflict and trade levels, while ignoring explicit measures of welfare gains. Though trade levels and welfare gains are obviously related, the correlation is by no means perfect, so that omitting welfare gains can bias the trade-conflict estimates. On the other hand, as shall be shortly illustrated, including welfare gains estimates enables a more substantial test of the model's validity.

Incorporating welfare gains is difficult, as there are no current data directly measuring gains from trade. One must obtain them implicitly as consumer and producer surpluses computed as the area under import-demand and over export-supply curves. The more inelastic the import-demand and export-supply curves the greater the levels of consumer and producer surplus. The greater these surpluses the smaller the incidence of conflict, holding trade levels constant. For this reason inelastic import-demand and export-supply curves should serve to decrease conflict just as does greater trade. This being the case, less conflict and more cooperation should be observed for trading partners exhibiting relatively small import demand and export supply curves. While this result may appear obvious, to our knowledge there are no empirical test of this proposition. Yet such a test is important because verification of this latter result adds credence to our proposed dyadic conflict model.

To best test the conflict-trade model, commodity specific supply and demand elasticities are needed for each country pair. Despite the importance of these estimates, no such data have been computed on a regular systematic basis. This leaves two options: (a) to compute elasticities or (b) to piece together whatever elasticities have already been compiled. Both options are taken in turn. Nevertheless, simplification is still necessary because of remaining data limitations. First the ensuing analysis concentrates solely on demand elasticities, and ignores supply curves. Second, only aggregate demand curves are considered, thereby omitting consideration of specific commodities. Finally there are limitations concerning the number of countries and country pairs that are considered.

4.4.1 Import Demand From the Rest of the World and the Trade/Conflict Relationship

Data limitations force certain simplifications: First, aggregate import demand curves are used rather than commodity specific demand elasticities. Second, an actor's demand from the rest of the world is used rather than dealing with dyadic bilateral demand, though this latter simplification will be eliminated in the next section when we incorporate elasticities computed by Jaime Marques.[29]

A country's import demand from the rest of the world can be specified as

$$\log(m/MUV)_{it} = \alpha_{i0} + \alpha_{i1}\log(MUV/CPI)_{it} + \alpha_{i2}\log(GDP/CPI)_{it} + \varepsilon_{it} \qquad (4.19)$$

where m is imports (in millions of US dollars); MUV is the import unit value index; and i and t are country and time subscripts ranging from 1 to N and 1 to T respectively; CPI is the consumer price index; GDP is gross domestic product (in local currency units), and ε_{it} is an error term.

The dependent variable (m/MUV) is import value computed as import expenditures divided by an index of import prices. The independent variables are real import prices (MUV/CPI), and a national income deflated by the consumer price index (GDP/CPI). The CPI was used instead of more appropriate measures, such as the GDP deflator because complete series were available for a greater number of countries when using this measure. The equation is estimated log-log form so as to directly obtain elasticity estimates. Price and income elasticities are α_{i1} and α_{i2} respectively. These equations are estimated using yearly time series data for 1963-1977.[30] Import expenditures and GDP data are from the International Monetary Fund's *International Financial Statistics* for various years. Import consumer price data are obtained from the *Supplement on Price Statistics,* 1981. Adjustments for autocorrelation were made using the Corchorane-Orcutt and Prais-Winsten methods.[31] To check the plausibility of these estimates alternative import price elasticities for various countries with available data were examined.[32] The correlation coefficient between both is .29 thereby least partially corroborating the elasticity estimates.

Lower import demand elasticities imply greater levels of consumer surplus and hence greater welfare gains from trade. Similarly greater quantities of imports holding the import demand elasticity constant also implies greater consumer surplus, and hence a larger welfare gain from trade. Consequently, importing countries with the most inelastic import demand should exhibit the least amounts of hostility. This is the proposition that is now tested.

Regressions were run looking at the relationship between import demand elasticities, levels of trade, country attributes, and a measure or relative conflict (Table 4.7). Unlike the paper's previous sections since bilateral trade elasticities were not computed, countries are used as the basic data points rather than dyads. The number of observations falls considerably to approximately 50 countries for which import demand elasticities were computed and for which the trade and attribute data were available. Still the results are strong. Despite drastic aggregation, a statistically strong positive association between conflict and the import demand elasticities emerge. Further the inverse trade/conflict relationship's statistical significance strengthens considerably. As before, the elasticity of conflict with respect to trade remained in the 0.15 range, only slightly less than previously obtained. These results are important because they unambiguously strengthen the conflict theory hypothesized in this paper.

In this sense, this section's empirical results are not directly comparable to the previously carried out analysis. For this reason we disaggregate somewhat by next considering dyadic data points.

TABLE 4.7

The Conflict-Trade Relationship Enhances
(t-values in parentheses)

	(1)	(2)
Constant	-11.30 (4.4)	-1.13 (0.1)
Import Elasticity of Demand	1.91 (2.2)	13.47 (1.4)
Trade Level	-7.99 (3.4)	-8.69 (1.9)
R^2	.57	.19

1) Dependent variable proportion of weighted conflict 1963-77; other Independent Variable long and short term capital flows and export commodity concentration.

2) Dependent variable net conflict 1948-1978; other independent variables rest of world demand for exports.

4.4.2 Bilateral Import Demand Elasticity Estimates and the Trade/Conflict Relationship[33]

Recent empirical work by Jaime Marquez (1988) used the IMF Directions of Trade data to compute dyadic import elasticities based on the imperfect-substitute model of Goldstein and Kahn (1985). Income (both long term and short term), price and cross-price elasticities were computed by Marquez based on the following equation using 1970Q4 to 1984Q4 data

$$\ln (M_{ks}/e_s P_s^w)_t = \alpha_0 + \alpha_{1ks} \ln Y_{kt}^p + \alpha_{2ks}(\ln Y_{kt} - \ln Y_{kt}^p) + \sum_j \alpha_{3ksj} \ln P_{ks\ t-j} + \quad (4.20)$$

$$\sum_j \alpha_{4ksj} \ln P_{kq\ t-j} + \alpha_{5ks} (\ln M_{ks}/e_s P_s^w)_{t-1} + \delta D + U_{kst}$$

where

$M_{ks} \equiv$ dollar value of imports of country k from country s.

$e_s \equiv$ exchange rate (dollars/foreign currency).

$P_s^w \equiv$ export price of country s in domestic currency.

$Y_k^p \equiv$ potential income of country k based on a Cobb-Douglas production function.

$Y_k \equiv$ real income of country k.

$P_{ks} \equiv$ relative import price in country I from country s.

$P_{kq} \equiv$ overall world price of imports.

$D \equiv$ dummy variable for one-time events.

$U_{kst} \equiv$ normally distributed non-autocorrelated error.

t denotes a time subscript.

Eight country groups to match the Federal Reserve Board Multi-country Model were considered: Canada, Germany, Japan, United Kingdom, United States, Other Industrial Countries, OPEC, non-OPEC developing countries, and the rest of the world. The "other industrial countries" category was further disaggregated, but because of the turbulent oil crises of the 70s, the OPEC countries were deleted.[34] The disaggregation yielded 178 dyads. The elasticities were adopted from Marquez. To conserve space they are not reported here, but instead will be made available upon request.[35]

Table 4.8 contains regression results for the conflict/trade model using the Marquez elasticities. Country trade and attribute data for 1973 are used to maintain some degree of time period comparability. As before, trade is inversely related to conflict, but the magnitude of the relationship is far stronger than before. A ten percent rise in imports leads to a five percent reduction in conflict. For a ten percent rise in exports, conflict is reduced by 2-1/2 percent. Import demand elasticities also remain a strong deterrent. As before a 10 percent more elastic demand is associated with a five percent lower level of conflict. Here imports appear more powerful than exports as a deterrent to conflict. Using an oil crisis year may be reason, but this will have to be investigated further.

To enhance the gains from trade argument, the difference in actor target GNP is used as an exogenous proxy for differences in factor endowment. If actor and target GNP differences (GNPDIF) imply actor/target factor endowment differentials, then larger "GNPDIF" should raise the gains from trade and diminish conflict. Again the regression result (i.e., the -.056 coefficient) is consistent with this hypothesis.

TABLE 4.8

The Conflict-Trade Relationship Enhanced by Dyadic Trade Elasticities

Variable[1]	Mean[1]	Coefficient[2]	Elasticity[3]
Constant		-50.49 (3.12)	
Dyadic Trade Elasticity	0.83 (.04)	37.62 (2.63)	0.47
Exports (billions US dollars)	4.13 (.67)	-4.49 (-4.47)	0.28
Imports (billions US dollars)	4.02 (.67)	-8.21 (-6.86)	0.50
GNP (actor)	232.8 (26.1)	0.0178 (0.46)	
GNP (actor) - GNP (target)	3.93 (39.0)	-.056 (2.20)	.003
Net Conflict	-66.68 (9.66)		
R^2		0.35	
Observations		178	

[1]Standard error of mean in parentheses.
[2]t-values in parentheses.
[3]Computed at mean variable values.

4.5 Conclusions

Political conflict between nations is an important topic. Though widely studied among political scientists, it is widely ignored by economists as there are few economics based models of conflict and cooperation. The approach outlined in this paper, though with roots back to the 18th Century differs, from the few current studies in that a price theoretic approach is taken to analyze cross-sectional differences in the incentives for cooperation.

Basic to the model are that trade patterns emerge because heterogeneous factor endowments necessitate a division of labor based on comparative advantage. If conflict leads to a cessation (or at least more unfavorable terms) of trade, then those countries with the greatest welfare losses face the highest indirect implicit costs of conflict, and engage in the least conflict and greatest cooperation.

Currently there are no measures that adequately portray the welfare gains associated with trade. Thus in this paper two elements affecting welfare are used: (1) trade levels, which are positively associated with welfare; and (2) import demand elasticities, which are negatively associated with welfare gains. Conflict measures, taken from events data culled from forty-eight newspapers taken over 30 years are statistically related to these two factors affecting welfare gains from trade.

Despite many statistical and data problems, there is a strong and robust negative association between conflict and trade. Country pairs engaged in the most trade have the least conflict. Similarly, as predicted, there is a positive association between import demand elasticities and conflict. Countries with the most elastic import demand curves have the smallest gain from trade, and hence the least incentive for cooperation.

The work set out in this study is obviously not complete, and should not be construed as a final product. Instead this project is an ongoing research effort, and the work presented in this paper, though highly suggestive, has many avenues to which one may turn for additional elaboration and extension. To save space, only a couple will be mentioned.

Gains from trade should be subsumed in import demand and export supply elasticities. However, unduly extensive aggregation as well as other statistical estimation problems may imply biased estimates of the consumer and producer surpluses. If such is the case, other factors might be important in adequately ascertaining true trade gains. These include such factors as the degree of competition in the international market for the goods in question, the domestic production possibilities for these goods, the availability of substitute commodities, as well as other factors.

Little consideration has been given to the appropriate functional form governing the conflict/trade relationship. In this paper (at least in the theoretical section) only qualitative results were considered. Yet in the empirical implementation, strong evidence exists favoring nonlinear functional forms governing the trade conflict relationship. One reason for this may be that welfare gains are inadequately represented by trade alone. Another, however, may be that the framework of analysis is oversimplified in that coalition behavior is ignored. Yet coalition behavior may be a consideration for the hyperbolic trade/conflict relationship. On the other hand, competition may induce conflict between nontrading nations; and coalition behavior may yield cooperation. As such, this and other aspects of coalition behavior may be important.

In summary, this paper can be viewed as an initial exploration applying an economic framework to an analysis of international relations. Strong results were obtained, and it is hoped that these results will become even more powerful as the work progresses.

Footnotes

*Earlier versions of this chapter have been presented at various professional meetings and academic seminars. I wish to thank Ed Azar for originally stimulating this research, Walter Isard for much continued encouragement, Mark Gasiorowski and Judith McDonald for collaboration over the years, and Steve Suzzan and Jeffrey Beliveau for research assistance.

[1] *Economic Report of the President,* (February 1988), Table B-77, pp. 338-9.

[2] Trade wars deal not with international relations, but the effect of trade on the domestic economy.

[3] Burton (1946, 521).

[4] ibid.

[5] de Montesquieu (1900, 316).

[6] Polachek (1978; 1980, 85-78); Gasiorowski and Polachek (1982,709-729) and Polachek and McDonald (1991).

[7] Obviously, as will be shown later, the relationship between international trade and conflict is simultaneous. Trade enhances cooperation, but at the same time political

conflict reduces or at least makes trade more expensive. See Pollins (1988) for an interesting analysis exploring how political interaction influence trade. See Lois Sayrs (1990) for an analysis of econometric issues in estimating the conflice trade relationship.

[8]Indeed Lionel Robbins finds special interest groups to be unimportant in the formulation of policy so that an aggregate welfare function is viable.

[9]We assume no direct costs of conflict. However, incorporating direct costs will not alter the results.

[10]The positive slope results from the second derivative of the bracketed term.

[11]For detail on the pros and cons of events data, see Kegley (1975).

[12]A description is contained in Azar (1980).

[13]It is interesting to note that such a measure of relative conflict has precedence in the literature. The father of arms race models, Lewis F. Richardson, states: "Usually both threats and cooperation are going on simultaneously; so that as we have restricted ourselves to a single variable for one group, that variable must represent the net result, the excess of threats over cooperation." (Richardson 1960, 30).

[14]The International Trade and Related Statistical Branch of the Statistical Office of the United Nations possesses data tapes containing annual dyadic commodity trade for 1962 to 1983 and quarterly data since 1975, but these data are not readily available.

[15]Banks (1973).

[16]Gillespie and Zinnes (1971).

[17]Analysis of particular country pairs indicates that the negative relationship varies in magnitude depending on the specific countries. Indeed for some country pairs a positive relationship emerges. My future research will analyze differences in the trade-conflict relationship by pairs of countries.

[18]For alternative tests comparing COPDAB and WEIS data, see Howell (1983) and Vincent (1983).

[19]For example, see Seiglie (1988).

[20]Because of missing data values the sample is 204.

[21]Richardson (1960).

[22]Richardson (1978).

[23]See Pollins op. cit. for stronger evidence that conflict decreases trade.

[24]Much of this section is based on Gasiorowski and Polachek (1982).

[25]Theil (1971, 138-9).

[26]Lagged conflict and a time trend are included in the regression to purge serial correlation and to detrend the data.

[27]See Polachek and McDonald (1991) for further elaboration on how trade elasticities can be derived and used in the context of the trade-conflict model.

[28]The same holds true for diminished trade occurring when conflict merely alters the terms of trade.

[29]Marquez (1988).

[30]To conserve space these elasticities are not reported here but are available upon request.

[31]Maddala (1979, 217-291).

[32]These estimates are obtained from Stern et. al. (1976).

[33]Judith McDonald and Jeffrey Beliveau were instrumental in carrying out the research for this section.

[34]Future work will incorporate the OPEC countries, but for now we concentrated on Austria, Belgium, Canada, France, Germany, Italy, Japan, Mexico, the Netherlands, Norway, South Korea, Sweden, and Switzerland so that comparisons could eventually be made with the International Monetary Fund "World Trade Model" to be described.

[35]Another recent source of bilateral import demand elasticity data is the "World Trade Model" (WTM) described in Haas and Turner (1988). From the WTM disaggregated manufacturing, agricultural, and raw materials elasticities can be

computed. The countries contained in WTM are Austria, Belgium-Luxembourg, Canada, Denmark, France, Germany, Italy, Japan, Netherlands, Norway, Sweden, Switzerland, U.K., and the U.S.

References

Arad, S. and Hirsch, R. (1983). *The economics of peacemaking: focus on the Egyptian-Israeli situation*. New York: St. Martins Press.

Arat, Z. (1984). *The viability of political democracy in developing countries*. unpublished Ph.D. dissertation, State University of New York at Binghamton.

Armington, P.S. (1969a). A theory of demand for products distinghished by place of production. *IMF Staff Papers*, 16, 159-178.

Armington, P.S. (1969b). The geographic pattern of trade and the effects of price changes. *IMF Staff Papers*, 16, 179-199.

Armington, P.S. (1970). Adjustment of trade balances: Some experiments with a model of trade among many countries. *IMF Staff Papers*, 17, 488-526.

Azar, E. E. (1980). The conflict and peace data bank (COPDAB) project. *Journal of Conflict Resolution*, 24, 143-152.

Banks, A. (1973). Cross-national time-series data. Center for Comparative Political Research, State University of New York at Binghamton.

Blainey, G. (1973). *The causes of war*. New York: Free Press.

Bloch, P. (1986). The politico-economic behaviour of authoritarian governments. *Public Choice*, 51, 117-28.

Brough, W.T. and Kimenyi, M.S. (1986). On the efficient extractions of rents by dictators. *Public Choice*, 48, 37-48.

Burton, J.H. (1946). *Life and correspondence of David Hume, Vol. II*. Edinburgh: William Tate Publishers.

Carlson, E. and Lundborg, P. (1987). An econometric analysis of superpower influence in the United Nations. Trade Union Institute for Economic Research Working Paper.

Cuzan, A. (1980). Authority, scope and force. *Public Choice*, 35, 363-69.

Deardorff, A. V. and Stern, R.M. (1986). *The Michigan model of world production and trade: Theory and applications*. Cambridge, Massachusetts: MIT Press.

Ellyne, M. (1986). The economic determinants of alliance cohesion in eastern Europe. Paper Presented at the Eastern Economic Association Meetings, Philadelphia, April 1986.

Gasiorowski, M. and Polachek, S. (1982). Conflict and interdependence: East-west trade and linkages in the era of detente. *Journal of Conflict Resolution*, 26, 709-729.

Gastil, R. (various years). *Freedom in the world*. Westport,Connecticut: Greenwood Press.

Gillespie, J. and Zinnes, D. (1971). Military expenditures data: 1948-1970. University Consortium for Political and Social Research, University of Michigan.

Goldstein, M. and Kahn, M. (1985). Income and price elasticities in foreign trade. in R. Jones and P. Kenen (eds.), *Handbook of International Trade, Vol. II*. Amsterdam: North-Holland.

Haas, R.D. and Turner, A.G. (1988). The world trade model: Revised estimates. International Monetary Fund Working Paper, WP/88/50, Washington, D.C., June 1988.

Hirschman, A.O. (1945). *National power and the structure of foreign trade*. Berkeley: University of California Press.

Howell, L. (1983) A comparative study of WEIS and COPDAB data sets. *International Studies Quarterly*, 27,149-59.

Hug, A.M. Abdul. (1988). *The global economy: An information sourcebook*. New York: Oryx Press.

International Monetary Fund (IMF). (various years). *International financial statistics*. Washington, D.C.

International Monetary Fund (IMF). (various years). *Direction of trade statistics yearbook*. Washington, D.C.

Isard, W. (1988). *Arms races, arms control, and conflict analysis*. New York: Cambridge University Press.

Kegley, C. (ed.). (1975). *International events and the comparative analysis of foreign policy*. Columbia, SC: University of South Carolina Press.

Lundborg, P. (1987). *The economics of export embargoes*. London: Croom Helm Publishers.

Marquez, J. (1988). Income and price elasticities of foreign trade flows: Econometric estimation and analysis of the U.S. trade deficit. Board of Governors of the Federal Reserve System International Finance Discussion Papers, Number 324, Washington, D.C., June 1988.

Masson, P., Symansky, S., Haas, R. and Dooley, M. (1988). MULTIMOD: A multi-region econometric model. International Monetary Fund Working Paper, WP/88/23, Washington, D.C., March 1988.

McClelland, C. (1977). World event/interaction survey (WEIS product), 1966-1977. University Consortium for Political and Social Research, University of Michigan.

McGuire, M.C. (1986). Factor migration, trade, and welfare under threat of commercial disruption. Paper Presented at The American Economic Association Convention, 1986.

McGuire, M.C. and Shibata, Hirofumi. (1988). Protection of domestic industries vs. defense against trade disruptions: Some neglected dimensions. Paper Presented at the Third World Congress of the Peace Science Society (International), College Park, Maryland, 1988.

de Montesquieu, Baron. (1900). *The spirit of laws*. translated by Thomas Nugent. New York: Collier Press.

Polachek, S. (1978). Dyadic dispute: An economic perspective. *Papers, Peace Science Society (International)*, 28, 67-80.

Polachek, S. (1980). Conflict and trade. *Journal of Conflict Resolution*, 24, 55-78.

Polachek, S. (1985). Review of the economics of peacemaking. *Southern Economic Journal*, 51, 1273-4.

Polachek, S. and McDonald, J. (forthcoming). Strategic trade and incentives for cooperation. in *Disarmement, Economic Conversion and the Mangagement of Peace*, M. Chatterji and L. Forcey (eds.), Praeger.

Pollins, B. (1988). Does trade still follow the flat? A model of international diplomacy and commerce. (May 1988), mimeo.

Pollins, B. (1989). Conflict, cooperation and commerce: The effect of international political interactions. *American Journal of Political Science*, 33, 737-61.

Read, D. (1967). *Cobden and Bright: A victorian political partnership*. London: Edward Arnold.

Richardson, L.F. (1960). *Arms and insecurity: A mathematical study of the causes and origins of war*. Chicago: The Boxwood Press, Pittsburgh and Quadrangle Books.

Richardson, N. (1978). *Foreign policy and economic dependence*. Austin: University of Texas Press.

Richardson, N. (1980). Trade dependence and foreign policy compliance: A longitudinal analysis. *International Studies Quarterly*, 24,191-222.

Robbins, L. (1968). *The economic causes of war*. New York: Howard Fertig Press.
Sayrs, L. (1985). The correlates of trade: An extended model of conflict and cooperation. Paper Presented at the International Studies Association, Washington, D.C., March 1985.

Sayrs, L. (1990). Expected utility and peace science: An assessment of conflict and trade. *Conflict Management and Peace Science* (Spring 1990), 17-44.

Scully, G. (1988). The institutional framework and economic development. *Journal of Political Economy*, 96, 652-62.

Seiglie, C. (1988).   International conflict and military expenditures: An externality approach. *Journal of Conflict Resolution* , 32:141-61.

Srinivasan, T.N. and Whalley, J. (ed). (1986). *General equilibrium trade policy modeling.* Cambridge, Massachusetts: MIT Press.

Stern, R., Francis, J. and Schumacher, B. (1976). *Price elasticities in international trade, an annotated bibliography.* London: Macmillan Press, Ltd.

Tullock, G. (1986). *Autocracy.* Boston: Martinus Nijboff Press.

Usher, D. and Engineer, M. (1987). The distribution of income in a despotic society. *Public Choice,* 54, 261-76.

Van Marrewijk, C. and van Bergeijk, P. (1990).   Trade uncertainty and specialization: Social versus private planning. *De Economist* (1990) 15-32.

Vincent, J.E. (1983). WEIS vs COPDAB: correspondence problems. *International Studies Quarterly,* 27, 161-8.

Economics of Arms Reduction and the Peace Process
W. Isard and C.H. Anderton (Editors)
© 1992 Elsevier Science Publishers B.V. All rights reserved.

Chapter 5

ON MODELING THE IMPACT OF ARMS REDUCTIONS ON WORLD TRADE

Jeffrey H. Bergstrand

University of Notre Dame[*]

[The basic work of Polachek focusses on fundamental aspects of the general relation between trade and political conflict. But at any particular point of time, major shocks in the world economy may occur which can lead to drastic change in trade among many countries. Such was the oil shock of 1973. Today, the shock is the demise of the Warsaw Pact Organization and the economic collapse and democratization (political demise) of the old Soviet totalitarian regime.

As we have seen, Klein/Gronicki/Kosaka have addressed the impact of arms reduction in Eastern European countries and the Soviet Union upon their internal economies. But it is also important to examine the impact of major arms reduction in a number of Western powers upon trade in general. While neoclassical and Keynesian theory suggest several different kinds of effects that may come about, Bergstrand looks to empirical materials to identify: (1) the relation of arms trade to aggregate trade; (2) the relation to nonarms trade of the share of real GDP going to military expenditures in importing and exporting countries; and (3) the economic determinants of arms trade. (eds.)]

5.1 Introduction

The historic opening of the Berlin Wall in East Germany in 1989 and subsequent developments in Eastern Europe and the Soviet Union in 1990 have motivated proposals for future substantive reductions in military expenditures in the United States and the USSR, as well as in many of their respective allies. The potential economic implications of large changes in the volume of arms spending are extensive and complex. For instance, the 9.0 percent and 7.6 percent increases in real military expenditures in the United States in 1982 and 1983, respectively, have been given some credit for raising the U.S. economy from the trough of the 1981-1982 recession, and the strength of the subsequent U.S. economic expansion. But these military expenditure increases have also been partially credited for the substantive enlargement of the U.S. federal budget and international trade deficits.

Military expenditures have long been considered to be economically intertwined with world trade. The *SIPRI* (Stockholm International Peace Research Institute) *Yearbook* reports regularly on arms trade. Recent yearbooks note that the total world volume of arms transfers have flattened in the past decade. This flattening was not attributed to international detente but rather to "serious economic problems currently experienced in the world, particularly in the Third World." (SIPRI 1984; p. 175, italics added). Thus, political and economic factors jointly influence the amount of military spending and arms trade.

The purpose of this paper is to offer one approach toward modeling the impact of arms reductions on the volume of world trade. Section 5.2 describes the motivation for the methodology pursued. Section 5.3 briefly outlines some theoretical issues underlying the methodology, although technical details will be omitted here. Section 5.4 summarizes the methodology. Section 5.5 describes the data. Section 5.6 details the empirical results for aggregate and non-arms trade. Section 5.7 details results for arms trade. Section 5.8 provides conclusions and policy implications of the results.

5.2 Motivation

Recent events in Eastern Europe and the USSR have generated proposals for substantive reductions in military spending by the United States, the USSR, and their allies. Both the Bush Administration and the U.S. Congress have proposed cuts in defense spending over the 1990s, with the latter proposing significant decreases in real terms. NATO has revamped its defense strategy in light of these events. On the assumption that there is no reversal of such developments, what implications do these potential arms spending reductions portend for world trade? At first, one might expect that fewer resources devoted to arms implies more resources available to produce and export non-arms commodities, including consumer and investment goods. Such an argument suggests a decrease in world arms trade but an increase in world non-arms trade; aggregate world trade need not change. To the extent that resources are diverted to investment in non-military plant and equipment, the possibility for enlarging world production and aggregate world trade is enhanced. Also, to the extent that uncertainty and economic and political trade barriers are reduced, world trade should be enhanced.

However, consider the alternative argument. If defense spending reductions are concentrated in research and development (R & D), such cuts could have a negative impact on private commercial research and development, such as high-definition television and x-ray lithography (see *N.Y. Times*, November 16, 1989).

Reductions in military spending of this type would induce declines in nonmilitary production and investment in plant and equipment, would tend to reduce world production, and might well diminish world trade.

Empirical evidence on the benefits to (nonmilitary) productivity of military expenditures is mixed. Henderson (1990) notes that cross-country comparisons of industrialized economies suggest that military spending and productivity growth are negatively related, supporting the notion that defense cuts could spur world production and trade in the long run. However, time-series studies have shown that the slowdown in productivity growth and the decline in military expenditures' share of output have coincided, using data prior to the 1980s, suggesting that defense cuts might curtail world production and trade in the long run.

Recognizing that political and economic influences on trade might well be highly "complementary," Summary (1989) estimated the effect on U.S. non-arms trade of certain political factors -- namely, actual arms transfers with each trading partner, an index of the degree of political freedom in the trading partner, the number of civilian U.S. government employees in the trading partner, and the number of foreign agents of the trading partner registered in the United States -- after taking into account important economic considerations. The economic factors expected to influence U.S. non-arms exports to (imports from) country j were j's gross domestic product (GDP), j's population, and the distance between the economic center of the United States and country j -- economic variables that typically compose a "gravity equation" in international trade, which will be discussed in Section 5.4.

Summary (1989) found that U.S. non-arms exports to country j in 1978 and 1982 were significantly related to economic variables that typically explain trade flows, but were also significantly related to some of the political variables. On the economic side, U.S. non-arms exports to j were (significantly) positively related to j's GDP as a proxy for j's expenditure capability and negatively related to the distance between the United States and country j as a proxy for transportation costs. On the political side, U.S. non-arms exports were positively related to arms trade between the two countries, the number of civilian U.S. government employees in j, and the number of j's agents registered in the United States, reflecting the "complementarity" between political and economic interests shared by the countries.

Summary (1989) found that U.S. non-arms imports from country j in 1978 and 1982 were also significantly related to both traditional economic and the novel political variables. On the economic side, U.S. non-arms imports from j were (significantly) positively related to j's GDP as a proxy for j's production capacity and negatively related to the in distance as a proxy for transportation costs. On the political side, U.S. non-arms imports from j were positively related to arms trade between the two countries and the number of j's agents registered in the United States, reflecting again the "complementarity" of political and economic interests shared by the countries.

The results in Summary (1989) imply that the volume of world trade may be significantly reduced by a decline in arms trade. These results also *suggest* that reductions in military expenditures may well lower the volume of non-arms, as well as arms, trade flows.

As a first step toward evaluating the potential impact of arms reductions on world trade, consider the relative magnitudes of world arms and world aggregate (merchandise) trade. According to the SIPRI (1984), the value (in current prices) of world exports of major weapons in 1983 was estimated at $34 billion. However, the value (in current prices) of world exports of all goods in the same year was estimated by the IMF at $1682 billion. According to these estimates, arms trade makes up only 2 percent of world trade.

Consider also the relative magnitudes of world military expenditures and world GDP. Because of an absence of reliable data on world GDP, consider the 24 countries composing the Organization for Economic Cooperation and Development (OECD), most of which are also in NATO. OECD military expenditures in 1981 (in current prices) were estimated at $320 billion. OECD nominal GDP in 1981 was $7617 billion. Thus, military expenditures make up only 4 percent of OECD total expenditures.

Such figures are considerably below comparable U.S. magnitudes. U.S. major-weapons exports in 1983 (in current prices) were estimated by SIPRI at $13.4 billion, which was almost 7 percent of its aggregate merchandise exports of $201 billion. U.S. military expenditure of $225 billion in 1983 estimated by SIPRI was also almost 7 percent of its gross domestic product of $3356 billion. Thus, studying U.S. exports and imports alone as in Summary (1989) might bias somewhat the effect of arms spending reductions on arms and non-arms trade.

5.3 Theoretical Issues

One approach to consider in analytically understanding these ramifications is a conventional synthesis of (short-run) Keynesian and (long-run) neoclassical frameworks. In the short run, arms spending reductions would (ceteris paribus) reduce aggregate demand in the U.S. economy. The fall in aggregate demand for military goods would tend to reduce employment and prices in this sector (or, in a dynamic context, slow their inflation rate). The fall in employment and national income in the short- and medium-run would tend to reduce aggregate demand for consumption and investment (non-military) goods. Prices for these goods would tend to fall, tending to lower the general level of prices in the U.S. economy. Real and nominal GDP would tend to be depressed. Some firms producing military goods and others producing non-military goods would go out of business. Interest rates would decline as the supply of Treasury securities to the market is curbed, as money demand slows due to the slowing of national spending, and as the real money supply expands as prices (or the inflation rate) fall.

In the long run, however, the fall in interest rates will stimulate aggregate demand, tending to restore employment and output. The interest rate decline will make consumer durable purchases and investment in plant and equipment cheaper by lowering the cost of capital. Real GDP will tend to be restored to its level preceding the military expenditures cut, with a smaller share of output in military-goods-producing industries.

The reason for ambiguity surrounding the new long-run real GDP level is the uncertain impact of the changed composition of real GDP on its level. The lower cost of capital should raise private investment in plant and equipment. The additional capital available to each worker should make each laborer more productive, enlarging world production (i.e., non-arms production rises more than proportionately to the fall in arms production).

However, as noted earlier, if most military spending cuts are on R & D which has strong "spillover" effects on the civilian economy, long-run real GDP could decline. Military (and space) R & D have made important contributions to the commercial jet aircraft, computer, semiconductor, communications, and nuclear power industries. These contributions have taken the form of spillover of the research itself as well as cost reductions generated by economies of scale in the application of the R & D, the sharing of manufacturing facilities for civilian and military products, and learning curves. Consequently, large military R & D expenditure cuts could tend to raise private production costs, such that non-arms world production would rise less than proportionately to the fall in arms production, decreasing world production on net.

Consider now the international trade implications of reduced military spending in a major arms producer and exporter, such as the United States.[1] Exports of arms will likely decline, as the level of military spending in a major arms supplier is probably an important determinant of its arms exports. However, the volume of non-arms exports is likely to rise. There are several reasons for this. Foremost, the consequent lower cost of capital (discussed earlier) will tend to raise non-arms production and their potential export supply. Second, as private investment enlarges the capital stock, raising the capital available to each worker, the production and export supply of non-arms goods will tend to increase, if such goods are capital intensive in production. Third, the defense industry is widely believed to be more "concentrated" than most other industries. A smaller share of national output in defense is likely to lower the costs of production in the exporting country, making the costs of non-arms production less relative to foreigners, expanding non-arms exports. If less military spending lowers the relative costs of production vis-a-vis other nations, this is tantamount to a real depreciation of its currency, or an increased international competitiveness. Complementing this last channel, suppose military spending is largely on nontradable items. Some economists view the real exchange rate as the relative price of tradables to nontradables. Reduced military spending by the exporter will lower the relative demand for nontradables, raising the relative price of tradables to nontradables, which is tantamount to a real depreciation of the exporter's currency, tending to increase non-arms (tradables) exports. Moreover, to the extent that the exporter's interest rate declines, this would generate a net capital outflow, a nominal depreciation of its currency, and a further real depreciation. All of these influences suggest reduced military spending will tend to augment non-arms exports.

On the other hand, some factors suggest non-arms exports might decline as military spending is cut. First, in the short run, military spending reductions diminish arms and, via the multiplier, non-arms output, tending to contract non-arms export supply. Second, if military spending cuts curtail important spillovers for civilian production, the rise in non-military production costs will tend to reduce production and export supply of non-arms goods. Third, as arms exports decline, the "tie-in" with non-arms goods will tend to reduce non- arms exports.

Note that this Keynesian/neoclassical framework ignores the dynamic potential for "free trade pacts" arising as an outgrowth of reduced political-military uncertainty. In fact, some trade pacts have already been signed to reduce artificial trade barriers between Western and Eastern European economies. Two years ago, the European Community (EC) signed trade pacts easing trade barriers bilaterally between members and Hungary and Czechoslovakia. Such an agreement was reached in November 1989 with the USSR. Since these pacts are similar to the pact between EC members and members of the European Free Trade Association (EFTA), it is likely that trade flows will be enhanced significantly as such pacts proliferate at the same time that arms reductions spread. There exists strong empirical evidence that custom unions and free trade areas significantly enhance trade flows.

Now consider the import side. The seemingly most prominent importers of arms are Third World countries. Almost 70 percent of USSR arms exports are to these countries. But only half of U.S. arms exports are to the Third World; the other half is supplied to other industrialized countries. Reductions in military expenditures will reduce the imports of arms by these countries from the major suppliers.

The impact of military spending reductions in a country on its non-arms imports is also ambiguous, although there are several reasons to suggest that such reductions will diminish non-arms imports. Foremost, the consequent decline in interest rates and the cost of capital from lower aggregate demand will tend to raise non-arms production in the long-run, thus decreasing import demand for non-arms goods. Second, as military spending reductions curtail the relative costs of production vis-a-vis trading partners, due say to less "concentration" in the importer, relatively cheaper domestic non-arms production will be substituted for foreign non-arms production, lowering non-arms import demand. Complementing this channel, if military spending is largely on nontradables, military expenditure cuts will lower nontradables prices, raising the relative price of tradables to nontradables. This real depreciation of the importer's currency will tend to curtail non-arms import demand. Moreover, to the extent that the importer's interest rate declines, this would generate a net capital outflow, a nominal depreciation of the importer's currency, and a further real depreciation. Also, as arms imports are curbed, "tie-ins" will lead to accompanying reduction in non-arms import demand. All of these influences suggest reduced military spending will tend to diminish non-arms imports.

However, non-arms import demand could rise with reduced arms expenditures. If non-arms production rises more than proportionately to the fall in arms production, say because of greater productivity of workers, import demand for non-arms goods may rise on net, if the "income effect" dominates the "substitution effect."

As before, however, arms reductions will likely be accompanied by the creation of more "trade pacts." The proliferation of such preferential trading arrangements will tend to enhance the volume of non-arms world trade by stimulating import demand.

5.4 Methodology

The effects of arms reduction on world trade are estimated here with a frequently used empirical approach, like in Summary (1989). World trade flows between pairs of countries in any given year have long been explained empirically in the international trade literature using a reduced-form function commonly referred to as a "gravity equation." Walter Isard (1954a,b) first suggested the suitability of a gravity-like model for analyzing international trade flows. Tinbergen (1962) first applied a gravity equation to cross-sectional bilateral trade flow data; Linneman (1966) extended Tinbergen's work.

The typical gravity equation in international trade is estimated using the formula:

$$PX_{ij} = (\beta_0)Y_i^{\beta_1}Y_j^{\beta_2}(Y_i/N_i)^{\beta_3}(Y_j/N_j)^{\beta_4}D_{ij}^{\beta_5}R_{ij}^{\beta_6}e_{ij} \tag{5.1}$$

where PX_{ij} is the U.S. dollar value of aggregate imports of country j from country i, Y_i (Y_j) is the U.S. dollar value of gross domestic product in country i (j), N_i (N_j) is population in country i (j) so that Y_i/N_i (Y_j/N_j) is per capita GDP, D_{ij} is the distance from the economic center of i to that of j, R_{ij} is any other factor(s) either aiding or resisting trade between i and j, and e_{ij} is a log-normally distributed error term. The log-linear version of this equation is usually estimated by ordinary least squares (OLS).

Several authors recently have provided formal microeconomic foundations for this equation in the context of either a Cobb-Douglas expenditure system (cf., Anderson, 1979), a general equilibrium model of imperfect competion (cf., Helpman and Krugman, 1985), or a neoclassical factor-proportions model (cf., Bergstrand, 1985 and 1989). In my work, exporter and importer GDP's can be interpreted as exporter i's productive capacity and importer j's expenditure capacity, respectively. Exporter i's per capita GDP can be interpreted as i's capital-labor endowment ratio[2], a higher exporter per capita GDP will tend to be associated with a higher (lower) level of exports from i to j if the bundle of goods is capital (labor) intensive in production on average. Importer j's per capita GDP influences its demands; a higher importer per capita income will tend to be associated with a higher (lower) level of imports to j from i if the bundle of goods are luxuries (necessities) on average. Distance between i and j can be interpreted as transportation costs. R_{ij} represents a number of factors that can aid or retard trade between the two countries, including measures of price competitiveness, custom unions or free trade agreements, and -- as Summary (1989) showed -- political factors that might enhance or deter trade.

In my previous work, I have emphasized that measures of relative price competitiveness can be important determinants of bilateral trade flows in cross-section gravity models of international trade, as relative wage levels have been found to be important determinants of migration flows in that literature. However, here such indices are suppressed to focus on these other issues and to be able to relate my results to those in Summary (1989). Yet, I will show how measures of the importance of military expenditures in countries may well be representing their relative cost structures, and hence their relative international competitiveness.

In this study, GDPs, per capita GDPs, military expenditures as a share of GDP, and some other minor variables are considered as factors potentially influencing arms and non-arms world trade flows. First, I reexamine the Summary (1989) hypothesis that the level of arms trade between two countries influences their level of non-arms trade. In light of the observation made earlier that world arms trade is a much smaller share of world trade than U.S. arms trade is of U.S. aggregate trade, I consider 272 bilateral trade relationships among 17 OECD countries. Summary (1989) found that U.S. non-arms exports to (imports from) various trading partners was significantly positively related to the level of arms transfers between them, implying that military and economic interests were tied. Ideally, one would want to consider whether this relationship between arms and non-arms trade held for a wide sample of bilateral trading relationships. Unfortunately, disaggregate bilateral trade data on arms shipments is unavailable for most of the world. However, the OECD publishes bilateral trade flows for members for Standard International Trade Classification (SITC) 95, War Firearms and Ammunition Therefor -- the only category reflecting arms trade. Thus, the first set of results examines this relationship for several OECD countries.

Second, I examine more directly the link between military spending and non-arms trade flows. Since previous empirical analysis of bilateral trade flows in cross section suggests that the level of exporter i's and importer j's real GDPs are key determinants of the trade flow from i to j, I examine whether the share of military expenditures in national expenditures as well as per capita income in the two countries might influence non-arms trading behavior.

Third, I examine the economic determinants of arms trade. While analysts have recognized that economic factors influence arms trade, I formally estimate how much variation in arms trade flows can be explained by purely economic factors, using a gravity equation. Surprisingly, as much as a quarter of the variation in these flows across countries can be explained by economic determinants.

5.5 Data Considerations

Since data on bilateral arms trade flows is reported only by OECD countries, I limit the analysis here to 17 OECD countries for the years 1975 and 1985. The 17 countries were chosen based upon already compiled data on other economic variables, including real GDPs, populations, distances between countries' economic centers, and dummy variables for adjacency and preferential trading arrangements. The countries examined include Canada, the United States, Japan, Belgium, Denmark, France, (West) Germany, Italy, the Netherlands, the United

Kingdom, Austria, Greece, Norway, Portugal, Spain, Sweden, and Switzerland. The list, of course, maintains no illusion of being comprehensive. Rather, it should be viewed as an extension of the data examined in Summary (1989), but preliminary to further research in this area. Yet, as one-half of U.S. arms exports are shipped to other industrialized countries, the sample is representative to a large extent.

Bilateral arms and non-arms trade flow data, measured in nominal U.S. dollars, are from the OECD's *Foreign Trade by Commodities - Series C*. Real GDPs are measured in "international" dollars, and are extracted from the Heston and Summers International Comparisons Program (ICP), cf., Heston and Summers (1988). Work by Kravis, Heston and Summers in the ICP has shown that cross-country comparisons of gross domestic products using exchange rate conversions are misleading. For instance, in 1985 the price level in Greece was three-fifths that of the United States for the same basket of goods. Using purchasing-power conversions, the ICP has calculated real GDPs for most countries that are internationally comparable, measured using "international" dollars. Populations are also from Heston and Summers (1988). Military expenditures as a share of gross domestic product are from the *SIPRI Yearbook* (1984, 1988).

For distance, sea distances are from U.S. Naval Oceanographic Office's *Distance Between Ports* and land distances are from the *Rand McNally Road Atlas of Europe*. Land distances were multiplied by a factor of two following Gruber and Vernon (1970). On this adjustment, see further supporting evidence in Isard (1989).

Several dummy variables were also appended. Dummy variables captured the presence or absence of a common land border, common membership in the EC, common membership in the EFTA, and membership in either the EC or EFTA to represent the benefits of the EC-EFTA free trade pact.[3]

5.6 Empirical Results

Table 5.1 presents the results of regressing aggregate and aggregate non-arms bilateral trade flows among numerous OECD countries on several economic variables for 1975 and 1985. First, columns (2) and (3) provide the results from estimating a typical gravity equation, such as described by equation (5.1). The gravity model explains about 85 percent of the cross-country variation of their aggregate bilateral trade values. All of the right-hand-side (RHS) variables are statistically significant at conventional levels with anticipated signs for trade among primarily industrialized countries. Exporter i's and importer j's real GDPs are positively related to the aggregate trade flow from i to j. A higher exporter GDP expands the productive capacity of i to export to j; a higher importer GDP expands the expenditure capacity of j to import from i.

For a given level of national output in exporter i, a higher exporter per capita income raises the trade flow from i to j. In the context of a two-factor world, this might be interpreted as a higher capital-labor endowment ratio in the exporter (see footnote 2), tending to expand the export supply of relatively capital-intensive products from i to j, for a given level of national output.

TABLE 5.1

Coefficient Estimates of Cross-Sectional Determinants of Aggregate and Non-Arms Bilateral Trade Flows

(1)	Aggregate Trade		Non-Arms Trade	
RHS Variables	(2) 1975	(3) 1985	(4) 1975	(5) 1985
Exporter Real GDP	0.79 (20.96)	0.90 (24.60)	0.79 (20.95)	0.90 (24.40)
Exporter Per Capita Real GDP	0.75 (5.84)	0.70 (5.91)	0.75 (5.83)	0.71 (5.92)
Importer Real GDP	0.65 (17.31)	0.86 (23.29)	0.65 (17.30)	0.86 (23.07)
Importer Per Capita Real GDP	0.37 (2.86)	0.71 (5.97)	0.37 (2.85)	0.72 (6.05)
Distance	-0.45 (-6.47)	-0.55 (-8.85)	-0.45 (-6.46)	-0.55 (-8.77)
Adjacency Dummy	0.77 (5.95)	0.67 (5.35)	0.77 (5.96)	0.66 (5.28)
EC Dummy	0.83 (5.52)	1.04 (8.14)	0.83 (5.51)	1.04 (8.09)
EFTA Dummy	0.98 (5.75)	1.33 (7.52)	0.98 (5.74)	1.33 (7.45)
ECEFTA Dummy	0.71 (6.10)	1.01 (8.42)	0.71 (6.10)	1.00 (8.31)
Constant	-11.19 (-7.08)	-17.02 (-10.73)	-11.17 (-7.07)	-17.21 (-10.76)
Adjusted R-squared	0.84	0.87	0.84	0.87
Standard Error	0.618	0.589	0.618	0.594
No. of Observations	272	272	272	272

Notes: t-statistics are in parentheses. Critical t values are 1.65, 1.96, and 2.58 for the 10, 5, and 1 percent significance levels, respectively (two tails).

For a given level of national expenditures in importer j, a higher importer per capita income raises the trade flow from i to j. In the context of a two-good world, this might be interpreted as the trade flow containing largely "luxury" goods, assuming a nonhomotheticity of tastes causes industrialized countries' income elasticities of import demand for other industrialized countries' products to exceed unity.

The other RHS variables are statistically significant as well. Distance, as a proxy for transportation costs, deters trade. Adjacency, as a proxy for cross-border trade, enlarges trade. All three preferential trading arrangements significantly enhance trade, with the trade volume gains from common membership in EFTA being the greatest. Moreover, the enhancement to the volume of bilateral trade from such common memberships increases from 1975 to 1985.

Second, the same economic variables have virtually identical impacts on the volume of aggregate non-arms bilateral trade flows, as shown in columns (4) and (5). This is not surprising since arms trade composes only 2 percent of world merchandise trade.

Table 5.2, columns (2) and (3), reveal that the addition of bilateral arms trade flows to the model significantly enhances the volume of non-arms trade. This result confirms the finding in Summary (1989) that political and economic foreign interests appear "complementary." However, the coefficient estimate in columns (2) and (3) for the arms-trade variable is only one-twentieth that found in Summary (1989). Thus, the impact of reducing arms trade on non-arms trade might not be as severe as suggested in that study. One possible explanation for the larger coefficient estimate in Summary (1989) is the absence of dummy variables for preferential trading arrangements, the effect of which might have been captured by arms trade in that study.

When the shares of military expenditures in the GDPs of the exporting country are appended to the model, several interesting results emerge, as columns (4) and (5) of Table 5.2 show. First, consistent with most of the literature on defense spending and the macroeconomy, the results for exporter's military share of real GDP are mixed. The coefficient estimate for exporter's military share of real GDP is negative in 1985 and positive in 1975.

As suggested under theoretical issues, the expected effect of exporter's military share of real GDP on non-arms trade was ambiguous. For 1985, the negative coefficient estimate is consistent with the neoclassical notions that a reduction in defense spending's share of real GDP will augment non-arms production as the cost of capital falls and will lower the relative cost of non-arms goods vis-a-vis trading partners (improving the exporter's international non-arms price competitiveness), both effects tending to raise export supply. For 1975, the positive coefficient is consistent with: (i) the Keynesian notion that reduced defense spending will have a multiplied impact upon non-defense production, curtailing export supply, (ii) the spillover notion that reduced military expenditures will curtail important technology and cost spillovers to non-arms production raising their relative cost, curtailing exports, and (iii) the tie-in notion that reduced arms production will diminish arms exports, and consequently decrease non-arms exports because of "tie-in" arrangements discussed in Summary (1989).

Although stability of this coefficient across the two years might first seem desirable, there are two feasible explanations for the instability of the coefficient estimate of exporter's military share of real GDP on non-arms bilateral trade. First, 1975 was a year of worldwide economic recession and extreme excess capacity among industrialized countries following the first OPEC oil crisis of 1973-74. In the presence of excess capacity and high unemployment, it is conceivable to expect that the Keynesian explanation would have more relevance. A higher share of real GDP on military spending would have the typical Keynesian multiplier impact on non-arms production and export supply. By contrast, 1985 was three years after the previous recession and the degree of excess capacity and unemployment was much less worldwide than in 1975. One might expect the neoclassical explanations to be more relevant in 1985 than in 1975. Second, "spillovers" to civilian productivity from military R & D expenditures have been documented to have been much greater in the mid-70s (fifteen years ago) than more recently; see Rosenberg (1987). Consequently, the spillover hypothesis could be expected to have been more relevant for 1975 than for 1985. These explanations are consistent with a positive coefficient estimate for exporter's military share in real GDP in 1975, but a negative estimate in 1985.

While both of these explanations are plausible, the empirical result remains that the effect of a reduction in the exporter's military share of real GDP was associated with a decline in non-arms bilateral trade in 1975, but a rise in non-arms bilateral trade in 1985. Nevertheless, two empirical points are worth emphasizing. First, the more recent data (1985) are consistent with military spending reductions being associated with non-arms trade expansion. Second, the positive coefficient estimate for 1975 is not statistically different from zero at the 5 percent significance level. The negative coefficient estimate for 1985 is statistically different from zero at the 5 percent and 1 percent significance levels.

The effect of importer's military share of real GDP on non-arms bilateral trade is consistently positive for 1975 and 1985. This greater stability, relative to the previous coefficient estimate, perhaps reflects a greater "compatibility" of various

J.H. Bergstrand

explanations for this relationship. Unlike previously, the neoclassical and Keynesian explanations suggest the same, not opposite, relationships. In the neoclassical view, reduced military spending in the importing country will lower the cost of capital, raising production of non-arms goods in the importer, which would

TABLE 5.2

Coefficient Estimates of Cross-Sectional Determinants of Non-Arms Bilateral Trade Flows

(1) RHS Variables	(2) 1975	(3) 1985	(4) 1975	(5) 1985
Exporter Real GDP	0.76 (19.12)	0.88 (21.92)	0.74 (19.24)	0.92 (22.88)
Exporter Per Capita Real GDP	0.73 (5.64)	0.68 (5.67)	0.82 (6.14)	0.54 (4.47)
Importer Real GDP	0.62 (15.62)	0.83 (21.03)	0.58 (15.19)	0.82 (20.75)
Importer Per Capita Real GDP	0.36 (2.82)	0.75 (6.23)	0.62 (4.71)	0.84 (6.90)
Distance	-0.42 (-6.01)	-0.54 (-8.53)	-0.34 (-4.86)	-0.55 (-9.03)
Adjacency	0.76 (5.88)	0.65 (5.19)	0.88 (7.00)	0.63 (5.19)
EC Dummy	0.86 (5.71)	1.04 (8.12)	0.93 (6.46)	1.06 (8.38)
EFTA Dummy	0.94 (5.56)	1.28 (7.10)	0.97 (6.02)	1.28 (7.42)
ECEFTA Dummy	0.69 (6.04)	0.97 (7.90)	0.75 (6.78)	0.98 (8.26)
Arms Trade Flows	0.01 (2.19)	0.01 (1.72)	0.01 (2.22)	0.01 (1.11)
Exporter's Military Share of Real GDP	–	–	0.04 (1.77)	-0.09 (-3.84)
Importer's Military Share of Real GDP	–	–	0.13 (5.17)	0.06 (2.35)
Constant	-10.35 (-6.42)	-16.68 (-10.27)	-14.09 (-8.14)	-16.42 (-10.18)
Adjusted R-squared Standard Error No. of Observations	0.84 0.614 272	0.87 0.592 272	0.85 0.585 272	0.88 0.570 272

Notes: t-statistics are in parentheses. Critical t values are 1.65, 1.96, and 2.58 for the 10, 5, and 1 percent significance levels, respectively (two tails).

tend to reduce import demand for such goods. Moreover, reduced military spending -- either by lowering relative demand for skilled workers or reducing "concentration" in the economy -- could lower the cost of non-arms production in the importer relative to other countries, improving the importer's international competitiveness, and lowering non-arms import demand. In the Keynesian view, reduced defense spending will lower income, aggregate demand, and demand for non-arms, as well as arms, imports. Moreover, if tie-ins are present, reduced military spending, by lowering arms import demand, will tend to curtail non-arms import demand. All these explanations are consistent with the estimated relationship that a reduction in the importer's military share of real GDP lowers non-arms bilateral trade volume.

An interesting consequence of the change in these two coefficients between 1975 and 1985 is that a one percent reduction in both countries (exporter's and importer's) shares of real GDP spent on military reduces the volume of non-arms bilateral trade in 1975, but increases this trade in 1985. A one percent reduction in both countries' military shares in real GDP -- using 1975 estimates -- lowers non-arms trade by 0.17 percent, but -- using 1985 estimates -- raises non-arms trade by 0.03 percent.

As noted earlier, military spending reductions do not likely occur in a vacuum. The reduction of potential conflict may well occur simultaneously with establishment of preferential trading arrangements or granting of "most favored nation" status. Thus, to the extent that political-military uncertainty is reduced, trading pacts will likely emerge as arms reductions spread. While the formation of customs unions might seem overly optimistic, free trade pacts -- such as the European Free Trade Association (EFTA) -- might become prominent, as recent pacts signed between Hungary and the EC and between Czechoslovakia and the EC demonstrate.

To allow for this, we consider the effect of reduced military spending in both countries along with the creation of an EFTA-like pact. In the case of 1985, the impacts are complementary; a reduction of both countries' military shares of real GDP raises non-arms trade and the institution of a free trade pact (like EFTA) raises non-arms trade. In the case of 1975, even though the impacts are opposite, the net impact of arms reduction on non-arms trade is likely positive. Using the coefficient estimates in column (4) in Table 5.2 for 1975, even if any two countries were to reduce their shares of military spending by three percentage points -- which was their average shares in 1975 -- the resulting negative effect on non-arms trade (-0.51) would be less than the positive impact on such trade of the creation of a free trade pact (0.75).[4]

Note also for 1985 that the inclusion of exporter and importer military shares of real GDP erode the statistical significance of the arms trade coefficient estimate.

Since, as will be shown, arms trade flows are statistically significantly related to military shares, the arms trade flow variable in Summary (1989) perhaps reflected the exporter's and importer's military shares of real GDP.

TABLE 5.3

Coefficient Estimates of Cross-Sectional Determinants of Non-Arms Bilateral Trade Flows with Military Expenditures as Variables

(1) RHS Variables	(2) 1975	(3) 1985
Exporter Non-Military Real GDP	0.58 (6.83)	1.15 (12.39)
Exporter Military Expenditures	0.16 (2.23)	-0.24 (-3.21)
Exporter Per Capita Real GDP	0.79 (6.24)	0.57 (4.80)
Importer Non-military Real GDP	0.19 (2.29)	0.61 (6.72)
Importer Military Expenditures	0.40 (5.58)	0.21 (2.84)
Importer Per Capita Real GDP	0.54 (4.26)	0.82 (6.87)
Distance	-0.31 (-4.39)	-0.55 (-8.82)
Adjacency	0.90 (7.13)	0.64 (5.16)
EC Dummy	0.89 (6.23)	1.05 (8.39)
EFTA Dummy	0.96 (5.94)	1.29 (7.43)
ECEFTA Dummy	0.72 (6.57)	0.98 (8.27)
Arms Trade Flows	0.01 (2.30)	0.01 (1.19)
Constant	-10.83 (-7.03)	-16.63 (-10.63)
Adjusted R-squared	0.86	0.88
Standard Error	0.584	0.570
No. of Observations	272	272

Notes: t-statistics are in parentheses. Critical t values are 1.65, 1.96, and 2.58 for the 10, 5, and 1 percent significance levels, respectively (two tails).

The empirical results in Table 5.2 might be interpreted as constraining world production unrealistically. That is, the effect of a unit reduction (one percentage point) in the exporter's military share of real GDP is estimated holding constant exporter real GDP; that is, the effect is estimated assuming exporter non-arms production rises endogenously to maintain a constant level of real GDP. I also estimated the effects on non-arms trade of arms reductions holding constant only the levels of non-arms national outputs. Table 5.3 presents the results of reestimating the model separating (exporter and importer) real GDPs into components non-military GDP and military expenditures. The results are generally consistent with those in Table 5.2. Notably, a reduction in exporter military expenditures lowers the level of non-arms trade in 1975, but raises the volume of non-arms trade in 1985. A reduction in importer military expenditures lowers non-arms trade flows in both years. And for 1985, a one percentage point reduction in exporter and importer military expenditures raises the volume of their non-arms trade flow by 0.03 percent, as in Table 5.2.

5.7 Economic Determinants of Arms Trade

Given the relative success of the gravity equation for explaining across country pairings aggregate and non-arms bilateral trade flows, the model was considered for gaining insight into the economic determinants of arms trade flows. A priori my expectations were limited; I anticipated that the model would fare poorly with arms trade, expecting such trade to be determined largely by political, military or other non-economic factors. Surprisingly, the gravity framework explained about 25 percent of the variation across countries in bilateral arms trade flows.

Table 5.4, columns (2) and (3), present the results of using the basic gravity specification (equation 5.1) for estimating variation in the value of arms flows across country pairings. At the 5 percent significance level, exporter GDP, importer GDP and distance are statistically significant with the anticipated positive, positive and negative, respectively, coefficient estimate signs in 1975. In 1985, exporter and importer GDPs and per capita GDPs are statistically significant (along with distance). The positive coefficient estimate for exporter per capita GDP, interpretable as a proxy for its capital-labor endowment ratio (see footnote 2), suggests that arms exports tend to be capital intensive in production, which is feasible. The negative coefficient estimate in 1985 for importer per capita income suggests that arms tend to be "necessities" in consumption, i.e., that their income elasticities of import demand are less than unity.

Column (3) in Table 5.4 also reveals for 1985 that common membership in the EFTA, or if one country was in the EC and the other in the EFTA, would significantly increase arms trade flows, but not so for common EC membership. The lack of statistical significance for adjacency suggests that cross-border trade does not contribute much to the volume of arms trade.

TABLE 5.4

Coefficient Estimates of Cross-Sectional Determinants of Bilateral Arms Trade Flows

(1) RHS Variables	(2) 1975	(3) 1985	(4) 1975	(5) 1985
Exporter Real GDP	2.62 (5.81)	2.69 (6.79)	–	–
Exporter Per Capita Real GDP	2.39 (1.54)	2.68 (2.10)	–	–
Importer Real GDP	2.67 (5.92)	2.45 (6.17)	–	–
Importer Per Capita Real GDP	0.63 (0.41)	-2.45 (-1.91)	–	–
Exporter Military Expenditures	–	–	2.23 (5.83)	2.12 (6.39)
Importer Military Expenditures	–	–	2.15 (5.62)	1.86 (5.58)
Distance	-2.46 (-2.96)	-1.32 (-1.98)	-1.07 (-1.30)	-0.74 (-1.07)
Adjacency	1.22 (0.79)	1.30 (0.97)	3.25 (2.08)	2.67 (1.95)
EC Dummy	-2.37 (-1.31)	-0.03 (-0.02)	-1.08 (-0.59)	-1.17 (-0.83)
EFTA Dummy	2.91 (1.43)	5.15 (2.70)	2.41 (1.17)	3.94 (2.03)
ECEFTA Dummy	0.99 (0.71)	3.82 (2.95)	1.40 (1.00)	2.70 (2.07)
Constant	-72.70 (-3.84)	-53.98 (-3.15)	-30.85 (-3.94)	-27.45 (-3.70)
Adjusted R-squared	0.23	0.25	0.19	0.19
Standard Error	7.405	6.363	7.622	6.617
No. of Observations	272	272	272	272

Notes: t-statistics are in parentheses. Critical t values are 1.65, 1.96, and 2.58 for the 10, 5, and 1 percent significance levels, respectively (two tails).

Finally, I replaced exporter and importer real GDPs in these regressions by exporter and importer military expenditures, respectively (and deleted per capita GDPs). The results are presented in columns (4) and (5) of Table 5.4. While I anticipated improvement of the results, in fact the adjusted R-squared values deteriorated in both years. Yet the coefficient estimates did not change noticeably.

Thus, while earlier sections of the paper indicate that military expenditures and arms trade appear to significantly influence the volume of aggregate non-arms trade between countries, this section reveals that about 25 percent of the variation across country pairings in their arms trade can be explained by economic factors.

5.8 Conclusions and Implications

Events in Eastern Europe and the Soviet Union over the past year have raised widespread expectations of reductions in military spending by the United States, the USSR, and their allies, as well as reductions in economic and political trade barriers among all these countries. This paper attempted to offer an analytical framework for understanding the potential implications of these dramatic changes for the path of world trade.

Using 1975 data, the empirical model suggested that reductions in military expenditures would tend to reduce exporters' supplies of *non-military*, as well as military, products and reduce importers' demands for non-military, as well as military, products. However, to the extent that arms reductions will likely be accompanied by trade liberalization -- witness bilateral trade pacts last year signed between Hungary and Czechoslovakia with the European Community and a recent similar pact signed between the USSR and the EC -- the volume gains to world trade from such liberalization would tend to offset the losses because of military cuts.

Yet using 1985 data, the empirical results suggested that reductions in military expenditures by exporting countries would tend to *increase* the volume of non-arms trade, by enhancing non-arms export supply. And even though military reductions in importing countries, by enhancing the share of those countries' national production in non-military goods, would tend to reduce non-military import demands, this effect was estimated to be small. Combined with an even larger estimated effect of trade liberalization on trade creation in 1985 relative to 1975, the 1985 data suggest that *the long-run implications for world trade from arms reductions and consequent trade liberalization are quite favorable.*

Footnotes

*An earlier version of this paper was presented at the Allied Social Science Association annual meeting in Atlanta, December 29, 1989 and at a conference on "Economic Issues of Disarmament" sponsored jointly by the University of Notre Dame and Economists Against the Arms Race. I am grateful to the Center for Research in Business and the Center for Research in Banking, both at the University of Notre Dame, for financial support.

[1] The following is intended neither to be an exhaustive nor a formal discussion of how military spending affects arms and non-arms world trade flows. The presentation is intended to be illustrative, to motivate the inclusion of the military's share of national output in a well-established empirical model of trade flow determinants. For a more thorough summary, see, for example, Adams and Gold (1987).

[2] In a cross-country regression of 34 countries' per capita GDPs on their respective capital-labor endowment ratios, the capital-labor ratio explained 96 percent of the variation in the per capita incomes.

[3] The use of dummy variables to capture the presence or absence of a preferential trading arrangement is common, and its precedent was set in Tinbergen (1962) in the first estimation of an international trade gravity equation. By contrast, recent work in the "conflict resolution" literature of international relations hypothesizes that the level of conflict between a pair of countries is inversely related to its bilateral trade volume. To the extent that a preferential trading arrangement between two countries reflects a low level of conflict, this literature suggests that the presence of a preferential trading arrangement is a function of the level of bilateral trade. Such causality is, of course, the converse of that suggested by the typical gravity model. In reality, these two variables are both endogenous and influenced by common (unspecified) exogenous variables, and suggests the use of a simultaneous equation system. However, addressing this issue is beyond the scope of this paper. On this issue, see Polachek (1988).

[4] This conclusion was drawn by summing the coefficient estimates for the exporter and importer shares of military expenditures in national GDP, multiplying the sum (0.17) by negative three to arrive at an estimated impact on trade of -0.51, and comparing it to the estimated effect of creating an EC-EFTA- like trade pact on trade (0.75).

References

Adams, G. and Gold, D. (1987). Defense spending and the economy. Defense Budget Project at the Center on Budget and Policy Priorities, Washington, D.C., July 1987.

Anderson, J.E. (1979). A theoretical foundation for the gravity equation. *American Economic Review*, 69, 106-116.

Bergstrand, J.H. (1989). The generalized gravity equation, monopolistic competition, and the factor-proportions theory in international trade. *Review of Economics and Statistics*, 71, 143-153.

Bergstrand, J.H. (1985). The gravity equation in international trade: some microeconomic foundations and empirical evidence. *Review of Economics and Statistics*, 67, 474-481.

Deardorff, A. (1982). The general validity of the Heckscher-Ohlin theorem. *American Economic Review*, 72, 683-694.

Gruber, W.H. and Vernon, R. (1970). The technology factor in a world trade matrix. *The Technology Factor in International Trade*. New York: NBER.

Helpman, E. and Krugman, P. (1985). *Market structure and foreign trade.* Cambridge, MA: MIT Press.

Henderson, Y. (1990). Defense cutbacks and the New England economy. *New England Economic Review*, July/August 1990, 3-24.

Heston, A. and Summers, R. (1988). A new set of international comparisons of real product and price levels estimates for 130 countries, 1950-1985. *Review of Income and Wealth*, 34.

Isard, W. (1954a). Location theory and international and interregional trade theory. *Quarterly Journal of Economics*, 68, 97-114.

Isard, W. (1954b). Location theory and trade theory: short-run analysis. *Quarterly Journal of Economics*, 68, 305-320.

Isard, W. (1989). On bilateral trade matrix projection. mimeo.

Linnemann, H. (1966). *An econometric study of international trade flows.* Amsterdam: North-Holland.

Polachek, S. (1988). Nations in conflict: an economics approach to international interactions. mimeo.

Rosenberg, N. (1987). Civilian spillovers from military R & D spending: the U.S. experience since world war II. in S. Lakoff and R. Willoughby (eds.), *Strategic Defense and the Western Alliance.* Lexington, MA: Lexington Books.

SIPRI (1984). *SIPRI Yearbook, 1984.*

SIPRI (1988). *SIPRI Yearbook, 1988.*

Summary, R.M. (1989). A political-economic model of U.S. bilateral trade. *Review of Economics and Statistics*, 71, 179-182.

Tinbergen, J. (1962). *Shaping the world economy: suggestions for an international economic policy*. New York: The Twentieth Century Fund.

Economics of Arms Reduction and the Peace Process
W. Isard and C.H. Anderton (Editors)
© 1992 Elsevier Science Publishers B.V. All rights reserved.

Chapter 6

THE NEW STRATEGIC ENVIRONMENT AND
ECONOMIC FACTORS IN THE FUTURE OF NUCLEAR DEFENSE

Martin C. McGuire

University of Maryland

[The papers of Arrow, Klein/Gronicki/Kosaka and Bergstrand have provided insights and findings on how changes in military expenditures impact on an economy, its trade and via trade on other economies. But one wants to know what determines the level and composition of military expenditures --- from which arms escalation or deescalation proceeds --- and which at any point of time are dependent upon many political and economic factors. Clearly, the recent revolutionary political developments in Europe require reexamination of national security, defense strategy, and perceived requirements of weaponry and military expenditures, to whose discussion we now turn.

There is the view that understanding why a nation engages in nuclear or other weapon development requires one to understand the nature of war itself. The rationale for this view is clearly brought out in McGuire's deep and fundamental analysis of the new strategic situation regarding nuclear defense in the next years, if not decades --- analysis which no serious student of this subject can afford to overlook. Has the allocation and operations game changed from an essentially non cooperative one to a cooperative one --- to one of coordination? Are strategic defenses now obtainable with newly developing technology so that damage threatening and damaging limiting objectives can be treated separately --- and, consequently, is such treatment on the rise? If so, what then is the nature of the new economic tradeoffs, especially given that the cost of retaliation has increased since the Cold War period? Do such economic tradeoffs take center stage in multi-national security policy? McGuire addresses these and other vitally important questions. (eds.)]

6.1 The New Strategic Environment

Even as the elation for the watershed events of 1989-90 grew, many began to ponder just what might be the function and disposition in the new world order of the massive strategic forces accumulated in NATO and the WTO over the preceding four decades. With progressive (be it limited) nuclear disarmament between the super powers on the horizon, what remains of the doctrines of deterrence, mutual assured retaliation and destruction, or of the notion of the nuclear umbrella, trip-wire defenses, limited war, or extended deterrence?

The topic of this paper concerns a special corner of the residual of the super power strategic competition, namely what might become of the decades old efforts hitherto truncated by feasibility and cost to build defense systems which actually defend populations from nuclear devastation. This subject is of interest not merely for its importance in the ongoing although moderating conflict between East and West, but also for its eventual value and interest as a global public good. Since the anti-missile-defense push of the late 1960's analyses of defense against nuclear attack have concluded that any meaningful defense was fraught with difficulties and possibly beyond economic capability. The reasons for this included; (1) missile defense may be technically unworkable; (2) even if it could be made to work it would undermine the stability of deterrence and thereby incite the very disaster it is intended to prevent; (3) even if it could be made to work without undermining deterrence, the protection which it yields could be much more cheaply defeated than it cost to produce thereby negating the defense initiative; (4) even if none of the above obtained the cost is simply too great. In the new strategic context is that old will 'o wisp objective of regaining control over one's own national survival more or less desirable, more or less feasible, more or less dangerous than in the bad old days of bi-polar hegemony? (See Kent and Thaler, 1990). Although some Communist governments may collapse, Russian military forces most probably will not, meaning that these issues will prove no less momentous under the new dispensation than they were during the cold war.

The thesis of this paper is that the new era of superpower cooperation may change both the economic feasibility and strategic desirability of strategic defenses, and that evaluation of this potential has a weighty economic component. Although strategic choices and strategic forces often seem driven by technology, engineering analysis alone can not make sense out of the strategic utilization of its own discoveries. This is because technological capability is only one ingredient necessary to understanding strategic defense. The others which must be incorporated in analysis are; (a) the strategic goals, utility, or preferences of nations which might invest in strategic defense; (b) the absolute and relative resource costs of strategic defense and offense; (c) values of alternative resource utilization subject to overall resource scarcity in relevant countries; (d) and finally the strategic, interactive, interdependence between the choices and decisions of two countries simultaneously striving to use their technologies and resources to achieve their goals. Each of these components is familiar to economists and central to economic analysis of strategic defense.

What is there in the new strategic environment that makes strategic defense worth reexamination? Amidst the diversity and novelty of the ongoing upheaval in global security three changes stand out as crucial to the argument of this paper that strategic nuclear defense may have a viable place in the new order.

a. The first of these changes is behavioral: strategic force levels, compositions, and operations will no longer be determined primarily by independent competitive decisions on either side of the Iron Curtain. The allocation and operations "game" has changed from being essentially non-cooperative to cooperative -- a game of coordination. The meaning of this change is that through mutual coordination the level of attack each country might have to neutralize to successfully defend itself and protect its population from annihilation has been reduced to manageable proportions.

b. The second of these changes is technical: weapons systems have evolved over the past three decades such that now different categories of forces are becoming dominant for damage threatening and damage limiting objectives. Unlike weapons configurations in the l960's and l970's, in the future *different* systems will inflict and deflect damage; therefore effective choices between the two objectives may become possible, whereas they used not to be. Another crucial implication of this trend -- that offensive and potentially defensive systems are becoming more separate -- is that the linkage between strategic defense and possible instabilities in deterrence is weakening. Those instabilities derived from mutual incentives to (relative benefits from) strike first rather than wait, leaving the decision up to the adversary. It has been widely thought that such destabilizing mutual incentives would be exacerbated by strategic defenses, but that now seems increasingly unlikely.

c. The third of these three crucial changes is simply narrowly economic: the relative costs of offense vs. defense have been shifting slowly so as to favor the offense/attack somewhat less than two decades ago.

Not only can it be argued that strategic defenses have become feasible as a result of the above factors, but also that the individual great powers may find them more desirable. At least one lesson worth pondering of the Mid-East crisis of 1990-91 and war in the Persian Gulf is how useful it can be to a country to be able to apply its own coercive, destructive military force with impunity. With little or no effective risk of meaningful retaliation from an enemy, countries which are able to pursue their objectives will do so. (This principle applies equally to conventional and nuclear powers). Any great power which -- by dint of research, development, and luck -- found it within its means to achieve a posture of nuclear invulnerability vis a vis the nuclear powers would indeed find itself in a singular position. With the implications of this possibility obvious to the major economic powers one might reasonably expect (at a minimum) modest research and development efforts to continue for the foreseeable future in Star Wars programs, in any country which can afford it. Even if the immense national benefits from such a weapons breakthrough did not make it highly unlikely that the issue of strategic defense will go away, the relevance of such protective technology to the provision of nuclear security as an international public good via creation of larger security associations of governments insures its continued relevance.

6.2 Economic Infeasibility of Strategic Defense in Cold War Environment

As the existence of nuclear weapons, deliverable in great numbers over great distances with short tactical warning time became a permanent fact of life, it was soon recognized that a country's sovereignty over its very existence was removed from the control of its leaders and instead placed in the control of leaders of other countries. These developments naturally produced great political and military counter-pressures to recapture sovereign control over national survival at least in the two superpowers -- in the US culminating to this date in our Star Wars adventure. In the end, technical trends unfavorable to strategic defense simply overwhelmed leaders desires to assert/retain control over national survival. In place of that objective, mutual assured destruction was ultimately accepted by both superpowers. If the thesis of this paper proves correct, it is ironic that just as the hostility between the two superpowers is abating, the possibility of reciprocal improvements in assured survival are on the rise. Furthermore, new discoveries may in the future reverse or moderate the technical dominance of attack over defense; it would be unwise at least to assume this was impossible. Moreover, it may not be true that technical development is exogenous. Good technical advance may happen only if scientists look in the right places, and this requires concepts of what are desirable technologies. To understand how such developments as these may reinvigorate strategic defense it is essential to understand why such initiatives failed in the Cold War era.

6.2.1 Similarity of offensive vs defensive technologies and forces

The first element in any explanation of the failure to deploy strategic defense is the merger of the two types of forces -- offensive and defensive. If weapons developments had allowed offensive and defensive forces to be concretely and operationally separated, then one dilemma characteristic of strategic force build up early during the cold war might have been avoided. That dilemma -- not commonly the focus of adequate attention -- derived from the fact that the very same forces which might be used to *limit* damage from strategic attack were the most effective for *inflicting* damage either in attack or retaliation. Thus, for example, highly accurate MIRVed (multiple independently-targetable reentry vehicle) ICBMs (inter-continental ballistic missiles) while a crucial component in the strategic retaliatory posture, in the early days also promised to be the first most effective damage limiting weapon among all the alternatives contemplated. As ICBM accuracies increased dramatically and ICBMs were then fitted with multiple independently targetable re-entry vehicles, it became obvious that their ability to destroy enemy land based missiles gave them a high damage limiting or assured survival effectiveness. Similarly, ballistic missile defenses not only protect a country's population, they also protect a country's land based weapons and command and control systems. But this enhances their effective retaliatory assured destruction capability.

This merger of offensive with defensive technologies has, I believe, three generic origins. First is the focus on piecemeal engagements between offensive and defensive forces. It has been as if the absence of a bullet proof vest compels one to aim at the incoming bullets. Second is the corresponding vulnerability of defensive weapons to offensive attack-- the defensive gun itself is vulnerable. Thus it is sometimes claimed that even if SDI (Strategic Defense Initiative) interceptors were effective at destroying attacking missiles, the SDI system itself is highly vulnerable to very similar missiles. Third, this vulnerability of weapons generates a corresponding vulnerability of population. (Contrast this with bubbles over cities vs. space-based offensive forces, where defense need not destroy offensive weapons at all, or if it does, produces zero collateral damage against the valued assets of the attacker).

In a technical environment where the two technologies are completely merged and a strategic/behavioral environment where adversaries compete rather than collaborate, choices *between* deterrence and defense cannot, in fact, be seriously considered or weighed at all. In this environment independent decisions to increase damage limiting capabilities would always increase retaliatory capabilities *pari passu*. Figure 6.1 gives a simple illustration. Suppose there are two countries 1 and 2. D_1 and D_2 denote damage or loss in the event of war in the two countries respectively. Let the "strategic" budget of both countries be fixed. If there is some flexibility for choosing between reducing own damage and imposing damage on the enemy, country 1's budget opportunity set could be represented by curve B_1^o, and 1 would choose a point on this budget set *depending on its strategic preferences*. A strategy which placed greater weight on assured destruction than assured survival would favor points toward the North East, while a strategy which gave more weight to self protection would indicate points along the South West stretch of B_1^0. (A strategy which required more of D_2 *and* less of D_1 would of course require a greater budget). Note however that with no flexibility to choose between own and enemy damage, curve B_1^0 will degenerate to a single point. The result in this case is that the choice of the mix between D_1 and D_2 is not influenced by strategic "preferences" at all. On the contrary however, technical developments which did allow separate systems for damage limitation (or assured survival) in contrast to damage infliction (or assured destruction) -- as represented by curve B_1^0 would not only allow but require that tradeoffs be considered even if the adversary is a non-cooperative competitor. Bubbles over cities defending populations against space based countervalue weapons could partition choices between defending one's own population and damaging another country's value.

   If such technically based distinctions between offensive and defensive systems ever emerge, then the role of preferences in the economic analysis of how to choose which will be appropriate and crucial. (For further development of the interaction between opportunities and preferences in the choice between deterrence and defense see McGuire (1967, 1987).

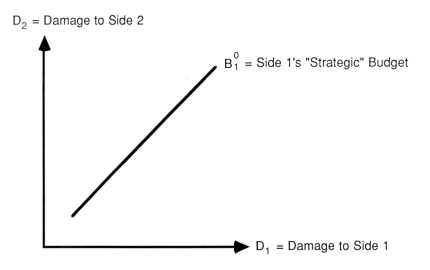

Figure 6.1: Side 1's Budget Opportunity Set

   Not only did a merger of offensive and defensive technology render choices between assured destruction and assured survival moot, it also was a source of confusion between the desirability of deterrence, and the stability of deterrence. If assured destruction and assured survival systems employ essentially the same weaponry, when increasing the latter capability a country will necessarily increase the former capability in step. Thus the merger of the two technologies means it is virtually impossible for the outcome of a second/retaliatory strike to be strongly preferred to that of a initiating/first strike. Although such preference order is not strictly necessary for stability of deterrence it is strongly instrumental to such stability. In fact the stability of deterrence has been increasingly threatened by weapons developments over the past two decades. Serious operational problems in Cold War stability have not arisen primarily because of the saturation of the system with weapons. The huge increase in number of strategic weapons (RVs) on both sides since 1965 has meant that war outcomes are calculated to be almost equally horrendous under first and second strike. As a specific instance it might be calculated that a country looses 95% in striking second but "only" 90% from striking first. In this case a country will endure much greater provocation and uncertainty as to the intentions of its adversary to attack or wait, and will withstand much greater pressure to strike first itself, than if the losses from going second were 50% say, but from striking first reducible to only 10%. In other words as both side's capabilities really approach overkill so that who strikes first matters very little the temptation to be trigger happy vanishes.

A nominal example of this merger of offense and defense is shown in Table 6.1. That table portrays a rough conjecture of the relative number of reliable, deliverable warheads (RVs) which could have been purchased and operated in the strategic force structure for $X billion dollars in 1965 for the two main categories of missile forces, under two war contingencies -- first strike and second retaliatory strike.

TABLE 6.1

Relative Number of Reliable, Deliverable Warheads Potentially Purchased and Operated for $X billion in 1965 (rough conjecture)

	ICBMs	SLBMs
Damage Limiting Ist Strike	10	4
Retaliatory 2nd Strike	7	3

As the table is meant to illustrate, in the 1960's the cost advantage clearly lay with ICBMs whether regarded as first strike damage limiting or second strike retaliatory weapons. The same ICBMs best served both purposes, dominating SLBMs (submarine-launched ballistic missiles) (as well as other alternatives not included in the above table). This situation essentially obviated the possibility of any choice between the two objectives of punitive retaliatory capability vs damage limiting self protection capabilities. (See Kent, 1964).

6.2.2 Relative costs of assured survival vs. assured destruction

From the inception of the Cold War a second crucial feature in the evaluation of offensive vs. defensive forces and strategies has been the relative costs of the two systems in competition with one another (McGuire, 1967 and Schelling, 1967). Since the deployment of ICBM's, technology and costs have greatly favored the offense. This was not easily accepted especially by defense planners. A superiority of defense over offense is not historically unprecedented; epochs in warfare favoring the defense have not been uncommon. Thus, early in the Cold War defense in the form of sheltering and population evacuation was thought to be a viable and relatively cheap way to defeat nuclear attack. This belief was dominant for a time in the Soviet Union. The reality throughout the period, however, has been that it is cheaper to defeat defensive systems than the costs of the systems themselves (Kent, 1964). Moreover, diminishing returns to further expenditures on defense and offense yield the result that this relative cost disadvantage borne by the defense becomes greater the higher the absolute amount of protection a country strives to achieve. For example to limit damage to "only" 10% of national assets might cost a country twenty times the amount it would cost an enemy to inflict 10% destruction; whereas "limiting" damage to 50% might cost "only" twice what it would cost an enemy to cause that 50% assured destruction. Under these circumstances unless one party to an offense-defense arms race is orders of magnitude richer than the other, even the strongest determination to protect one's population and other assets of value will be overcome by an adversary's moderate insistence on an assured retaliatory capability.

6.2.3 The cold war: a non-cooperative allocation game

These cost factors could change, gradually or suddenly, thereby making concentration on defense relatively more attractive and sustainable. But in a competitive environment between the superpowers such as existed throughout the cold war, the degree of cost change required might have been very large. Thus the third of the three major forces combining against strategic defense in the cold war was the absence of coordinated offensive weapons limitations. Without serious limits the incentives to overwhelm expensive strategic defense with cheap offenses dominated the system and defense was rejected. The over all status of the choices possible between deterrence and defense in the cold war years is also easily summarized in a diagram. Figure 6.2 shows the range of war outcomes measured by damage to each of two sides 1 and 2, D_1 and D_2, as dependent on the relative allocations between damage creating and damage limiting weapons by the two sides. (See McGuire, 1967 and 1987, for details on the construction of this figure and others to follow). Figure 6.2 shows this range of outcomes for fixed "strategic" budgets on both sides -- the variable of choice being the division of these budgets between expenditures on offense and defense. The diagram shows how each side, by changing its allocation, can very easily increase the damage it does to its adversary, but can reduce the damage done to itself only by very little. The situation is symmetric, and the only result accomplished by mutual budget increases as shown by Figure 6.3 is to increase the scope for higher damage levels. Figure 6.2 also depicts, the Nash-Cournot type equilibrium in this allocation game, wherein each side chooses its allocation assuming it will not change the other's similar decision. This non-cooperative behavior results in higher potential damage levels than would be most agreeable in a negotiation (where Pareto preferred outcomes should likely emerge). In fact, throughout the cold war period, the possibilities for mutual destruction increased toward total reciprocal annihilation.

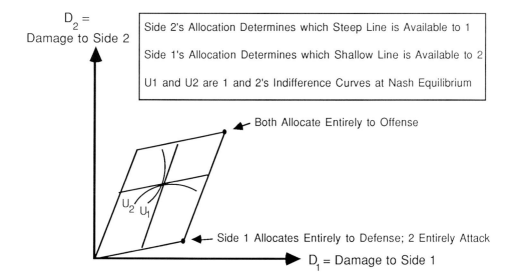

Figure 6.2: Cheaper to Attack than to Defend

M.C. McGuire

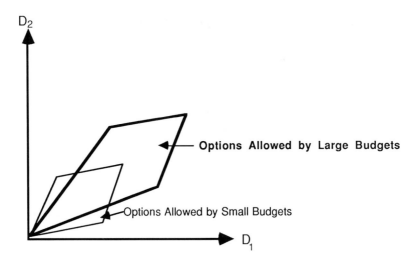

Figure 6.3: Options Allowed by Small and Large Budgets

For comparison, Figure 6.4 depicts the hypothetical situation where costs of defense are relatively low and of attack relatively high, and the associated Nash equilibrium. In this latter case Nash-Cournot result is *less* potential damage than negotiators might agree to.

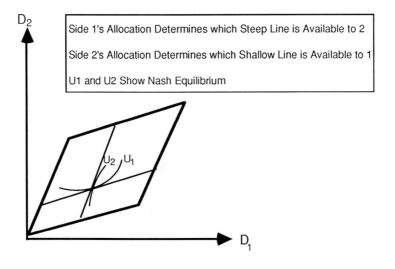

Figure 6.4: Defense Cheaper than Attack

6.3 Strategic Defense in the Post Cold War Era

6.3.1 Relative costs of defense vs. offense and separation of defense and offense technologies

The gradual evolution of weapons development proceeding mostly independent of the East-West rapprochement has placed an increasing reliance on SLBM's in the arsenals of both superpowers. Due to the increased accuracy of land based ICBMs and fitting MIRVs on these weapons, their second strike capabilities have diminished dramatically (see Kent and Thaler (1990)). Moreover with the shift to sea based missiles, forces now dominate the inventory which do not pose much greater first strike risks to the adversary than they provide second strike capability to their owners. A nominal example of this effect is shown in Table 6.2. The table portrays the relative number of reliable, deliverable warheads (RVs) which could have been purchased and operated in the strategic force structure for $Y billion dollars in 1990, for the two main categories of missile forces, under two war contingencies -- first strike and second retaliatory strike.

Table 6.2

Relative Number of Reliable, Deliverable Warheads Potentially Purchased and Operated for $Y Billion in 1990

	ICBMs	SLBMs
Damage Limiting/lst Strike	6	5
Retaliatory/2nd Strike	1	4

As these conjectural numbers suggest, a choice of sea based deterrence by the US means that an adversary who defends himself against our first strike has not provided himself with a very much more effective defense against our second strike, and therefore has not been provided with a strong incentive to strike first himself. On the contrary however, a choice of ICBMs today provides any adversary desiring to defend itself with a strong incentive to strike first since his defenses then will have so few retaliators to deal with. In the absence of ICBMs therefore, a rather strong separation of offense from defense would be achieved. SLBMs can not attack and destroy each other (except boats in port) and strategic defenses a la Star Wars adds very little to the protection of weapons. Moreover, absent ICBMs, the cost of retaliation has increased in comparison with the cold war period and with this the relative cost of defending against a first strike has decreased.

6.3.2 Shift in the character of the arms race: more collaboration-less competition

The above arguments suggest how technical weapons developments could generate rationales under which strategic defense might become viable even between wealthy, determined countries pursuing an adversarial competition. More likely for the present, however, are scenarios wherein rich countries prefer to coordinate and collaborate in their deterrence/defense or assured survival/destruction decisions. In this environment strategic defense could dominate offense by choice and restraint, despite unfavorable technological and cost factors such as just itemized. In fact, it appears at the present that collaboration among great powers could produce stable equilibria at very low levels of assured destruction, ie, very high levels of assured survival as between the major players (see Kent and Thaler, 1990). Restraint on each side with respect to offensive forces in this environment makes assured survival possible at a tolerable total cost even though relative cost factors are unfavorable. Political instabilities in the Soviet Union, or whatever emerges therefrom should it collapse, probably mean that strategic collaboration of this sort is not imminent, but it is a possibility for the future not hitherto available.

Under this set-up for example each of the "superpowers" might maintain verified inventories of say 50 SLBM's with 500 verified warheads and adequate defenses to intercept an expected 99.9%, requiring say 1500 to 2000 interceptors. If the probability of a successful launch and kill from a single one-on-one engagement were 90% then to achieve 99.9% expected kills would require three interceptors to be targeted against each attacker. With a shoot-look-shoot capability the average number of interceptors per attacker would be less. Since present SDI-related studies analyze defenses against *10,000* incoming RVs the numbers in the several hundreds to a thousand should be technically entirely manageable. Assuming such success probabilities were achievable at possibly high but tolerable cost would have very profound and very interesting implications for great power relations. Among such would be:

a. Any economic power desiring to guarantee its own assured survival without threatening others could do so. The mutual restraint among superpowers being an international public good, would allow any rich countries to defend themselves against nuclear devastation (assuming any rich country could provide itself with strategic defense).

b. Lesser economic powers and non-powers would be in a *less* desirable situation than today or during the cold war, in as much as nuclear powers would not have the overriding constraint of their fears of an apocalypse initiated by intervention of *other superpowers* into their conflicts with lesser countries.

c. The chances of conventional conflict among great powers and even among the superpowers might well increase as the apocalyptic threat recedes.

6.3.3 Strategic Preferences

The possibility that countries may actually face the choice of allocating resources between assured destruction and assured survival -- whether because of the evolution of technology and relative cost factors, or because of changes in the play of the resource allocation and strategic competition games among the great powers -- means that policy will have to attend much more closely than hitherto to preferences between these and other strategic goals. That is, one's policy will have to attend both to one's own preferences and to those of the other players. Thus to operate in an offense/defense environment, both in pursuit of one's own national objectives and of larger objectives of global peace and security may require a subtle appreciation of the adversarial partner's preferences and tradeoffs. Figure 6.6 gives an example of what I mean. Suppose line A shows the amount of damage a country "Y" could cause the undefended US at various levels of attack, shown on the x-axis. That country trades off its resource costs (increasing with greater levels of attack forces) against the benefits it perceives from being able to threaten so much damage. This trade-off is shown by country Y's indifference curve Uy. Now suppose the US can defend itself using either of two equal cost alternatives, B and C. B just shuts out a fixed number of enemy intruders, while C degrades all intruding forces by a given percent. Which of these two equal cost systems is better for the US? Obviously it depends on *Y's* tradeoffs. (see especially Schelling, 1967).

Not only should other players' objectives become of greater concern but a more coherent understanding of a country's own objectives should have to be articulated. The likelihood envisaged here is that policies will be driven less by one dominant technology, and more by political and economic preferences among alternative technologies. Strategic goals, preferences or utility may include such elements as power projection, war avoidance, damage limitation in the event of war, the ability to coerce by threatening destruction and many other desiderata including of course those foregone by allocating resources to strategic programs.

In the analysis of alternative preference patterns and of interactions among players economics may make a special contribution. If a country actually could choose between assured destruction, assured survival, or some mix of the two at different levels for different resource costs, which might it prefer? It may seem obvious to some that a strategic posture where the only force which prevents my country from suffering 90% damage is my guarantee that my adversary will suffer the same, is inferior to one in which neither side can threaten over 1/10% damage.

The argument in favor of this position, I suspect, might be made quite convincing in a two sided world, for then bilateral security of assets, borders, and populations is in fact global security. The situation could be quite different however in a multi-party world, of many countries. In that more complex and more realistic asymmetric world one side need not necessarily give up the ability to inflict punishment or to compel submission (see Schelling, 1966) as a cost of immunity from retaliation. In this environment the value of securing the politico-economic status quo versus favorable changes therein must be weighed, and the effectiveness of force versus cooperation in the achievement of a country's objectives calculated. In this context an ability to threaten 1% damage could just possibly be better than an ability to threaten only 1/10 %.

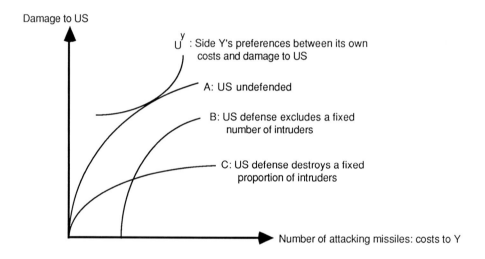

Figure 6.5: Importance of Anticipating Adversary's Preferences

References

Bailey, M.J. (1973). Strategic Interaction in Force Structure Planning. Carnegie-Mellon University Working Paper (Graduate School of Industrial Administration) November 15, 1973.

Kent, G.A. (1964). *Damage limiting: a rationale for the allocation of resources by the US and the USSR.* US Department Defense (Directorate of Defense Research and Engineering) undated ("secret" later declassified) Study.

Kent, G.A. and Thaler, D.E. (1989). *First strike stability and strategic defenses part I.* RAND Corporation Report R-3765-AF, August, 1989.

Kent, G.A.and Thaler, D.E. (1990). *First strike stability and strategic defenses part II.* RAND Corporation Report R-3918-AF, October 1990.

McGuire, M.C. (1965). *Secrecy and the arms race.* Cambridge: Harvard University Press.

McGuire, M.C. (1967). The structure of choice between deterrence and defense. in R.N. McKean (ed.) *Issues in Defense Economics.* New York: Columbia University Press.

McGuire, M.C. (1987). Economic considerations in the comparison between assured destruction and assured survival. in C. Schmidt and F. Blackaby (eds.) *Peace, Defense, and Economic Analysis.* International Economic Association, London: Macmillan.

Schelling, T.C. (1966). *Arms and Influence.* New Haven: Yale University Press.

Schelling, T.C. (1967). The strategy of inflicting costs. in R.N. McKean (ed.) *Issues in Defense Economics.* New York: Columbia University Press.

Economics of Arms Reduction and the Peace Process
W. Isard and C.H. Anderton (Editors)
© 1992 Elsevier Science Publishers B.V. All rights reserved.

Chapter 7

COMPETING OPTIMA IN THE GULF WAR

*Murray Wolfson, *Sergio Gutierrez, *John Traynor, and **Robert Smith‡

*California State University-Fullerton

and

**Coastline Community College

[At this point in this book, it is profitable and most interesting to pursue a tangent to the main theme. Thus far, the papers have discussed topics having in mind the recent upheavals in Eastern Europe and the Soviet Union. However, there has been a recent event, the Gulf War, which allows an analyst to look at another area of peace economics, namely the costs of war itself as perceived by key political decision makers prior to the outbreak of war, and as can be objectively estimated after the event. The costs considered in this chapter go beyond the costs of maintaining a stock of weaponry for the damaging threatening and damaging limiting objectives discussed by McGuire.

Wolfson, Gutierrez, Traynor and Smith come forth with a unique contribution. First they attempt to formulate appropriate cost functions for the Gulf War, a task interesting in itself. Next, they utilize the best available published data to estimate relevant magnitudes of total, fixed, variable and marginal costs as well as the value of a life based on experts' estimates. With such estimates they then analyze the efficacy of the goals (desired policies) of the several different parties and decision makers involved in the Gulf War. Whether or not the reader is in agreement with their method of analysis, clearly they have significantly advanced the state of art on the costing and valuing of different policies (scenarios) associated with the question of "economic sanctions *or* war", and if war, ways of engaging to minimize costs inclusive of the value of lives lost. (eds.)]

7.1 Introduction

Like every decision to allocate resources, the conduct of war reflects the valuations of benefits and costs as perceived by various decision makers. This paper will operationalize the contending valuations operative during the Gulf War, and compare the policies which alternative criteria generated. It will not attempt to evaluate the larger question of gains from forcing Iraq to relinquish its hold on Kuwait, but will focus on the Desert Storm military operation as a means of doing so.

This study will analyze the goals of the participants in terms of the length of the bombing campaign prior to the ground attack (Section 7.2), their valuations of the lives of allied service personnel saved by bombing (Section 7.3), and the distribution of the economic costs of the attack. These elements will appear as part of a formal model (Section 7.4) which will reproduce the actions of the participants (Section 7.5). Section 7.6 will consider quantitative information which will permit some approximate measures. Section 7.7 re-evaluates the sanctions versus ground attack controversy that preceded the decision to wage war, and Section 7.8 concludes by putting the problem in the perspective of choices for the future.

7.2 Competing Goals

We will focus on the US air and ground forces whose use was sanctioned by the United Nations. The special character of the war was that these forces were thrown into action sequentially. Those in authority had to decide how long to conduct the air war before starting the ground attack, such that they would defeat the Iraqi army, and such that the human and material cost of the war would be minimized. That is to say, the air war was to proceed until it would inflict enough damage on Iraq to at least ensure the later military victory on the ground. But, as we shall see it might continue until the marginal benefit of bombing equalled its marginal cost. The bombing campaign might turn out to be longer or shorter than the minimum time required to ensure victory. When the ground forces finally did launch their attack on February 23, the war ended almost immediately.

There were several individuals and entities on the UN side as well as in Iraq, each with its own concept of benefits and costs. They might be identified schematically as follows:

(1) The UN Security Council professed goal was to force Iraq's army to withdraw from Kuwait.

(2) President Bush aimed at accomplishing more than the UN goal. He proposed also to establish "the security and stability of the Persian Gulf." Operationally that seems to have meant the security of the world oil supply, the removal of Saddam Hussein from power, and the destruction of Iraq's offensive military capability. At the same time, the President evidently believed that security and stability required that he not destroy Iraq as a political entity, its capacity to defend itself against its neighbors, or its role as a player in the Middle East balance of power.

(3) General Norman Schwarzkopf's goal was to destroy as much of Iraq's army as he could up to some optimum level consistent with the value of US human life

that would be lost in the process. The optimum would be where the marginal cost to the US equalled the marginal benefit.

Clausewitz[1] would advise professional military leaders such as Schwarzkopf to think in extreme terms:

> If you are to force the enemy, by making war on him, to do your bidding, you must make him literally defenseless or at least put him in a position that makes this danger probable. It follows, then, that to overcome the enemy, or disarm him--call it what you will--must always be the aim of warfare." [Clausewitz, p.77].

(4) The goal of the US allies was to destroy as much of the Iraqi army as was consistent with the marginal cost of their contribution to the war effort.

(5) President Saddam Hussein's goal was to inflict a prohibitive cost on the UN in order to prevent or defeat an attack.

(6) Senator Sam Nunn's strategy expressed in his interchange with General Colin Powell (Powell, 1990) was to force Iraq to withdraw from Kuwait by means of sanctions.[2] This was the view of former members of the Joint Chiefs of Staff given as testimony to the Senate Armed Services Committee.

The model we will develop will show how each of these decision makers came to a different conclusion. In actuality, it was George Bush who made the final decision for the UN within technical military constraints, even though he might not have represented the valuation schemes of the other parties who shared both the costs and benefits of Desert Storm.

7.3 Competing Valuations of Human Life

Our benchmark (w^*) in valuing lives lost or saved during Desert Storm is the Value of Statistical Life (VSL) in the United States. VSL was developed for cost-benefit analysis to assist in the evaluation of public and private programs that reduce the probability of death (industrial safety, pollution control, etc.) and to settle legal claims for wrongful death. The VSL literature was extensively reviewed by Fisher (1989) and included in a more comprehensive study by Jane Hall et. al. (1989).

The estimates of VSL are computed from "wage-risk studies" where the willingness of individuals to accept a higher risk of death is presumed to be compensated by wage differentials. The literature puts the acceptable range of VSL between $1.7 and $9.2 million.[3] The lower range of estimates tend not to correct adequately for the bias that results when risk takers select themselves into dangerous occupations. As the literature has developed, the estimates have tended to rise from the lower to the higher end of the range. They are much higher than the old capitalized expected value of income lost. Income loss estimates are made at the margin of choice, and therefore do not include the intra-marginal consumer's surplus involved in the "all-or-none bargain" implicit in losing one's life.

VSL only represents the social cost of life to the extent that the social welfare functions of decision makers reflect individuals' own valuations. Those in authority may place different values on human life than individuals. In particular, national civilian as well as military leaders value the lives of their enemies--particularly their military personnel--much lower than they do.

The competing goals of the decision makers may be ranked in terms of their valuations:

The UN Security Council (1) which wished simply to expel Iraq from Kuwait, presumably reflected the highest value on Iraqi life. In contrast, General Schwarzkopf (3) following Clausewitz's dictum that the conduct of war should be aimed at destroying the enemy's army, probably placed the lowest value on Iraq's military personnel--indeed it must be a negative number. Sensitive to political considerations at home and in the likely postwar balance of power in the Middle East, President Bush (2) and Senator Nunn (6) are likely to have evaluated Iraq's military life somewhere between the two. Probably European, Japanese and Middle Eastern allies (4) felt much the same, although, as we shall see, their economic cost structure was different. Judging by his actions, Saddam Hussein's evaluation of the life of his personnel was lower than their own estimate.

The same set of decision makers had to evaluate the life of the US military personnel. It is reasonable to assume that President Bush (2) and General Schwarzkopf (3) placed the Statistical Value of Life on US soldiers. It is reasonable to assume that the UN (1) members who had not committed sizeable ground troops evaluated US soldiers at less than these American decision makers; allied countries (4) that had substantial forces probably valued them much as did the US. Some military officials of UN members such as the Soviet Union scoffed at the American sensitivity to casualties.

Senator Nunn and other congressional opponents of an early ground war (6) probably placed a higher value on military casualties. That is not to say they necessarily had a higher level of sympathy than other US decision makers, but sensitive to the experience in Viet Nam, they seemed to feel that the cost of substantial casualties as reflected in the Social Welfare Function implicit in American public opinion would exceed even the valuation of the volunteer army soldiers themselves. The "no blood for oil" opponents of the war exhibited just this evaluation.

Finally we should mention the pacifist position expressed by Senator Mark Hatfield (R-Ore.) who regarded the value of human life on either side of the conflict as greater than any benefit that might accrue from war.

Undoubtedly Saddam Hussein's valuation of American life was negative, but the analysis will show that his conjecture was that the US evaluation would be high, and that he could enforce his low evaluation of his own personnel to the point where that cost would be excessive.

7.4 The Model

7.4.1 Destruction function (Figure 7. 1)

Letting X stand for the number of air sorties[4] and Y for the amount of Iraqi military capital destroyed, we can write the Destruction Function as:

$$Y=\beta X^\alpha \tag{7.1}$$

where the constants $\beta>0$ and $1>\alpha>0$. The boundaries on the constants imply that the marginal destruction of bombing is positive and subject to diminishing returns. Although there may be regions of increasing returns, bombing is an extractive industry and certain to become increasingly ineffective as targets are destroyed.

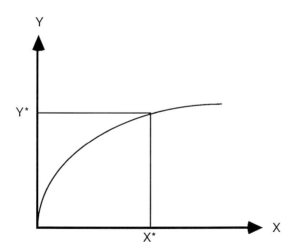

Figure 7.1: Destruction Function

7.4.2 *Iraqi Casualties* (Figure 7.2)

Iraqi casualties (C) as a result of the bombing and in the subsequent ground campaign are an increasing function of (Y), the amount of their capital destroyed. This function is likely to exhibit diminishing returns up to some point and then increasing returns to bombing. The reason for this has to do with the public good nature of soldiers' behavior.   In every military action, soldiers are trained to fire on the enemy, thus exposing themselves to fire. The rationale for this action is that if they collectively behave in this fashion more than the enemy, he will not be able to fire back effectively; the unit maintaining the fire will then be mobile and the enemy fixed in place.   Mobility permits flanking and other offensive maneuvers which, combined with firepower, lead to the destruction of the enemy and the preservation of one's own life.

In this way each individual soldier maximizes his chances of survival by exposing himself to death as long as he believes that his comrades will do likewise. He gains an external benefit from the collective utility of the unit. Military discipline has as its purpose the substitution of conditioned response in the place of atomistic utility maximization in the psychology of armies. Discipline prevents individuals from "free-riding" on the exposure of their comrades by hiding, deserting or failing to fire on the enemy. But if soldiers no longer believe they can hold their own in a fire fight with their enemy, then individual utility maximization takes over, the conditioned response of discipline collapses, and each soldier runs for his life.   In the ensuing rout, the collective protection fails, and casualties mount on an increasing scale. It is at this point that armies are defeated.

We can model this effect as a cubic equation whose point of inflection is this breaking point. Letting n and L represent the Y and C coordinates of that point, and m a positive constant, we have the Iraqi Casualty Function:

$$C=m(Y-n)^3+L \tag{7.2}$$

Since from (7.1):

$$X=(Y/\beta)^{1/\alpha} \tag{7.3}$$

a ground attack consistent with the UN position aimed at causing the enemy to run away would take place at $X^*=(n/\beta)^{1/\alpha}$ sorties. Let us call this the capitulation point, it being understood that resistance might continue past that point, but it would become progressively less effective.

The essential aspect of this function for our purposes is behavioral. When do the troops revert to individual utility maximization based on their private valuation of their own lives as opposed to the social valuation required for effective collective action? The behavior of individuals determines the breaking point, even though it is a technical military question that measures the number of casualties endured. The solid graph in Figure 7.2 displays the revealed behavior of the Iraqi troops, breaking at Y*, while the dashed graph shows the expectations of Hussein and perhaps the fears of Senator Nunn that the point might be at Y**.

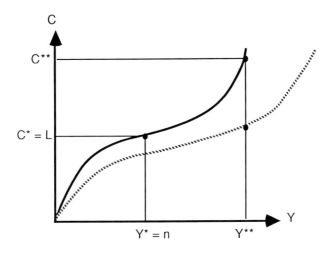

Figure 7.2: Iraqi Casualty Function

Clearly the discontinuity in behavior represents a break in behavior that is difficult to predict since it has its roots in the complex social, political, religious and ideological nature of Iraqi society, as well as the training, indoctrination and discipline of soldiers. Clausewitz explains:

If you want to overcome your enemy you must match your effort against his power of resistance, which can be expressed as the product of two inseparable factors, viz. *the total means at his disposal and the strength of his will.* The extent of the means at his disposal is a matter--though not exclusively--of figures, and should be measurable. But the strength of his will is much less easy to determine and can only be gauged approximately by the strength of the motive animating it. Assuming you arrive in this way at a reasonably accurate estimate of the enemy's power of resistance, you can adjust your own efforts accordingly...But the enemy will do the same; competition will again result and, in pure theory it must again force you both to extremes." [Clausewitz, p.77].

7.4.3 Cost of bombing (Figures 7.3a, 7.3b)

We treat the bombing campaign as a means of reducing the cost of US and allied lives that would be lost when the ground campaign began. Therefore it is a factor of production, whose ultimate output is US lives saved on the ground. Consequently the cost curves should be understood to be total and marginal factor cost curves.

The total cost of bombing $\pi(X)$, consists of the variable costs $\rho(X)$, as well as fixed and sunk costs F, as shown in equation (7.4). Marginal costs are, of course $\rho'(X)$.

$$\pi(X)=\rho(X)+F \tag{7.4}$$

There were special circumstances to this operation that bear on its the cost structure (Figure 7.3):

(1) The military equipment used against Iraq was designed and stockpiled by the US (as well as the UK) to fight a land war in Europe against the USSR. Now that the possibility of such a conflict has become so remote, and the US intends to drastically reduce the size of its armed forces, a great deal of this accumulated materiel represents a sunk cost. Much of the military infrastructure had already been put in place in Saudi Arabia against the possibility of a Soviet thrust southward toward the oil fields. With the diminution of that threat, much of the materiel used up in the Gulf would not have been replaced; it would have depreciated without extensive maintenance; and would in any case be replaced by more modern equipment. In the absence of alternative uses, F must have been very large.

(2) Even though not high compared to the total cost of the war, the variable costs to the US differ from those of its allies. One might expect that the rate of change in variable costs (marginal costs) to rise with bombing due to the law of diminishing returns. Since the United States was to be compensated for its incremental costs by its allies, its marginal costs would be low and would not rise as long as it did not have to expend resources on new equipment beyond the compensation by its allies.

Consequently there are two marginal cost curves in Figure 7.3b. The upper curve represents the marginal cost to the allies, and is smoothly upward sloping in response to the increasing opportunity cost of allied production that will be transferred to the United States by the subsidy.[5] The lower curve is the US marginal cost curve. It is horizontal up to the point X'--never reached--in which the US would have to produce more war materiel, transport facilities, air bases, recruit and train new troops, and so on. At that point there would be a sharp discontinuity in the marginal cost curve corresponding to the kink in the US total cost curve in Figure 7.3a.

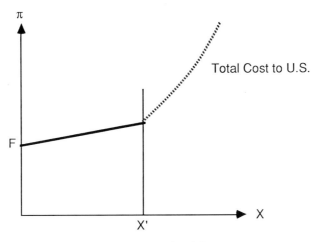

Figure 7.3a: Total Cost

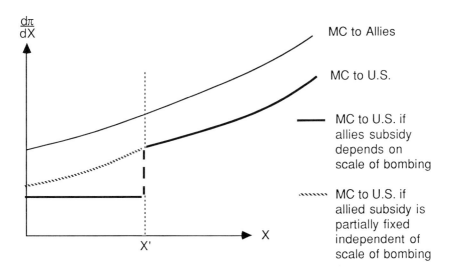

Figure 7.3b: Marginal Cost of Bombing

The degree to which the US bore the variable costs depended on the terms of the subsidy. To the extent that the subsidy was a fixed amount, it would not enter into a marginal cost calculation and hence would not subsidize the US variable costs.[6] In suggesting that the subsidy entered in a significant way into variable costs, we are assuming that implicitly or explicitly they were related to the scale of operations. Since the structure of the aid would influence US decisions, we show an intermediate US marginal cost curve in the diagram.

7.4.4 UN Casualties (Figure 7.4)

US and other UN casualties (I) that would be suffered during the ground attack must be a decreasing function of the Iraqi military capital destroyed during the preceding bombing. A reasonable specification is, for some positive constant H, and positive weighting parameters δ and ε:

$$I^\delta Y^\varepsilon = H \tag{7.5}$$

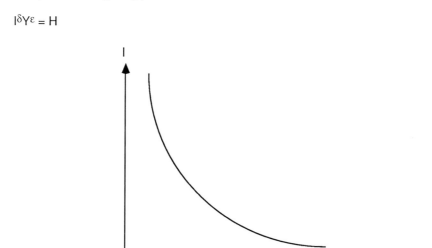

Figure 7.4: U.S. Casulaties and Destruction of Iraqi Military Capital

Taking the derivative of (7.5) with respect to Y, $dI/dY = -\gamma I/Y$, where $\gamma = \varepsilon/\delta$. γ is the elasticity of casualties saved with respect to destruction of Iraqi military capital. The negative sign means that casualties are reduced by Y and hence are saved. From the destruction function (7.1):

$$dY/dX = \alpha\beta X^{\alpha-1} \tag{7.6}$$

Multiplying by X and dividing by Y, the elasticity of the destruction function is simply α. By the chain rule the marginal product of bombing MP_X is:

$$dI/dX = (dI/dY)(dY/dX) = -\alpha\gamma I/X \tag{7.7}$$

The elasticity of the effectiveness of bombing in saving US lives is simply $\alpha\gamma$. It is the elasticity of the effectiveness of bombing in destroying Iraq's military capital times the elasticity of US-UN lives saved by that destruction.

The actual shape of I as a function of X can be derived easily from (7.7) by integration of $dI/I = -\alpha\gamma dX/X$ to yield a weighted hyperbola. Substituting (7.1) into (7.5), the curve is

$$IX^{\alpha\gamma} = K \tag{7.8}$$

where $K = H^{-\delta}\beta^{-(\delta+\epsilon)}$. Its slope, the MP_X once more is found by substituting for I from (7.1), (7.5), (7.6) and (7.7) to get:

$$MP_X = -\alpha\gamma\beta^{-\gamma}H^{1/\delta}X^{-(1+\alpha\gamma)} \tag{7.9}$$

Then $(MP_X)(X^{(1+\alpha\gamma)}) = -\alpha\gamma\beta^{-\gamma}H^{1/\delta}$ and is a more steeply sloped weighted hyperbola than (7.8).

The derived demand for bombing, the Value of its Marginal Product is found by multiplying the Marginal Product by w, the value placed on the life of a US soldier. Changing the sign in (7.9) to indicate US lives saved, VMP_X is simply w times MP_X, and is the rectangular hyperbola:

$$(VMP_X)(X^{(1+\alpha\gamma)}) = w\alpha\gamma\beta^{-\gamma}H^{1/\delta} \tag{7.10}$$

Interestingly, VMP_X slopes downward even though there might conceivably be increasing returns to the destruction of military capital by bombing if $\alpha > 1$.

7.5 Competing Choices

The VMP_X of bombing, then, is a downward sloping function of X, but which shifts inward or outward radially as w is lower or higher. In Figure 7.5 the VMP_X is superimposed on the marginal costs in Figure 7.3b, permitting us to study the optima chosen by the participants. For simplicity we display only the VMP_X associated with two contrasting values of w: the Statistical Value of Life in the United States $VMP_X(w^*)$; and the value associated with hopes of Hussein and the fears of Nunn, $VMP_X(w^{**})$. The reader can interpolate other values.

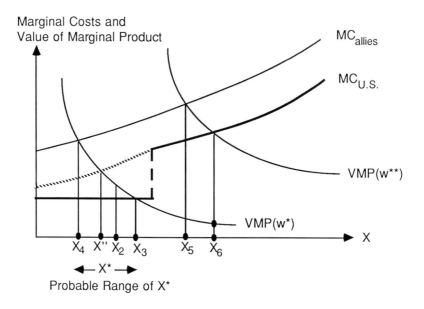

Figure 7.5: Optimal Bombing Points at the "Statistical Value of Life" to U.S.

$VMP_X(w^*)$ intersects the graphs of all three marginal costs of bombing. Given the goals and valuations we have imputed to him, General Schwarzkopf would rationally wish to drive to X_3 where the Marginal Factor Cost to the US equalled the Value of the Marginal Product of continued bombing. The allies might well have accepted the US evaluation of human life lost in a ground action, w^*, since their troops were involved as well. But since they bore a higher Marginal Cost would have launched the attack sooner, at X_4. This difference was expressed in political terms and resolved at some point intermediate between them, perhaps close to President Bush's choice X_2. The intermediate bombing, X", represents the length of bombing that Schwarzkopf would have chosen if some portion of the support given by allies entered into the marginal cost calculation.

$VMP_X(w^{**})$ intersects two Marginal Cost curves, the actual marginal cost of the operation associated with the allied contribution and the lower marginal cost to the US, given the subsidy. From the Nunn point of view the US might have had to go on to X_6 if the alliance held, or to X_5 if it did not as Hussein hoped. Given that length of bombing, and the associated economic expense, they debated whether the operation would be worthwhile, or be seen to be worthwhile by the public in the US and abroad.

The cost-prohibitive level of bombing at X_5 or X_6 depended on Iraq behavior as well as US valuation of human life. These points could be reached under the w^*

Statistical Value of Life as well as w**. Suppose the Iraqi soldiers were willing to fight up to some level Y** in Figure 7.2, corresponding to some X* in Figure 7.5 in the neighborhood of X_5 and X_6. In this case both Marginal Cost curves representing the factor cost of bombing would exceed the $VMP_X(w^*)$ and the ground campaign would not be undertaken.

In these cases, the appropriate strategy would have been sanctions and economic warfare rather than military attack. In actuality, war broke out due on one side to the preference of President Bush for military action, his political adroitness, the suitability of high technology US air-land doctrine to the terrain and the brevity of the campaign; and, on the other, Saddam Hussein's political and military ineptitude, the inability of Soviet-style military doctrine and technology to counter the US on this terrain, and the perhaps anticipated unwillingness of Iraq's soldiers to maintain collective behavior in the face of fire.

Consequently X* turned out to be somewhere between X_4 and X_3 in Figure 7.5. But where? Could it have been somewhere to the left of X_3, so that the US continued to attack even after Iraq was unable to offer organized resistance? *A priori* one would expect that since the US was the effective decision maker, considering only its own utility it would bomb up to the point where its VMP_X equaled is marginal factor cost at General Schwarzkopf's point X_3. Since the marginal cost was extraordinarily low due to the special circumstances we have described, and the US evaluation of allied lives and Iraqi lives was as described, the US would rationally have bombed "too much" compared to the evaluations of others. It would have inflicted further destruction on the enemy and would have saved more US and allied lives if it bombed to, say, point Y** in Figure 7.2 with C** the corresponding level of Iraqi casualties along the solid-line actual Iraqi Casualty Function.

7.6 Measurement: The Elasticity of Saving Lives Through Bombing

In the face of the paucity of data which makes it impossible to estimate the parameters of the system of equations in the model, we attempt a point estimate of the elasticity of US casualties saved with respect to sorties. A low elasticity implies that the bombing was carried on to the extent that further air attacks would yield only a small percent reduction in casualties when the ground war started.

From equation (7.7):

$$(dI/dX)(X/I) = -\alpha\gamma \tag{7.11}$$

Multiplying by the value of life, w and changing the sign again:

$$VMP_X(X/I) = w\alpha\gamma \qquad (7.12)$$

At equilibrium the VMP_X of another sortie equals its MC. Substituting and dividing by w we get the point elasticity of lives saved with respect to bombing to be:

$$(MC/w)(X/I) \qquad (7.13)$$

We make rough high and low estimates of the elasticity in Table 7.1. Each estimate is made both with and without the allied subsidy. The components of (7.13) are measured as follows:

(1) MC is approximated locally by Average Cost as the per-sortie Total Variable Cost (TVC) of Desert Storm. Since only aggregate point data are available, it is our only measure. Nevertheless it is consistent with the theory which suggests that the US was operating in a constant returns environment.

TVC is reported in different ways by various agencies. We shall rely on data contained in the report of Richard Darman, Director of the Office of Management and Budget to the Congress (Darman, 1991). OMB estimates that what it calls the Total Incremental Cost of Desert Storm to finally be $60 billion when the operation is phased down and the troops are returned home. As of the end of February $31.574 billion was spent. *The Wall Street Journal* (Wessel, 1991) reports that the General Accounting Office estimates the cost of Desert Storm to have been much lower, $40 billion on a similar incremental basis. With a few adjustments, we will use the OMB figures to derive the elasticities in Table 7.1.

For our high estimate of Total Variable Cost we only subtract from the $60 billion the $1.220 billion reported by OMB for aircraft and vehicles destroyed since they came from stock (OMB p.8), and the $2.1 billion estimate of the ground campaign itself by *US News and World Report* (March 11, 1991, p.74).

Our low estimate includes all of the OMB Total Incremental Cost for January-February 1991 even though that includes the ground campaign that took place between February 23 and February 27. To this is added half of the remaining incremental costs, since the attack force was doubled from the approximately 200,000 troops for the defensive Desert Shield Operation, to over 400,000 for the offensive Desert Storm. This measure, which we consider still to be an overestimate, turns out to approximate the GAO figure.

(2) The value of life is taken to be the Statistical Value of Life. In light of the trend of its estimates over the years, w*=$6 million seems reasonable for a volunteer army.

(3) The total number of US sorties, X, is reported by *Time* (March 4, 1991, p.32) to be 94,000.[7]

(4) US killed in action casualties, I, is subject to fine definitional problems. In actual fact the number of Americans killed in the ground campaign proper was very small, excluding as it does the casualties incurred by the Scud attack on the barracks in Riyadh, and losses of air personnel. There may have been as few as 4 persons killed on this narrow definition. However, in this analysis we are concerned with choices that by definition must have been made *ex ante* before the ground attack was launched. According to *Newsweek* (March 18, 1991, pp. 37-38), the plan of attack was carried out under assumptions given by computer simulations conducted by General Schwarzkopf which showed an expected casualty rate of 5,000 killed.

In Table 7.1, we compute three elasticity estimates for the high and low values of TVC: (1) if the US had received no subsidy; (2) if the subsidy was limited to the amount that actually has been collected by the date of the OMB report; and (3) if all the subsidy were collected, corresponding to the OMB estimate of incremental cost when the whole operation is wound up.

TABLE 7.1

Incremental Costs and Elasticities of Bombing (Costs in Billions of Dollars)

	High	Low
Gross US Incremental Costs	60	39.193
Adjustments	-3.32	0
Net US Incremental Costs	57.68	39.193
Elasticity Without Subsidy	1.92	1.31
Contributions Received	36.1	36.1
US Costs after Receipt	21.58	3.093
Elasticity after Contributions Received	0.7193	0.1031
Contributions Received and Promised	54.56	54.56
US Cost after Contributions	3.12	-15.367
Elasticity after Contributions	0.104	-0.512

Sources: OMB 4-27-91; *US News and World Report* 3-11-91; *Newsweek*, March 4, 1991 p.32 and March 11, 1991 p.74.

These results suggest that the "over-bombing" had been carried out to an extreme margin, just as one would expect from the theoretical analysis. For the lowest of the estimated costs, it seems that even if all the promised contributions do not come in the US seems to have earned a positive quasi-rent and probably a profit on the venture.

7.7 Ground Attack Versus Sanctions

However crude, these estimates seem sufficiently robust to justify the conclusion that the US carried out the bombing campaign until there was nothing at all to be gained by continuing further. It could do so because of two special factors that reduced the marginal cost of the action to virtually zero: the war was fought out of inventory, much of which was either obsolete or not to be replaced; and, the subsidy by allies more than covered the variable cost.

This approach is in line with the position most closely associated with the post-Viet Nam views of General Colin Powell that one does not "fool around" with war by following a piecemeal program of graduated response or one-dimensional air or economic war which allows the opponent any opportunity to adapt.[8] Powell regarded the decision to wage offensive war as a political one to be made by the President. But once that decision was made, his approach was Clausewitzian: the maximum multi-dimensional air-land-sea assault power available is to be brought to bear on the enemy to completely destroy his capacity to fight. This approach was reiterated by General Schwarzkopf on the eve of battle, and which he and General McCaffrey[9] carried out until ordered to halt by the President.

The rush to early military action pressed by President Bush reflected what turned out to be a correct estimate of the costs. At very little sacrifice to the US, he hoped for the political advantages of his New Order in the Middle East, stabilization of the world's oil supply, and an object lesson to those who threaten the values he espouses.

Total wars of the past--the US Civil War, the two World Wars, and the Cold War now won--tested the production possibilities of nations. The Gulf War was not an economic war from the American point of view. It was largely fought with slack economic resources, within the US production possibility frontier. Until the cease-fire was ordered, it was seemingly a technical military war to the US, safely left to the experts to employ tactics and equipment designed to destroy a Soviet-style army. The decision not to apply sanctions amounted to a decision not to wage economic war during the hostilities, although it has since been conducted after the cease fire.

In the end the political decision to halt the attack illustrates the limitation of the purely military maximum assault approach which is simply turned on and then allowed to run its course. Even though the economic limitation did not apply to the

US in this case, political constraints continued to matter and to influence the course of war. War can never be a purely technical military question left to military leaders any more than the operation of a business enterprise can be left to its engineering staff.

The question we consider in retrospect is: If the military campaign was a model of systems designed to defeat the Soviet Union, could the economic war, which actually did defeat the USSR, have been directed toward Iraq (Wolfson, 1991)? Would sanctions have worked? As Senator Nunn remarked to General Powell: "We will never know."

Consider evidence on both sides of the proposition:

7.7.1 Sanctions and economic war would have worked

Iraq was in a severely debilitated situation as a result of the vagaries of world oil prices, the destruction and disruption of oil exports as a result of the 1980-1988 war with Iran, as well as the expense of that struggle. Real Gross National Product was halved during those years, and its per capita GNP reduced by almost two-thirds as Table 7.2 shows.

TABLE 7.2

Iraq Gross National Product 1980-1981 (Constant 1988 Dollars)

Year	GNP (billions)	GNP per Capita (dollars)
1980	124,600	9,441
1981	70,420	5,145
1982	67,880	4,785
1983	65,100	4,427
1984	68,740	4,509
1985	67,430	4,267
1986	56,870	3,472
1987	66,120	3,896
1988	65,790	3,742

Source: US Arms Control and Disarmament Agency (1990, 51).

Since oil makes up virtually all of the Iraqi exports, these could have been cut off, as they still are at this writing, either by the refusal of the rest of the world to buy or the closure of the pipeline terminals. Effectively this would have halted the importation of goods by closing off Iraq's supply of foreign exchange, without much effort at a naval blockade.

The dependency of Iraq on oil exports for its military program is illustrated in Table 7.3. The table shows the drastic decline in Iraq's exports during the Iran-Iraq war and the extremely large portion of arms imports compared to the export of petroleum. Exports fell from 30 per cent of GNP at the beginning of the war to 2 per cent at the end. At the start of the war, arms imports were only 9 per cent of the value of exports. By 1984 the value of arms imports reached 99 per cent of the value of all exports and never fell below 35 per cent throughout the war. To be sure some of Iraq's imports of arms was financed by transfer payments--from Kuwait among others--as well as its exports of oil. But with both these sources of finance eliminated, Iraq would have been unable to import military equipment as well as the other goods required to maintain its civilian economy.

TABLE 7.3

Iraq's International Trade in Arms (Constant 1988 Dollars)

Year	Imports	Exports	Arms Imports	Arms Imports/GNP
1980	19720	37180	3395	0.16
1981	26760	13590	5421	0.38
1982	26120	12430	8611	0.38
1983	14210	11430	8174	0.22
1984	12470	10380	10300	0.18
1985	11540	11320	5137	0.17
1986	10860	8032	6074	0.19
1987	7660	9311	5681	0.12
1988	12400	1300	4600	0.19

Year	Exports/GNP	Arms Imports/GNP	Arms Imports/Total Exports
1980	0.30	0.03	0.09
1981	0.19	0.08	0.40
1982	0.18	0.13	0.69
1983	0.18	0.13	0.72
1984	0.15	0.15	0.99
1985	0.17	0.08	0.45
1986	0.14	0.11	0.76
1987	0.14	0.09	0.61
1988	0.02	0.07	0.35

Source: *Ibid.* p.93.

In the long term, economic warfare might have destroyed the Iraqi military power. Military equipment is subject to depreciation and is in constant need of repair. The maintenance at the ready of a 4 million man army out of a population of 17 million imposes an intolerable burden on the economy.

7.7.2 Why sanctions might not have worked

Sanctions might not have imposed an unbearable cost on the Iraqi population. As both General Powell and Defense Secretary Cheney argued against Senator Nunn, Saddam appeared willing to inflict an enormous economic burden on his people in order to maintain his military strength (Table 7.2). In retrospect, he has shown himself able to enforce the compliance of his citizens even in the face of the destruction left by the war. This argument has its greatest force if sanctions were expected to starve the Iraqis out rather than cut off the supply of imports required to operate their military establishment.

In any case, sanctions and economic warfare are long term instruments of international policy. It was argued that Kuwait had to be relieved promptly before it was destroyed or depopulated. Furthermore, there was concern about the willingness of the international community to maintain sanctions in the face of economic incentives to buy Iraqi oil at concenssionary prices.[10]

Another reason is the danger, inherent in economic warfare, that the losing party may in desperation launch a pre-emptive nuclear or chemical strike--particularly at Israel--while it still had the capacity to do so (Wolfson, 1985). While such an attack would have ended in the unlimited destruction of Iraq in retaliation, that possibility could never be discounted. But the ability of the UN to disable these weapons by its own pre-emptive strikes, and the failure of Iraq to launch such weapons when the conflict was actually underway, suggest that this danger might have been over estimated if it was the basis for the allied decision.[11]

So there were uncertainties facing either course of action. President Bush chose to move quickly to technical military war. The low cost of conducting the military campaign as we have analyzed it, evidently compared favorably with the perceived uncertainties of long term econmic warfare. It was costly in Iraqi lives, saved some Kuwaiti lives, but to the US it was certain in its outcome and virtually costless in its conduct.

7.8 Conclusion

The issue of sunk costs is not so much about history as policy for the future. Would the US have conducted the Gulf action if it had to pay the full freight itself out of current expenditures? Should it plan to do this sort of operation again?

These are the questions that lie behind the military budget debates in Congress and elsewhere. The *Wall Street Journal* editorial (May 21, 1991) in criticizing the allocations of weaponry (although not the size) proposed by Congress assumes that the answer is yes.

The problem is that if the weapons are produced in one period, they enter into the stockpile of the next, where they become a sunk cost to the extent that they depreciate and obsolesce, or to the extent that they are not to be replaced in a third period. Then they do not enter into marginal cost and thereby encourage their use as they did in the Gulf.

The allocation of resources to research and development functions in the same way. It influences the nature of the national stock of technical knowledge, which, in turn determines the shape of the future production possiblity frontier. Fostering technical progress in the types and level of military capability in one period, cheapens the relative cost of war in the next (Wolfson and Shabahang, 1991).

The connection between the sunk cost problem and the allied subsidy problem is more tenuous. Nevertheless, there is a parallel since the alliances built up now, the mutual engagements agreed to, entail a *quid pro quo* that makes subsidies more likely, and lowers the marginal cost of future actions. That is to say, the expenditures that the US makes now in its alliance structure represents a form of political capital which it can draw upon in the future.

There is a "cobweb problem" of sorts at work here because the time lag between present actions and the ultimate stock of war fighting capacity is so long. Decisions made now strongly influence the attractiveness of war in the future. Consequently, the United States must make a fine distinction now about the kinds of wars it is willing to fight in the future. It should prepare for them. It should not prepare for wars it is not willing to fight.

The present budget reductions in armaments, and the view of US military planners that there will be at least a two year warning time before the USSR again might be a military threat, suggest that these considerations are under review (Tritten, 1991). The vexed question is whether even the reduced preparations for such an eventuality will continue to make other actions more attractive than they otherwise would be on the basis of current cost considerations.

Footnotes

‡We appreciate references provided by Mr. David Wessel of *The Wall Street Journal* and the advice and suggestions of Professors Robert Ayanian, Victor Brajer, Andrew Gill, Jane Hall and David Wong of the Department of Economics at CSUF. They are not responsible for our views or errors. We are particularly grateful to General Colin Powell for helpful criticisms of an earlier draft. It cannot be emphasized too strongly that he is not necessarily in agreement with any part of our analysis of the conflict or our statement of his position.

[1]Carl von Clausewitz, *On War* (1832-1837) trans. M. Howard and P. Paret, Rev. ed. (Princeton University Press, New Jersey, 1984). General Colin Powell explicitly cited Clausewitz in this connection in his testimony to the Senate Armed Services committee (December 3, 1990, p. 660).

[2]In private correspondence General Colin Powell denies the Robert Woodward contention in *The Washington Post* (May 2, 1991, p. 1 ff) and in his book *The Commanders* that he privately adhered to the Nunn position. His statement before the Senate Armed Services Committee (Powell, 1990) favored a quick and decisive military victory, which he regarded as certain to work, rather than what he saw as a problematic outcome of sanctions.

[3]It is a hotly debated point in the literature whether the value of life is higher for younger people such as those in the armed services than the those of average working age. Consequently we will not attempt an adjustment for the age factor.

[4]Sorties are really not homogeneous because their mission changed as the conflict developed. In the early stages of the air war, more of the sorties were directed at defending against Iraqi air capability. As the air attack developed, more sorties were directed against Iraqi ground warfare capital assets. Since at this point the bombing resulted in greater destruction of capital one might be tempted to say that there were increasing returns to bombing until those targets became increasingly scarce or required repeated attacks to destroy. At the present level of abstraction we will treat sorties as homogeneous and exhibiting diminishing returns. Somewhat surprisingly, it will turn out that this is not a crucial issue for the analysis.

[5]Professor Ayanian has suggested that the allied MC curve might not show diminishing returns in this interval and therefore should be drawn as horizontal, but still above the US MC. This would be in accord with our later treatment of variable costs as linear in the estimation of elasticities.

[6]We are grateful to Professor Robert Ayanian for bringing this fact to our attention.

[7]Allied sorties added to this figure. It turns out that for our linear approximation to cost this number cancels out, so that a precise segregation of US and allied sorties is not required.

[8]Reduction of the choice set of an opponent to measure zero is a very strong requirement more appropriate to chess than war. Certainly it is a sufficient condition for winning wars, but it is hard to imagine that it is necessary, since there may be a wide range of outcomes that will force an opponent to surrender (Wolfson and Shabahang, 1991, 53-55).

[9]*Los Angeles Times*, May 10, 1991, 9. A17.

[10]The influence of this political consideration on the military option can be seen in the exchange between Senator Nunn and General Powel (Powell, 1990):

NUNN: General Powell, you said waiting is not without cost. No one knows when sanctions will work...The whole question of time and whether time is on our side is to me enormously important.

General Schwarzkopf, our commander in the field, was quoted in the Los Angeles Times on November 29...as follows: "At the present, I think time is on the side of the world coalition. I really don't think there is ever going to come a time when time is on the side of Iraq, as long as the sanctions are in effect, as long as the United Nations coalition is in effect..."

POWELL: ...I think what General Schwarzkopf is saying is use as much time as you think is available...before the cost of using additional time is too high to bear. There were a lot of "as long as's" in his statement with respect to the coalition, with respect to other factors...We don't know if the sanctions will work. I hope, more than anyone, that they work quickly...We just don't know.

NUNN: If we have a war we are never going to know...the way you find out...is to give them enough time to work. (Hearings, December 3, 1990, p. 681).

[11]The war itself might be understood as a greatly enlarged surgical strike to be followed by sanctions to enforce compliance.

References

von Clausewitz, C. (1984). *On war.* Translated by M. Howard and P. Paret (rev. ed.). Princeton: Princeton University Press.

Darman, R. (1991). *United States costs in the persian guld conflict and foreign contributions to offset such costs.* Report #2 to Congress, Office of Management and Budget, April 27, 1991.

Fisher, A., Chestnut, L.G., and Violette, D.M. (1989). The value of reducing risks of death: a note on new evidence. *Journal of Policy Analysis and Management* , 8, 88-100.

Hall, J.V., et. al. (1989). *Economic assessment of the health benefits from improvements in air quality in the south coast air basin.* South Coast Air Quality Maintenance District Report (Contract 5685), California State University-Fullerton Foundation, June 1989, (pp 5-1--5-17).

Los Angeles Times, May 10, 1991, p. A17.

Newsweek, March 18, 1991.

Powell, C.L. (1990). Testimony, Senate Armed Services Committee, December 3, 1990.

Time, March 4, 1991.

Tritten, J. (1991). *America promises to come back: a new national strategy.* Report #NPS-NS-91-003A, U.S. Naval Postgraduate School, Monterey, California, May 13, 1991.

U.S. Arms Control and Disarmament Agency. (1990). *World military expenditures and arms transfers 1989.* Washington, D.C.

U.S. News and World Report , March 11, 1991.

Wall Street Journal, Editorial, May 21, 1991, p. A2.

Washington Post , May 2, 1991, p. 1ff.

Wessel, D. (1991). The US spent $31.5 billion on gulf war. *The Wall Street Journal,* April 30, 1991, p. A18.

Wolfson, M. (1985). Notes on economic warfare. *Conflict Management and Peace Science*, 8, 1-20.

Wolfson, M. and Shabahang, H. (1991). Economic causation in the breakdown of military equilibrium. *Journal of Conflict Resolution*, 35, 43-67.

Wolfson, M. et. al. (1991). *Essays on the cold war.* London: Macmillan.

Economics of Arms Reduction and the Peace Process
W. Isard and C.H. Anderton (Editors)
© 1992 Elsevier Science Publishers B.V. All rights reserved.

Chapter 8

DETERMINANTS OF MILITARY EXPENDITURES

Carlos Seiglie

Rutgers University

[Returning to a main theme of this book, Seiglie conducts research on the determinants of the level of military expenditures in a way which represents a major step forward. He tests a military expenditure function that explicitly treats *both* the supply and demand factors. Recall the statement made previously that the literature on peace economics comprises a helter-skelter of contributions. Thus we find Seiglie employing variables, for example to reflect political factors and level of trade, often different from those used by the previous contributors to this book. His contribution, however, lies in the comprehensive analysis involving a better balance of factors impinging on arms expenditure policy. (eds.)]

8.1 Introduction

There are two areas of research into the determination of military expenditures where economists have made significant contributions. The first is in the study of military alliances using the framework developed by Olson and Zeckhauser (1966) which emphasizes the public goods nature of defense. Examples of works in this area are Murdoch and Sandler (1982, 1984), Sandler and Forbes (1980) and Dudley and Montmarquette (1981). For the most part they have been interested in studying the NATO alliance and the degree of publicness of member countries' defense expenditures. For example, Murdoch and Sandler explore the implications of complementarity between *own* and the alliance's weapons and strategy and the implication of this for NATO's ability to achieve Pareto optimal levels of expenditures. Generally, these studies are concerned with how the demand for national security (and corresponding military expenditure function) is affected by member countries' expenditures.

The other area has been in the study of the dynamics of military interaction between adversarial countries or arms races. Notable examples in this literature are Brito (1972, 1975), McGuire (1965, 1977) and Isard (1988). Given the dynamic nature of many of these models, a major concern of the research is analyzing the existence and uniqueness of the equilibrium level of expenditures. Other studies emphasize the effects that resource, technological and informational constraints have on the dynamics of the armament process.

This paper combines aspects of both areas in deriving a military expenditure function by considering the actions of adversaries, as well as allies and by exploring how domestic and international factors impact on the character of these expenditures. That economists should be as interested in the demand for national security as they are for housing, electricity and other commodities should be evident by the data shown in Table 8.1. For the sample countries shown the share of national output accounted for by defense expenditures range from 32% to 0.5% and as a percentage of Central Government expenditures from 54.3% to 2.2%. That economists can delegate to political science the problem of explaining the allocation of up to 32% of GNP while concentrating on the remaining 68% seems unwise. It is inconsistent with the recent interest of economists in explaining the redistributive role of the State (Peltzman, 1980) which although large is still a smaller share of national output for most of the world.

There is a secondary interest for understanding the allocation of resources to defense which hinges on a debate in the economic development literature on whether military expenditure increases or retards the rate of economic development, e.g., see Benoit (1972, 1978), Deger (1986), Deger and Sen (1983), and Chatterhi (chapter 11 below). These econometric studies model the demand for military expenditures in an ad hoc fashion and proceed to explore the relationship between economic growth and these expenditures. Therefore, this paper may have some value to this problem by deriving the expenditure function from utility maxmizing behavior.

Finally, there is another area of research concerned with defense expenditures and that is the literature on large scale world econometric models for example, in the Leontief World I-O Model, the computable general equilibrium models and the LINK model (Leontief and Duchin (1983), Klein (1987) and Klein and Gronicki (1989)). All these employ military expenditure equations in investigating the impact that this component of aggregate has on the domestic and world economy. Given the prospects for major disarmament resulting from the improvements in East-West relations, a more comprehensive understanding of the factors affecting the military expenditure functions of nations may lead to a better understanding of the impact of disarmament on the performance of the economy in these large econometric models.

TABLE 8.1

Miliatry Expenditures (ME) as a percent of GNP and of Central Government Expenditures (CGE) for selected countries, 1978.

Country	Share of ME in GNP	Share of ME in CGE
Argentina	2.8	14.9
Canada	2.0	9.1
Chile	2.8	12.6
China	8.8	54.3
Congo	4.2	14.4
Dominican Republic	1.9	12.5
Egypt	12.2	30.5
Finland	1.4	5.7
France	3.9	18.3
Greece	6.4	26.1
India	2.9	15.1
Indonesia	3.1	13.4
Iran	14.6	27.4
Israel	23.4	35.7
Ivory Coast	2.1	6.3
Japan	0.9	5.5
Kenya	4.0	13.7
Luxembourg	0.9	2.2
Malaysia	4.5	14.3
Mexico	0.5	3.2
Nigeria	3.5	11.6
Pakistan	5.3	24.5
Peru	5.2	26.5
Quatar	32.0	14.6
Senegal	2.4	10.5
Singapore	6.2	26.3
South Africa	4.2	15.7
South Korea	6.3	32.6
Soviet Union	14.1	53.7
Spain	1.7	12.0
Sweden	3.4	8.2
Syria	14.3	35.6
United States	5.1	24.1
West Germany	3.3	21.8
Zimbabwe	6.7	20.2

The following two sections generalize a closed-economy, two-commodity model developed in Seiglie (1988a) by permitting countries to trade with the rest of the world, have allies as well as enemies, and produce capital goods (along with consumption and military commodities). The following section develops the production side of an economy producing these three commodities, two of which are assumed to be traded freely in world markets. Section 8.3 derives the demand, as well as military expenditure, functions of a country. To motivate some of the empirical aspects of the problem, a specific functional form for preferences is assumed and demand equations and military expenditure functions are derived for this form and later estimated.

Finally, section 8.4 presents the empirical estimates for the model, as well as some other important features of arms races. In particular, this section presents estimates for the military expenditure function derived in section 8.3 using cross country data from 1968 to 1976.

8.2 The Supply of Military Capability

We begin by deriving the production possibility surface (PPS) for the three commodity economy. The purpose for its derivation is that since countries are assumed to be open to international trade and face world prices the level of income is determined independent of demand. It is being measured by the intercept of the plane tangent to the PPS with a slope given by relative world prices. Given this income, the demand for each commodity will be derived in section 8.3, and in particular we derive the demand for defense. We note that in order to determine world trade patterns we will just take the difference between the amounts produced and consumed domestically of each commodity. Therefore, it seems appropriate that we present the supply side of the economy.

We assume CES production functions for M, military capability, Y, the consumption good and Z, the capital good, which depend upon the stocks of labor and capital employed in each of these sectors. The economy's endowment of capital at any moment in time is equal to the total amount of Z produced in the past minus any depreciation which has occurred. We assume that M and Y are traded freely at world market prices but that the capital good is not traded on the world market. Furthermore, if we assume that one commodity is always more capital intensive than the other at any factor prices (i.e., we rule out factor intensity reversals) and we assume competition both within and across sectors, then factor-prices will be uniquely determined. Therefore, the capital-labor ratios will also be uniquely determined for the two traded commodities, M and Y, as well as the non-traded capital good, Z. In other words, the international prices for the traded commodities uniquely determine the capital-labor ratios domestically for all three commodities. These capital-labor ratios determine fixed input coefficients for all the commodities (see Komiya (1967) for a proof).

Given the initial endowments of K and L, we have that the demands for each of these inputs by the several sectors must equal their endowment. If we denote a_{KM} as the proportion of capital employed in the M sector and define likewise, the other input coefficients, we have:

$$a_{KM} M + a_{KY} Y + a_{KZ} Z = K \tag{8.1}$$

$$a_{LM} M + a_{LY}Y + a_{LZ}Z = L \qquad (8.2)$$

Since we have two equations in three unknowns we need a third equation which is provided by assuming that the proportion of national income saved and invested is constant. Since investment is just the production of Z we have that the savings rate, s, is:

$$s = (P_Z Z) / (P_M M + P_Y Y + P_Z Z) \qquad (8.3)$$

or letting Z serve as the numeraire good we have,

$$-sP_M M - sP_Y Y + (1-s)Z = 0 \qquad (8.4)$$

This system can be solved for M, Y and Z, given the initial endowments of capital and labor and world prices for M and Y. To get the above equations in terms of the rate of capital accumulation we divide equations (8.1), (8.2) and (8.4) by K to get

$$a_{KM}(M/K) + a_{KY}(Y/K) + a_{KZ} i = 1 \qquad (8.5)$$

$$a_{LM}(M/K) + a_{LY}(Y/K) + a_{LZ} i = (1/k) \qquad (8.6)$$

$$-sP_M(M/K) - SP_Y(Y/K) + (1-s) i = 0 \qquad (8.7)$$

where $i = (Z/K)$ is the investment rate and k is the economy-wide capital-labor ratio.

Solving equations (8.5)-(8.7) for the military supply function, M^S, and rearranging we get:

$$M^S = \frac{\{[(1-s)a_{LY} + sP_Y a_{LZ}]k - [(1-s)a_{KY} + sP_Y a_{KZ}]\}L}{\Delta} \qquad (8.8)$$

where:

$\Delta = (1-s)(a_{KM}a_{LY} - a_{KY}a_{LM}) + s[(a_{KM}a_{LZ} - a_{KZ}a_{LM})P_Y + (a_{KZ} - a_{KY})P_M a_{LZ}]$.

To determine the long run equilibrium for the economy we assume that population (labor supply) growth is equal to n, that K depreciates at the rate δ and that the economy's investment rate, i, converges to the rate of population growth plus depreciation of the capital stock, i.e., $i = n+\delta$. In other words, we assume that the economy is in a steady state equilibrium. (For conditions required of such a system to converge to a steady state see, Findlay (1970) and Deardorff (1974)).

Again solving equations (8.5)-(8.7) for i and setting this equal to $n+\delta$ we can solve for the steady state capital/labor ratio, k^*,

$$k^* = (P_{Ma}k_Y - P_{Ya}k_M)/(P_{Ma}l_Y - P_{Ya}l_M - (n+\delta)\Delta) \tag{8.8'}$$

which when substituted into equation (8.8) yields the long run military supply function for the economy.

If savings are equal to zero and world prices happen to coincide with domestic prices prior to opening the economy then we would have the production equilibrium described in Seiglie (1988a). Yet, when domestic and world prices diverge the closed and open economy equilibriums would not coincide since countries can specialize in the production of the commodities in which they have a comparative advantage thereby serving to maximize their income. Once this production is determined, the representative individual maximizes utility subject to his share of national income. The next section considers this problem which leads to the determination of the demand for military capability under the assumptions outlined above.

8.3 The Demand for National Security

This section generalizes the demand for national security in Dudley and Montmarquette (1981) and Seiglie (1988a) in several directions. First, it introduces the possibility that expenditures by enemies decrease welfare just as those by allies increase welfare. Second, since the economy is open and in a steady state equilibrium, the budget constraint faced by individuals is altered. These extensions will be developed under the assumption that preferences take a particular functional form which generates military expenditure functions which are linear.

The amount of military capability produced or imported by a nation is not necessarily equal to the amount available for its consumption. Part of the difference is due in part to the public goods aspect of military alliances which has been discussed in the economic literature, the other part results from the fact that some proportion of an adversary's military capability spills over and *decreases* the effectiveness of the country's military defense, i.e., it reduces its national security. In the discussion that follows if we denote the adversary of Country 1 as Country 2 (and likewise its potential ally as Country 3) then the proportion of Country 2's weapon stock that reduces Country 1's national security will be denoted by a_{12}. Likewise, some proportion of Country 1's military capability reduces Country 2's national security. In the same manner denote this proportion a_{21}. These proportions differ for each country depending, for example, on the percentage of military spending directed towards offensive versus defensive purposes. If we represent the total amount of spillover from the adversarial Country 2 to Country 1 by M_{12}, and the positive spillover from the ally Country 3 by M_{13}, then the total consumption of national security by Country 1 is

$$m_1 = M_1 - M_{12} + M_{13} \tag{8.9}$$

where m_1 represents the total amount consumed and M_1 the total amount produced by Country 1.

By our previous assumption,

$$M_{12} = a_{12}M_2 + v_2 \tag{8.10}$$

$$M_{13} = b_{13}M_3 \tag{8.10'}$$

where M_2 is the total amount of military capability produced by Country 2 and therefore, some fraction of that total reduces the effectiveness of Country 1's military capability and v_2 is a measure of hostile actions by Country 2 which signal intentions and is assumed independent of M. A similar interpretation holds for the positive spillover, M_{13}, resulting from a military alliance.

Therefore, the total effective consumption of M for Country 1, m_1, is equal to:

$$m_1 = M_1 - a_{12}M_2 - v_2 + b_{13}M_3 \tag{8.11}$$

Likewise, for Country 2 which is assumed to be allied to Country 4,

$$m_2 = M_2 - a_{21}M_1 - v_1 + b_{23}M_4 \tag{8.12}$$

In the model, the coefficient, a_{ij}, is viewed as a measure of the degree of spillover embodied in the armament of the opponent. For example, if the weapons of the opponent were mainly offensive then a_{ij} would be high, but if the weapons systems of the opponent were mainly defensive then a_{ij} would be low. The other coefficient v_i can be viewed as a hostility signal. As such, it reflects the perception of threat or hostility directed towards Country i from other nations. Analogously, b_{ij} represents the "spill-ins" resulting from military alliances. The other coefficient, v_j can be viewed as a hostility signal. As such, it reflects the perception of threat or hostility directed towards Country i from Country j.

Let the representative citizen of Country 1 have preferences represented by the following Stone-Geary utility function:

$$\begin{aligned} U(c_1, m_1) &= (c_1 - \bar{c_1})^\alpha m_1^{1-\alpha} \\ &= (c_1 - \bar{c_1})^\alpha (M_1 - a_{12}M_2 + b_{13}M_3 - v_2)^{1-\alpha} \end{aligned} \tag{8.13}$$

where c represents consumption and $\bar{q}$ denotes a "minimum" subsistence level of consumption. We assume the economy is in a steady state with a capital/labor ratio, k^* and an average propensity to save, s^*. For the overall economy with N individuals,

$$I = \sum_{i=1}^{N} E_i + \sum_{i=1}^{N} s_i \, l_i \qquad (8.14)$$

where I denotes national income, E_i, the expenditure of the ith individual, l_i, his income and s_i, his savings rate.

Country 1's defense expenditure is equal to $P_M M_1$ where P_M is the world price of arms. For the ith individual his tax share to finance these expenditures will be denoted by τ_i, so that choosing consumption as the numeraire commodity his budget constraint is:

$$c_i + \tau_i P_M M_1 = (1-s_i) \, l_i = E_i \qquad (8.15)$$

Following Dudley and Montmarquette (1981), note that if the only tax rate, t, imposed by the government is proportional to income then

$$\tau_i = (t \, l_i) / \left(\sum_{i=1}^{N} t l_i \right) \; = \; l_i / \left(\sum (l_i/N) \right) N \; = \; (1/N) \, (l_i / \bar{I}) \qquad (8.16)$$

where $\bar{I}$ is average or per capita income.

Maximization of equation (8.13) subject to (8.15) yields the following first order conditions:

$$\alpha(c_1 - \bar{c}_1)^{\alpha-1} m_1^{1-\alpha} - \mu = 0 \qquad (8.17)$$

$$(1-\alpha)(c_1 - \bar{c}_1)^{\alpha} m_1^{-\alpha} - \mu\tau_i P_M = 0 \qquad (8.18)$$

which when substituting $m_1 = M_1 - a_{12}M_2 + b_{13}M_3 - v_2$ along with our budget constraint yields the following demand (reaction) function:

$$M_1 = (1-\alpha) \, [\, (1-s_i) \, l_i - \bar{c}_1] \, / \, (\tau_i P_M) + \alpha a_{12}M_2 - \alpha b_{13}M_3 + \alpha v_2 \qquad (8.19)$$

We can see from the above that the demand for defense is increasing in income with an income elasticity, η_M,

$$\eta_M = [(1-\alpha) \, (1-s_i) \, l_i \,] \, / \, [\tau_i P_M M_1] \qquad (8.20)$$

$$= [(1-\alpha)\ (1-s_i)\ l_i\ ]\ /\ [(1-\alpha)\ (1-s_i)\ l_i\ -\ (1-\alpha)\bar{c}_1 + \alpha a_{12}\tau_i P_M M_2$$

$$-\ \alpha b_{13}\tau_i P_M M_3 + \alpha \tau_i P_M v_2]$$

The effect of an increase in P_M on M_1 is

$$\partial M_1/\partial P_M\ =\ -(1-\alpha)\ [\ (1-s_i)\ l_i\ -\ \bar{c}_1]\ /\ \tau_i P_M^2 < 0 \tag{8.21}$$

so long as expenditures meet the minimum subsistence level of consumption, $\bar{c}_1$.

Several other results emerge from equation (8.19). Firstly, M_1 is increasing in the opponent's level of military weapons, M_2. Secondly, M_1 is also increasing in the "degree of aggression", v_2 of the adversary, i.e., increasing in the level of conflict with adversaries. Thirdly, the weapon stock is decreasing in the level of weapons of the ally. This tendency to *free-ride* off the ally is increasing in the degree that the ally's weapons have the non-rivalness property of a public good and in the strength of the alliance. This degree of non-rivalness is implicitly incorporated in b_{13}. This coefficient also captures the fact that an ally that is not very likely to intervene on behalf of Country 1 will not greatly reduce the latter's level of armaments. M_1 is also increasing in the threat of the adversary's weapons, a_{12}. For example, the proximity of the two countries geographically is important if the countries do not possess long range missiles or bombers so that the closer they are the higher is a_{12}, or if they are contiguous countries the mix of the weapon stock between offensive and defensive systems is important with an increase in offensive weapons implying a rise in a_{12}. Finally, M_1 is decreasing in the tax share, τ_i.

The military expenditure function for Country 1, ME_1, which is equal to $P_M M_1$ is the following

$$ME_1\ =\ (1-\alpha)\ [(1-s_i)\ l_i\ -\ \bar{c}_1]\ /\ \tau_i\ +\ \alpha a_{12} P_M M_2 - \alpha b_{13} P_M M_3 + \alpha P_M v_2 \tag{8.22}$$

$$=\ (1-\alpha)\ [(1-s_i)\ l_i\ -\ \bar{c}_1]\ /\ \tau_i\ +\ \alpha a_{12} ME_2 - \alpha b_{13} ME_3 + \alpha P_M v_2$$

which when substituting equation (8.16) for τ_i and assuming that each individual's savings rate is equal to the steady state rate, s^*, we get

$$ME_1\ =\ (1-\alpha)\ (1-s^*)l\ -\ [(1-\alpha)\ \bar{c}_1]/\tau_i\ +\ \alpha a_{12} ME_2 - \alpha b_{13} ME_3 + \alpha P_M v_2 \tag{8.23}$$

$$=\ (1-\alpha)l - (1-\alpha)s^*l - [(1-\alpha)\ \bar{c}_1]/\tau_i\ +\ \alpha a_{12} ME_2 - \alpha b_{13} ME_3 + \alpha P_M v_2$$

$$=\ \beta_1 l + \beta_2 S + \beta_3 (1/\tau_i) + \beta_4 ME_2 + \beta_5 ME_3 + \beta_6 v_2$$

where I is real national income, S (equal to s*I) is real national savings and

$$\beta_1 = (1-\alpha) > 0 ; \qquad\qquad \beta_2 = -(1-\alpha) < 0$$

$$\beta_3 = -[(1-\alpha)\,\overline{c}_1] < 0 ; \qquad \beta_4 = \alpha a_{12} > 0$$

$$\beta_5 = -\alpha b_{13} < 0 ; \qquad\qquad \beta_6 = \alpha P_M > 0$$

Several propositions emerge from this expenditure function, namely that military expenditures should be increasing in: 1) income, 2) the opponent's expenditures, 3) the level of conflict or aggression directed towards it from other nations and decreasing in: 4) allies' expenditures, 5) the savings rate, 6) the tax share, 7) the minimum subsistence level and, 8) the strength of the alliance, b_{13}.

Finally, the above assumes that countries trade at world market prices. Since the gains from trade are decreasing in distortions to world prices and since wars or international conflicts serve to raise the transaction costs involved in trade with the rest of the world, we expect that the more an economy is dependent on world trade and therefore, the greater the sum of consumers' and producers' surplus derived from this trade, the greater will be its military expenditures in order to protect these gains. Therfore, military expenditures should be increasing to the extent that an economy is open to world trade. Historically, large trading nations such as the U.S., England and Spain have developed large naval fleets to protect the gains resulting from world trade.

8.4 Estimates of the Military Expenditure Function

In this section, estimates are presented for the parameters of the expenditure function previously derived. For any Country i, the function to be estimated is now:

$$ME_i = \beta_0 + \beta_1 I_i + \beta_2 S_i + \beta_3(1/\tau_i) + \beta_4 ME_j + \beta_5 ME_k + \beta_6 V_j + \beta_7 O_i + \varepsilon_i \qquad (8.24)$$

where j denotes the adversarial country, k the ally, and O_i the degree of openness of the economy. We also introduce a constant, β_0 to the equation, as well as an error term, ε_i.

Let us briefly discuss the definitions of the variables and the expected signs to the estimated coefficients. Our dependent variable, ME_i, denotes the real military expenditures of Country i. As for our explanatory variables, I_i refers to the level of real GNP and S_i, to the level of real savings for Country i. From the model, the sign of income coefficient, β_1, should be positive and the savings coefficient, β_2, should be negative.

As for $(1/\tau_i)$, it is the inverse of the tax share of the representative individual (or median voter) in the country, which from equation (8.16) is equal to the inverse of the share of real income of the representative individual in GNP, $(1/\tau_i) = N(\bar{I}/I_i)$, where recall that N denotes population and $\bar{I}$ per capita income. Holding N constant, as the representative individual's income (I_i) rises above per capita (average) income, then $(1/\tau_i)$ falls. In other words, as the representative individual experiences an increase in income above the average individual or conversely, as individual income inequality rises, military expenditures should rise. A *political economic* explanation would be that as income inequality rises the smaller wealthier group is better able to control free riding amongst its members and therefore, its effectiveness in influencing the political decision on the amount of military spending the nation should provide increases. As discussed in Seiglie (1988b), the demand for national security increases with wealth since the potential loss from an attack by adversaries rises. Therefore, their greater influence would lead to their demand for greater security being met.

As a proxy for this variable we have used a Gini coefficient of sectoral inequality published by the World Bank. A better proxy would have been a Gini coefficient based on individual income or households but such a measure is unavailable for many of the countries in our sample. Although a comparison of the measure of inequality we use with another reported measure, the percentage of income going to the top ten percent of the population shows a strong correlation, we use the former because it is available for more countries in our sample. We therefore expect that as inequality increases (the Gini coefficient rises, i.e., τ_i rises and $(1/\tau_i)$ falls), the country's military expenditures, ME_i, should rise. Therefore, we expect the sign of its coefficient, β_3 to be positive (positive in τ_i, negative in $1/\tau_i$).

As for the other variables, ME_j represents the military expenditures of the adversarial nation which is chosen to be only one country throughout with one exception: the adversary for the NATO countries is assumed to be the Warsaw Pact countries and therefore, we employ their aggregate expenditures. We expect the coefficient, β_4 to be positive. Conversely, ME_k denotes the military expenditures of countries allied to Country i. For our study, we have only concentrated on the NATO alliance since our sample of countries does not include any Warsaw Pact countries due to the difficulty of obtaining data on their economies and in comparing these if they were available with the market economies in our sample of countries. We define ME_k to be equal to total NATO expenditures minus the contribution of the particular member country. This is intended to capture the spillin from the alliance's expenditures into the particular member country. Our model predicts the sign of this variable, β_5 to be negative due to the free-riding problem inherent in public goods.

For v_j, which measures the aggression from the rest of the world towards *Country i*, we expect its coefficient β_6 to be positive, i.e., increases in foreign aggression should lead to increases in expenditures. Likewise, v_i, which measures Country i's aggression towards the rest of the world should be expected to have a positive sign.

To arrive at a measure for the two aggression variables we have used the Conflict and Peace Data Bank (COPDAB) developed by Azar (1980a, 1980b). The COPDAB consists of approximately 500,000 international events which occurred from 1948 to 1978. Each event entry in the data base lists the actor and target nation, the issue involved, and the date of occurrence. This source of information is taken from close to 100 regional and international publications. The data base consists of a ranking of events according to a predetermined scale aimed at quantifying the intensity of the event ranging from the most cooperative given a value of 1, such as the voluntary unification of nation-states to the most conflictual which is given a value of 15, an extensive war act. In order to arrive at a level of aggression towards a country from the rest of the world (v_j) we have taken the average of the scaling of hostility from all countries in the data base towards that particular country during the year and conversely, to calculate the level of aggression of Country i towards the rest of the world (v_i). For example, if a country has had three international interactions in a particular year: 1) war was declared against it by a neighboring country (scale=15), 2) a country strongly attacked it verbally (scale=10), 3) it formed a major strategic alliance with another country (scale=2), then the index of hostility for the year would be 9, (15+10+2)/3. This index was calculated for all countries in the sample listed in COPDAB for each year.

We also employed the COPDAB to determine the main adversary for each country by looking at the mean aggression of each country towards others along with the number of interactions between them. In most cases, these adversaries were contiguous nations. For countries in the sample which were in NATO the main adversary was assumed to be the Warsaw Pact with the exception being Greece and Turkey where their adversarial role with each other dominates that of the Warsaw Pact. In the specifications of the model, v_i and v_j are entered separately since by the nature of how they are computed they are highly collinear. This is because in international relations the timing of events and who initiated them are difficult to ascertain.

As for the variable O_i, the degree of openness of the economy, it is measured as the share of imports in GNP. This standard measure used in international trade to measure the openness of an economy should be positively related to defense spending, i.e., the more open a country's economy is the greater the need to protect their gains from trade. Therefore, we expect β_7 to be positive.

Because of the possibility of heteroscedasticity when using cross-sectional data of countries of such divergent size (GNP) both the Goldfeld-Quandt and Breusch-Pagan tests were performed and the null hypothesis of homoscedasticity was rejected by both tests. We corrected for the presence of heteroscedasticity by weighting the regressions by the variable assumed to vary directly with the error variances, namely real GNP. Table 8.2 presents weighted least squares estimates of the coefficients of the military expenditure function given by the equation (8.24). We present estimates for average military expenditures for the years 1968 to 1971 and for average expenditures from 1972 to 1976. In addition, cross country estimates are presented for several years during the sample period dating from 1968 to 1976. Since the Gini index is unavailable annually we have included it only in the specifications which overlap with the computation of this variable. We have split the sample averages at 1972 because at that time there seems to be evidence that NATO's defensive strategy changed from a doctrine of *mutual assured destruction* to one of *flexible response*. Rather than deterring attack from the Warsaw Pact with nuclear weapons as the former doctrine emphasizes, the latter requires that NATO countries react in multiple modes in the case of an armed attack while attempting to avoid nuclear war. Therefore, this requires European nations to defend themselves more with conventional weapons and tactical nuclear weapons and rely less on the nuclear weapon deterrence from the nuclear allies of NATO which are the U.S., the U.K. and France. As Murdoch and Sandler (1984) have argued if we decompose military weapons by the allies into nuclear (tactical and strategic) and conventional, the shift in strategy during the early 70's created a complementarity in the production of defense between these two components which if strong enough can reduce the extent of free riding and even reverse it. Therefore, based on this shift in policy we should expect that the extent of free-riding in the alliance during the post 1972 period to have been reduced.

In fact this is what our estimates indicate. The coefficient for *Ally Spillover* is negative as expected, yet it decreases in magnitude as we approach the mid-1970's. In other words, the extent of free-riding in the alliance diminished from 1968 to 1976. Our results indicate that for the pre-1971 period this coefficient is statistically significant at the .05 level for every year up to 1973, although Table 8.2 only presents the results for 1968 and two other representative years, 1973 and 1976. In the case of average expenditures it is statistically significant at the .05 level for the 1968-1971 period but not for the 1972-1976 period. Again the size of the coefficient declines for the latter period, indicating a reduction in the extent of free-riding in the alliance. For example, a one million dollar increase in other NATO country's expenditures led in 1968 to a reduction of *own* expenditures of $50,000, in

1973 to $20,000 and by 1976 to only $4,000. A conjecture from this result is that during this time period we were moving from a Nash equilibrium (which is not Pareto optimal) to a Lindahl equilibrium (which is) among the NATO alliance.

As for the other estimates, the coefficient of real GNP is positive and significant as expected indicating that national security is a normal good. Elsewhere we have argued that as wealth increases the demand for protection of this wealth, i.e., national security increases. The estimates for this coefficient are remarkably stable over different specifications of the model, although the individual annual estimates indicate that there has been a decline in the marginal propensity to spend during the period. The implication is that in 1968 a one million dollar increase in GNP resulted in an increase in expenditures of $200,000, but by 1976 only $110,000 was diverted to defense. Using these estimates for the marginal propensity to spend on defense the income elasticity for national security for the United States in 1968 was 2.14, in 1973 it was 2.01 and in 1976 it was 2.07. Similarly, for the United Kingdom the estimates during this period are 3.73, 2.43 and 2.23, respectively.

The estimates for the variable measuring the openness of the economy is also positive as expected yet it is significantly different from zero in only the 1968-1971 period. We would expect that the greater the extent a nation relies on trade with the rest of the world and therefore, we presume the greater the extent of gains from trade, the greater the demand for national security to protect these gains, holding the benefits derived from the expenditures of allies constant. This latter assumption is important because ally's expenditures are in many instances a substitute for *own* expenditures. A case in point is the recent presence of U.S. warships during the Iraq-Iran War in the Persian Gulf attempting to insure the passage of oil although most of our allies, including Japan, are much more reliant on this trade.

Our estimates for the savings variable are negative as expected and also significantly different from zero. The inclusion of this variable allows us to determine to what extent increases in national savings are met by reduction in defense expenditures and to what extent by decreases in other public and private consumption. As the estimates show during the 1968-1971 period roughly 44% of an increase in national savings was met by reductions in defense, the remaining 56% being met by declines in private and/or public consumption. It is of note that the estimate for this variable has shown a decline during the sample period indicating that less of the increases in savings is being met by foregoing of national security and more by declines in public and/or private consumption. By 1976, the *crowding-out* of defense had been reduced to 31% indicating a greater willingness to reduce other forms of consumption.

TABLE 8.2

Weighted Least Squares Estimates for Average Real Military Expenditures for the Period 1968-1971, *ME6871* and 1972-1976, *ME7276*, Along with Estimates for Selected Years.

Dependent Variable	Intercept	Real GNP	Openness of the Economy	Gross National Savings	Ally's Spillover	Enemy's Military Expend.	Aggression Foreign	Aggression Domestic	Gini Index
1. *ME6871*									
a)	-21132.0 (3.28)	.17 (77.3)	14441.0 (2.27)	-.44 (36.7)	-.05 (8.16)	.08 (5.14)	1150.0 (1.55)		336.4 (3.85)
b)	-34037.0 (5.44)	.17 (83.6)	19242.5 (3.29)	-.43 (40.7)	-.05 (7.87)	.08 (6.06)		2873.0 (3.80)	362.8 (5.05)
2. *ME7276*									
a)	-25985.0 (5.06)	.12 (46.0)	6351.8 (1.05)	-.33 (23.8)	-.02 (1.64)	.025 (1.58)	2969.8 (3.85)		165.4 (2.30)
b)	-96363.0 (3.30)	.12 (37.8)	5755.9 (0.90)	-.32 (18.9)	-.005 (0.44)	.03 (1.68)		4239.9 (3.06)	220.1 (2.84)
3. *ME68*									
	277.7 (0.04)	.20 (51.5)	-8784.3 (1.08)	-.52 (25.5)	-.05 (6.90)	.06 (2.79)	148.6 (0.63)		
4. *ME73*									
	-25270 (9.37)	.12 (145.6)	7839.4 (2.27)	-.30 (55.1)	-.02 (3.70)	.01 (1.68)	663.4 (2.64)		
5. *ME76*									
	-172119 (5.06)	.11 (63.7)	7067.1 (1.30)	-.31 (27.2)	-.004 (0.44)	.001 (0.10)	285.8 (0.78)		

Sources: a) U.S. Arms Control and Disarmament Agency, *World Military Expenditures and Arms Transfers 1965-1979*, b) World Bank, *World Tables* (various years), and c) Azar, *COPDAB*.
Note: The sample of countries are the following: U.S., Canada, France, W.Germany, Dominican Republic, Jamaica, Mexico, Uruguay, Guatemala, El Salvador, Nicaragua, S. Korea, Paraguay, Colombia, Venezuela, Ecuador, Peru, Brazil, Chile, Argentina, Netherlands, Belgium, Switzerland, Portugal, Italy, Greece, Norway, Denmark, Mauritania, Ivory Coast, Ghana, Kenya, Morocco, Nigeria, Libya, Sudan, Turkey, Egypt, Syria, Israel, Saudi Arabia, Kuwait, Japan, India, Pakistan, Guyana, Thailand, Singapore, Phillipines, U.K., N. Zealand, Spain, Australia, S. Africa, Togo and Tanzania.
Notes: All relevant variables are in 1978 dollars. Real GNP was used as the weight in the regressions. The number of observations is 55 with the exception of regressions with Gini Index which was available for only 53 countries. Similar results are obtained with Domestic Aggression as an explanatory variable. The t-statistics are in parentheses below coefficients.

The estimates for the domestic and foreign aggression proxies are positive in all the cases with their statistical signifiance varying depending upon the sample period. The positive coefficients are as expected for both variables since in our model increases in foreign threats should lead to increases in military expenditures.

As for the measure of income inequality the coefficient is positive and statistically significant at the .05 level indicating that as a country's distribution of income becomes more equitable, i.e. the Gini coefficient falls, military expenditures also decline. It is of note that Peltzman (1980) finds that as income inequality diminishes in a country the size of government increases. Since here we find that the defense spending component of government spending declines his results imply that the increase in the size of government generated by greater equality is being met solely by an increase in the non-defense component which is largely composed of income transfer programs, in other words, by an increase in the redistributive aspect of the State.

Finally, the estimates for the opponent's military expenditures yield results which are consistent with our expectations. We would expect that increases in the opponent's expenditures should lead to increases in own expenditures. We find that all coefficients are positive and for the 1968-1971 period significantly different from zero at the 5% level and for the 1972-1976 period significantly different from zero at the 10% level. The strength of this result is surprising for several reasons. First, for each country in the sample we chose an enemy, but for many countries especially those who had gained independence only recently from the viewpoint of our sample years (this includes most African countries and Jamaica) the post-colonial boundaries were not drawn along tribal or kingdom lines but instead split tribes apart. This led to conflicts being manifested internally in these countries (Nigeria and the Biafran War during our sample years is a case in point), instead of with external countries. Next, even if this problem did not exist military expenditures may be a function of the opponent's expenditures but only after some lag. This may result from imperfect information on the opponent's contemporaneous actions or lags in the appropriation of funds by legislatures or other governmental bodies or by some delays in receiving (importing) arms from the relatively few world arms exporters.

There exists the possibility of some simultaneity in our model because some of the enemy countries' expenditures also appear as a dependent variable. If simultaneity is present, estimation of this military expenditure function by OLS will produce asymptotic bias, although it must be noted that for small samples so will all other alternative estimators. Furthermore, the OLS estimator has the advantage of having the minimum variance among these alternative estimators. Thus it is quite possible that OLS provides the minimum mean square error among all other alternative estimators. In addition, Monte Carlo studies have shown OLS estimators to be less sensitive than alternative estimators to the presence of multicollinearity, errors in variables or mis-specification particularly with small samples (see

Johnston, 1984). Nevertheless, Table 8.3 presents results using weighted two-stage least squares with the instrument being lagged expenditures, i.e., for *ME7276* it is *ME6871*, and likewise for other year's expenditures. As the results indicate, they conform very closely with our weighted least squares estimates.

TABLE 8.3

Weighted Two-Stage Least Squares Estimates for Average Real Military Expenditures for the Period 1968-1971, *ME6871* and 1972-1976, *ME7276*, Along with Estimates for Selected Years.

Dependent Variable	Intercept	Real GNP	Openness of the Economy	Gross National Savings	Ally's Spill-over	Enemy's Military Expend.	Aggression Foreign	Aggression Domestic	Gini Index
1. *ME6871*									
a)	-21144.0 (3.28)	.17 (77.3)	14449.07 (2.27)	-.44 (36.7)	-.05 (8.16)	.08 (5.14)	1151.0 (1.55)		336.6 (3.85)
b)	-34045.7 (5.44)	.17 (83.6)	19251.3 (3.29)	-.43 (40.7)	-.05 (7.87)	.08 (6.06)		2873.0 (3.80)	363.0 (5.06)
2. *ME7276*									
a)	-25976.1 (5.05)	.12 (46.0)	6347.0 (1.05)	-.33 (23.8)	-.02 (1.64)	.024 (1.57)	2970.5 (3.85)		165.1 (2.29)
b)	-96480.5 (3.30)	.12 (37.8)	5753.0 (0.90)	-.32 (18.9)	-.005 (0.43)	.03 (1.67)		4245.9 (3.00)	220.0 (2.84)
3. *ME68*									
	122.8 (0.02)	.20 (51.5)	-8787.7 (1.08)	-.52 (25.5)	-.05 (6.90)	.06 (2.78)	-602.0 (0.60)		
4. *ME73*									
	-25288.8 (9.38)	.12 (145.6)	7859.1 (2.27)	-.30 (55.1)	-.02 (3.70)	.01 (1.67)	3462.8 (8.28)		
5. *ME76*									
	-17209.7 (5.06)	.11 (63.7)	7073.2 (1.30)	-.31 (27.2)	-.004 (0.45)	.001 (0.10)	2333.2 (4.63)		

Sources: a) U.S. Arms Control and Disarmament Agency, *World Military Expenditures and Arms Transfers 1965-1979*, b) World Bank, *World Tables* (various years), and c) Azar, *COPDAB*.
Note: The sample of countries are the following: U.S., Canada, France, W.Germany, Dominican Republic, Jamaica, Mexico, Uruguay, Guatemala, El Salvador, Nicaragua, S. Korea, Paraguay, Colombia, Venezuela, Ecuador, Peru, Brazil, Chile, Argentina, Netherlands, Belgium, Switzerland, Portugal, Italy, Greece, Norway, Denmark, Mauritania, Ivory Coast, Ghana, Kenya, Morocco, Nigeria, Libya, Sudan, Turkey, Egypt, Syria, Israel, Saudi Arabia, Kuwait, Japan, India, Pakistan, Guyana, Thailand, Singapore, Phillipines, U.K., N. Zealand, Spain, Australia, S. Africa, Togo and Tanzania.
Notes: All relevant variables are in 1978 dollars. Real GNP was used as the weight in the regressions. The number of observations is 55 with the exception of regressions with Gini Index which was available for only 53 countries. Similar results are obtained with Domestic Aggression as an explanatory variable. The t-statistics are in parentheses below coefficients.

8.5 Conclusion

This recent year has marked dramatic improvements in East-West relations. These changes have elicited concern about the effect that disarmament will have on the performance of the world economy and the process of economic conversion in the directly affected countries. This study has indeed shown that reductions in tension reduce military expenditures but other factors are important as well. This paper's development of a military expenditure function which includes many of these factors may serve to improve the modeling of this sector in large world econometric models, as well as in the economic development literature concerned with the effects of military expenditure on the process of economic growth. These areas of research continue to be important not only because of the impact that East-West disarmament may have on the global economy, but because there is no reason to suspect that conflicts and wars which have characterized world history will cease to be a part of international interactions. Therefore, an understanding of the process of arming continues to be very important.

References

Azar, E.E. (1980a). The Code Book of the Conflict and Peace Data (COPDAB) : A Computer Assisted Approach to Monitoring and Analyzing International and Domestic Events, University of North Carolina, Chapel Hill (mimeo).

Azar, E.E. (1980b). The conflict and peace data bank (COPDAB) project. *Journal of Conflict Resolution*, 24, 142-152.

Benoit, E. (1978). Growth and defense in developing countries. *Economic Development and Cultural Change,* 26, 271-280.

Bergstrom, T.C. and Goodman, R.P. (1973). Private demands for public goods. *American Economic Review*, 63, 280-296.

Boulding, K.E. (1962).*Conflict and defense.* Boston: Harper and Row.

Brito, D.L. (1972). A dynamic model of an armament race. *International Economic Review* , 13, 359-375.

Brito, D.L. and Intriligator, M.D. (1985). Conflict, war, and redistribution. *The American Political Science Review* , 79, 943-957.

Brito, D.L. and Intriligator, M.D. (1977). Nuclear proliferation and the armaments race. *Journal of Peace Science,* 2, 213-218.

Connolly, M. (1970). Public goods, externalities and international relations.*Journal of Political Economy,* 78, 23-49.

Deger, S. (1986). Economic development and defense expenditure. *Economic Development and Cultural Change*, 35, 179-195.

Deger, S. and Sen, S. (1983). Military expenditure, spin-off and economic development. *Journal of Development Economics,* 13, 67-83.

Dudley, L. and Montmarquette, C. (1981). The demand for military expenditures: an international comparison. *Public Choice,* 37, 5-31.

Findlay, R. (1970). Factor proportions and comparative advantage in the long run. *Journal of Political Economy,* 78, 27-34.

Garfinkel, M. (1990). Arming as a strategic investment in a cooperative equilibrium. *American Economic Review,* 80, 50-68.

Intriligator, M.D. (1975). Strategic considerations in the Richardson model of arms races. *Journal of Political Economy,* 83, 339-353.

Isard, W. (1988). *Arms races, arms control, and conflict analysis.* New York: Cambridge University Press.

Johnston, J. (1984). *Econometric methods.* New York: McGraw-Hill Book Co.

Klein, L.R. and Gronicki, M. (1990). Tradeoffs between military and civilian programs in the Warsaw Pact. (mimeo).

Klein, L.R. and Gronicki, M. (1988). Defense spending among Warsaw Pact countries: implications for LINK simulations of the arms race. (mimeo).

Komiya, R. (1967). Non-traded goods and the pure theory of international trade. *International Economic Review,* 8, 132-152.

Leontief, W., and Duchin, F. (1983). *Military spending.* New York: Oxford University Press.

Murdoch, J.C. and Sandler, T. (1984). Complementarity, free riding, and the military expenditure of NATO allies. *Journal of Public Economics,* 25, 83-101.

McGuire, M.C. (1965). *Secrecy and the arms race.* Cambridge: Harvard University Press.

McGuire, M.C. (1977). A quantitative study of the strategic arms race in the missile age. *Review of Economic and Statistics,* 59, 328-339.

Olson, M. and Zeckhauser, R. (1966). An economic theory of alliances. *Review of Economic and Statistics,* 48, 266-279.

Peltzman, S. (1980). The growth of government. *Journal of Law and Economics,* 23, 209-87.

Sandler, T. and Forbes, J. (1980). Burden sharing, strategy, and the design of NATO. *Economic Inquiry,* 18, 425-444.

Sandler, T. (1977). Impurity of defense: an appilication to the economics of alliances. *Kyklos,* 30, 443-460.

Schelling,T.C. (1960). *The strategy of conflict.* Cambridge: Harvard University Press.

Seiglie, C. (1988a). International conflict and military expenditures. *Journal of Conflict Resolution,* 32, 141-161.

Seiglie, C. (1988b). The impact of technological progress on arms race. American Economic Association mettings, New York City, 1988.

SIPRI. (various years). *SIPRI yearbook: world armaments and disarmament.* London: Taylor and Francis Ltd.

United States Arms Control and Disarmament Agency. (various years). *World military expenditures and arms transfers.* Washington, D.C.

World Bank. (1976).*World Tables.* Baltimore: Johns Hopkins University Press.

Economics of Arms Reduction and the Peace Process
W. Isard and C.H. Anderton (Editors)

Chapter 9

DISARMAMENT NEGOTIATIONS AS AN EXERCISE IN MATURE RIVALRY

Robert E. Kuenne

Princeton University

[While we have examined factors that (1) determine the level and composition of military expenditures and their change, (2) the impacts of such expenditures on the economy and trade, (3) the costs of war, and (4) the goals of national security reflected in damage threatening and damage limiting weaponry, we have not yet treated another critical aspect of the peace problem, namely the reaching of decisions by key political leaders. Each leader of course, has a particular personality, possesses values of a specific political subculture, and is subject to all kinds of cognitive limitations. An extensive literature on decision making exists, as noted in the first chapter. In the present chapter within the framework of oligopoly theory Kuenne adapts his significant contributions on mature leadership to the possibility of disarmament decision making by key political leaders. He goes beyond a conceptual elaboration of the required interplay of both competitive and cooperative factors and begins to explore in a precise operational way desirable properties of such interplay. (eds.)]

9.1 Introduction

In a world of competitive political power struggle, disarmament negotiations are a rare occurrence. Given the history of modern warfare - at least since the American Civil War - one is led to ask why this should be. With the awesome loss of military and civilian life, the fearsome injuries inflicted, the scale of property damage sustained, and the huge resource cost of preparing and using military posture, the social cost far outweighs the social benefit. More relevant in an analysis of causation, the private gains to those who initiate hostilities are seldom long enjoyed if ever attained.

Some "explanations" offer little real insight. The Prisoners' Dilemma paradigm, for example, urges that what is in the joint interest of the involved nations cannot be achieved because the strategy required is not a rational choice for each nation in the absence of a credible agreement that all will abide by. But it is the failure to obtain such a cooperative agreement when negotiations are possible and motivation strong that constitutes the problem. Why, then, does the paradigm apply under conditions that should make it irrelevant? Seemingly, the prospective net cost of not cooperating should make the cooperative strategies dominant.

Similarly, the game of "Chicken" with its dual Nash equilibrium points that provide incentives to participants to threaten war to obtain their political goals can be relevant only if noncooperation can take advantage of opponents locked into a cooperative strategy. But building military posture is a long term venture impossible to conceal from those opponents long enough to prevent their responding in kind. Strategic surprise in the game of armament is not credible under modern conditions.

Among groups of interactive political powers with roughly equally productive economies and military potential, armed forces above requirements for credible deterrent threat, therefore, is not a rational strategy in economic benefit-cost terms. Since deterrence requirements are a function of relative strengths, simultaneous reductions in military capability at zero cost in terms of deterrence potential should be a preeminent political choice leading to fruitful political negotiations.

Yet, disarmament negotiations are not only rare but are tortuous, hard-fought and detailed. Part of the explanation, of course, is that security matters are concerned with the potential for national destruction. But business corporations are also involved with survival in the competitive process, yet they frequently succeed, without even formal negotiations, to attain informal understandings restricting the use of certain competitive strategies that are mutually harmful. That is, Prisoners' Dilemma or Chicken games are not serious threats to stability in many industries, but stability is attained without long and complicated formal bargaining and frequently only with rather subtle signalling. Why do these characteristics not develop in governmental relations?

I shall argue that one major reason is the greater difficulty that nation states have of achieving "mature rivalry", a term I will define in more detail in Section 9.2. Discerning the reasons for this retardation of a process which develops much more quickly in industrial relations may result in insights into policies or practices that will facilitate disarmament agreements.

9.2 Mature Rivalry

Individual agents in communities speedily recognize that their relationships, oriented about their goal-seeking, are mixtures of the competitive and the cooperative. Even in those communities where the rivalrous greatly outweighs the cooperative -- as in oligopolistic industries -- the dualistic nature of interdependence characterizes decision making in a large subset of cases. Because oligopolistic market structures provide the closest approach to the nature of international relations that one can find in the private economic sector with respect to the mixture of competition and cooperation that characterizes their coexistence, I shall draw upon oligopoly analysis as a point of departure.

By the very definition of the market structure, oligopolistic firms are similar to nation states in that they contend with identifiable rivals with whose modes of behavior they become familiar and which they must rationally incorporate into their own strategy choices. After a more or less lengthy period of coexistence in such industries there emerges the consciousness of most participants of a "rivalrous consonance of interests" -- which is to say, the recognition that although the dominant theme in their relationships with each other is competitive, they will fare better individually if they cooperate to some degree in their decision making. It is to their mutual advantage to take into account to a greater or lesser degree - perhaps calibrated to the degree of threat each rival affords - the welfare of opponents, and the manner in which their initiatives might adversely affect those rivals.

This cooperation, generally informal and tacit, but nonetheless real and effective, comes to characterize the industry and pervade its ethos. When this rivalrous consonance is recognized by at least all the major firms in the industry, and its stabilizing effects pervade the decision making of its incumbents, the industry has achieved what I have termed "mature rivalry".[1]

An industry, or to generalize, a community of decision makers, in that state is generally characterized by the following attributes, attitudes, or attainments:

1. The dominant actors at least have attained positions of assured continuance of pre-eminent importance in the community. Each may feel the possibility of short-run changes in fortune, good or bad, but a long-run threat is not foreseen.

2. The state of information flows concerning the actions of one's rivals is highly developed with rapidly obtainable and extensive information of changes in the status quo available. The intention to undertake initiatives which have important potential for the positions of participants may not be communicated, but the results of these decisions are quickly perceived.

3. Each rival is convinced of the ability of competitors to respond rapidly and effectively to initiatives that affect them adversely, and of the potential of reactive measures by those rivals to neutralize anticipated advantages or render them negative in prospect.

4. As the obverse of 3, each rival is assured that if it undergoes temporary setbacks which could be exploited by competitors with grave consequences for its

well-being those competitors will be restrained in their actions and stay within the limits of allowable rivalry.

5.   There exists an unwillingness of rivals to undertake initiatives that may directly or indirectly threaten their status in the community. Rivals' decision making, therefore, is characterized by "risk-averseness" with respect to actions with the potential for seriously harmful retribution.

6.   A sufficiently long period of coexistence has elapsed to give confidence to participants in the indefinite maintainability of the status quo in the absence of mutually acceptable changes and to confirm the conviction of the desirability of maintaining that status quo.

Rivalry is immature frequently when some of these conditions are not fulfilled. If one agent feels that another is vulnerable and that actions harming the rival would enhance his welfare, the status quo may be disrupted. In international relations if a nation feels an important challenge to its political or military power it may act to reduce the threat by preemptive war or such diplomatic measures as alliance. On the other hand a nation may believe it is possible to enhance its welfare at the expense of another and initiate hostile actions beyond the bounds of mutually acceptable rivalry. Israel's recent attack upon Iraq's nuclear reactor or its incursion into Lebanon furnish examples of the first situation, while Iraq's invasion of Iran and Kuwait are examples of the latter. The Middle East in general is a prime example of an area in which rivalry has not yet attained the stability of mature rivalry.

Western Europe since the end of World War II is an excellent case of a region which emerged after centuries of turmoil into a state of mature rivalry. The European Community provides a vehicle for cooperation as well as the formalization and supervision of member competition, and in 1992 will intensify interdependence and cooperation. Competitive disagreements can be intense and sacrifice of sovereignty painful, but each member feels a territorial and military security from hostile actions of other members that is still historically recent in the area and permits the recognition of rivalrous consonance.

Of course, the Cold War now ending was a preeminent study in immature international rivalry. Deep ideological commitment to antipodal social structures which contended for international allegiances; impeded information flows concerning rival intentions and actions; uncertainty concerning the potential success of each rival in offensive and defensive military actions with failure having the potential for national destruction; and a relatively short period of time to give confidence to each side that the hostility could be confined to ideological rivalry: these were keynotes in the relation.

The one condition of mature rivalry that was revealed was sourced in the very destructiveness of the military weaponry: unlike previous epochs it took little imagination to perceive the threat of mutual annihilation posed by nuclear weapons. This led both parties to extremely risk-averse attitudes that convinced them to avoid confrontations that had the potential for escalation to military conflict. Through the bluster and posturing of the Cold War period, this characteristic of the rivalry on both sides was quite apparent and to it the world may owe the preservation of the possibility of the recent approach to the achievement of full-blown mature rivalry.

9.3 Encouraging the Development of Mature Rivalry

The achievement of a state of mature rivalry by western liberal nations and the Soviet Union is complicated by the state of domestic political and economic turmoil the latter is currently experiencing. On the one hand it facilitates the process by placing a premium on calm and unthreatening external relations, the reduction of resource drains upon a struggling economy, and the prospect of economic assistance from former antagonists. Indeed, had the essential collapse of the economic system and the preoccupation with centrifugal nationalities problems not occurred, it is doubtful that the rapid progress we have experienced in the last five years could have happened at all.

But domestic turmoil and the retreat from empire set into motion forces opposing such progress as implementing policies threaten the status of entrenched bureaucracies and the military. Deeply implanted attitudes and allegiances as well as selfish interests of such establishments offer resistance to detente. Nor is such opposition confined to the Soviet side: the same groups for the same motives in the West urge caution in downsizing military posture or extending aid in the absence of "certain knowledge" of Soviet intentions.

In the face of these opportunities and obstacles, what steps can Western policy makers take to assure that progress continues to the desired end? The question is most germane because disarmament - especially in the area of strategic nuclear weaponry - must surely be considered the ultimate achievement of a state of mature rivalry. Such agreements involve voluntary limitations on nations' sovereign rights to exert lethal force to enforce their wills or, more compellingly, to defend themselves against or deter threats to their survival. These voluntary limitations are consistent with the condition that nations be risk-averse with respect to actions with the potential for seriously harmful retribution. As noted above, how might the establishment of other conditions for mature rivalry be facilitated?

Conditions 1 and 4 infer the desirability of avoiding seeming threats to the long-run eminence of the Soviet Union in the international economy and to giving assurances that strategic and tactical responses to its severe domestic stresses will be restrained. The short-run political and economic difficulties that nation is undergoing in what hopefully is a transition to a more liberal state should not be used in manners that would strengthen the position of those Soviet policy makers who point to military standdown as a symptom of national decline as a world power. The Bush administration was exemplary in this respect in ignoring strong domestic pressure to intervene in Eastern Europe at the time of the Soviet retreat and disarray. The restoration of most-favored-nation treatment and the extension of trade credits at the present time of goods scarcity also would be most advisable on the same grounds. Serious thought should also be given such steps as the inclusion of Soviet participants in Middle East peace initiatives at some point in the process of achieving the new status quo.

At the same time, however, Condition 3 asserts the desirability of the West to demonstrate its capability and its willingness to respond effectively to Soviet transgressions of the formal and informal rules of conduct of mature rivalry. This is particularly important, of course, in the case of violations of formal disarmament agreements. It also argues for the undesirability of complete disarmament which would deny all capacity for response on the part of both parties. In rivalrous cooperation it must not be lost sight of that the threat of punishment for excessively egoistic actions and the fear of such punishment play important roles in the maintenance of the relationship. In international relations, especially, where rules of justice are nonexistent or unenforceable, the dominance of the competitive vis a vis the cooperative should not be lost sight of, and least of all in the area of disarmament.

Perhaps the most readily providable and, in questions of military standdown, the most important prerequisite is Condition 2: the ability of both parties to obtain continuous, noncorruptible, and accurate data concerning actions of the rival that would seriously threaten the welfare of either party. Information flow, permitting verification of initial compliance with formal agreements as well as the monitoring of relevant rival actions, is a fundamental need of any mature rivalrous relationship. Certain knowledge that initiation of any such action will be discerned immediately by a rival and effective action taken to counter it both induces rivals to enter into such agreements and deters them from breaking them. Parties who are seriously interested in disarmament must be willing to provide ready access to such vital information with a substantial sacrifice of privacy, given the previous extreme confidentiality of such data.

Overriding all of the six conditions listed in Section 9.2 is a desire and willingness to cooperate that springs exclusively or nearly exclusively from selfish interest. Each rival must be convinced of the benefit to be derived for himself by substantial agreement to restrain the purely rivalrous aspects of the relationship to take into account the welfare of opponents. For effective cooperation is exactly that: initiating action both on the basis of its impacts upon one's own *and one's opponents' welfares,* with the motivation of such concern being the feedback from their reactions upon one's own welfare. Selfishness once removed motivated by prudent self-interest rather than altruism is the core concept of rivalrous consonance and its realization, mature rivalry. Workable disarmament agreements are the *ne plus ultra* of mature rivalry.

9.4 The Proposed START Treaty

To make these points clearer I may illustrate with a discussion and simple model of disarmament using the START agreement. On June 1, 1990, Presidents Bush and Gorbachev initialled an agreement to reduce strategic nuclear platforms and warheads by disappointingly small numbers, dramatically illustrating the early and tentative stages that strategic disarmament has now entered. Table 9.1 reveals data on delivery vehicles and warheads for both sides before and after the standdown if agreement on details is reached.

The warhead accounting in Table 9.1 is misleading because although bombers may carry up to 20 long-range cruise missiles, they are notionally perceived in the agreement as armed with only 8 or 10 missiles. If they are loaded with any number of short-range missiles or nuclear bombs they are accounted as carrying only one warhead. Sea-launched cruise missiles, at American insistence, are excluded from the body of the treaty, and hence not counted, although they will be limited by a non-binding and non-verifiable protocol. And, finally, missiles aboard out-of-service submarines are excluded from the number of "accountable" missiles as well. Hence, the actual number of warheads now possessed -- between 11,000 and 12,000 on each side -- will be reduced to about 9,500 for the U.S. and 7,000 for the U.S.S.R.

The treaty, therefore, once in force requires the scrapping of about 39 percent of Russian actual warheads and 21 percent of American, reducing their nuclear arsenals to approximately their 1980 and 1973 levels respectively. However, some aging missiles would have been scrapped because of obsolescence, and, moreover, both sides will be allowed over the 15-year lifetime of the treaty to modernize their missiles within the specified limits. When the heightened effectiveness of such "smart" weaponry is taken into account as well, the treaty may be seen to be a promising first step on the strategic nuclear warhead disarmament road, but only that.

Similarly, delivery platform reductions must be discounted because of normal obsolescence and serious doubts about whether they would not have been replaced even in the absence of START. The U.S. will be committed to scrapping about 100 Minuteman-2 missiles, 23 ballistic missile submarines, and 98 venerable B-52 bombers over the life of the treaty, while the U.S.S.R. will retire about 20 bombers and 50 submarines.

TABLE 9.1

Delivery Platforms and Warheads Possessed by U.S. and U.S.S.R. in 1990 and in Proposed START Reductions

System	1990 U.S.	1990 U.S.S.R.	Post-Agreement U.S.	Post-Agreement U.S.S.R.
1. Intercontinental Missiles	1,000	1,356	850	689
2. Submarine-Launched Missiles	560	930	378[a]	300
3. Bombers	263	162	224[b]	167
4. Warheads:				
a. Accountable[c]	8,457	10,407	5,903[ab]	5,893
b. Actual[c]	11,974	11,320	9,498	6,888

[a]Assumes 72 submarine missiles are exempted by "discounting" for submarines in port and hence not operational.

[b]Assumes 32 operational B-2 bombers.

[c]Warhead data depend on number of weapons estimated per bomber.

Source: London Economist, June 9, 1990, pp. 22, 25.

The treaty does require, however, a great deal of "openness" on the part of both nations for verifiability, and, in terms of the discussion of Section 9.2 this may be the greatest contribution it has to make to the establishment of mature rivalry and a more significant standdown. But deeper reductions in strategic nuclear capability will require long and detailed negotiations in the future, with progress accelerating as rivalry matures.

9.5   A Simple Model of Disarmament Negotiations

Proposing to model as complex a process as disarmament negotiations with a pretense to forecasting precision betrays an ambition that breaches the boundary of foolhardiness. Let me hasten to assert, therefore, that such is not the purpose of the simple scheme presented in this section. Rather, it is hoped through its construction and usage to illustrate some of the points made in Sections 9.2 and 9.3 and to gain elementary insights into the nature of the goals of the negotiators, the effects that different emphases upon such goals may have on the process, and the impacts which changes in such emphases may exercise upon results. This section, therefore, limits itself to seeking general hypotheses about the motivation of the principals, the immediate goals that spring from these motivations, and the manner in which the goals interact in a search for a resolution of conflicting interests. In no sense is the model presented as a framework that can be used to project the outcome of a specific disarmament process.

I shall continue to use the START negotiations as an example. Because of the extremely tight security surrounding the conferences one cannot calibrate relevant functions with historic data, and so where functions have been fitted with numerical data it must be understood to be notional, not actual. Frequently the data of Table 9.1 will be extrapolated or used as bases for speculation.

First, I assume that the negotiation set is determined by upper bound functions that both rivals determine before negotiations begin and which remain fixed during each finite *stage* of the talks. These *maximum* force functions I symbolize:

$$R^* = f_a(A_a; \tau) \tag{9.1}$$

$$A^* = f_r(R_r; \tau), \tag{9.2}$$

where R^* is the maximum size of the U.S.S.R. force (e.g., warheads) that the U.S. would accept given the projected size A_a of the U.S. force, and where correspondingly A^* is the maximum size of the U.S. force that the U.S.S.R. would accept given the projected size R_r of the U.S.S.R. force. The equations also incorporate a shift parameter τ which is assumed to be determined by the state of mature rivalry achieved, somehow measured. As these parameters rise with that state it is assumed that $\partial R^*/\partial \tau$ and $\partial A^*/\partial \tau > 0$, so that the negotiation set enlarges stage by stage as τ changes.

Treating the results of the START round in Table 9.1 as the end of stage 1, I have assumed specifications for equations (9.1) and (9.2) to fix ideas. One interesting insight is that if both rivals are willing to settle for the status quo and the maximum force functions in equations (9.1) and (9.2) are insufficiently concave they will have to do so because that solution will be the only point in the feasible region for armament reduction. For stage 2, I assume that both rivals would accept the new status quo at $[I_a, I_r]=[9,498, 6,888]$. Moreover, if either rival faced a hypothetical offer by the other to reduce force size to 0, I assume the other side would insist on maintaining some force size to confront potential threats from other adversaries (e.g., an Iraqi challenge or a Chinese threat.)

I have assumed arbitrarily that for $R^*=0$, A_a would equal 300, and for $A^* = 0$, $R_r =$ 200. Hence, the points [300, 0] and [0,200] lie on equations (9.1) and (9.2) respectively. Let $[A_a,A_r]$ be the U.S. proposals for U.S. and U.S.S.R. force levels respectively, and $[R_r,R_a]$ the U.S.S.R. proposals for own- and U.S. force levels. Fitting these points yields the following specifications for equations (9.1) and (9.2):

$$R^*=-221.1+.74A_a + .0000012A_a^2 \qquad\qquad (9.3)$$

$$A^*=-287.0+1.44R_r - .0000021R_r^2 \qquad\qquad (9.4)$$

These near-linear functions are roughly graphed in Figure 9.1 with the dash line depicting the maximum number of U.S.S.R. warheads the U.S. would permit for any number of its own warheads and the solid line the maximum force size the U.S.S.R. would find acceptable for U.S. strength as a function of U.S.S.R. force size. The two maximum force functions as I have hypothesized them, intersect approximately at the values set by the current START agreement.

The negotiation set under these conditions will be empty and no movement will be made from the status quo. Graphically this occurs because A^* lies everywhere to the left of R^* except where the curves join at the status quo. In terms of the process the difficulty is that neither nation is sufficiently yielding to the demands of the other. For every U.S. force level the maximum U.S.S.R. level it is prepared to accept is too small to induce the U.S.S.R. to acquiesce in the initiating U.S. force level proposal. On Figure 9.1, when $A_a=4,000$, $R^*=2,758$. But when $R_r=2,758$, A^* is only 3,669. Hence, an initial U.S. force level of 4,000 is mapped by equations (9.3) and (9.4) into a maximum allowable level of 3,669, and the proposed A_a is infeasible. Except for the status quo, even when the U.S. proposes for any desired force level the maximum U.S.S.R. level it is willing to accept, the U.S.S.R. declines to accept it as a response to the initiating U.S. offer. A similar statement holds for U.S.S.R. initiations. For example, as shown on Figure 9.1, a proposed R_r of 2,000 is mapped into an A^* of 2,585; but for the U.S. to find 2,585 acceptable, R^* would need to be 1,700. Thus the proposed offer of 2,000 is unacceptable to the U.S.

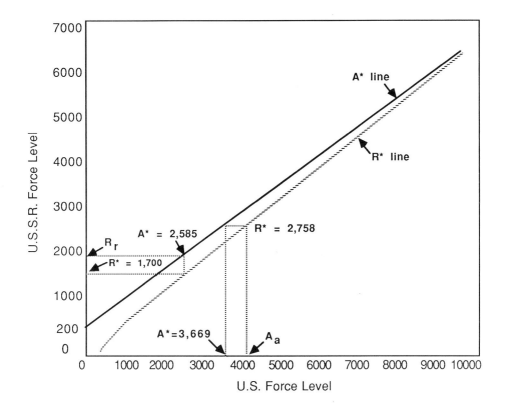

Figure 9.1: An Empty, Feasible Negotiation Region

Hence, the mere readiness of one rival to demand superior force levels and the willingness of the other to concede to those demands, as is apparent in Figure 9.1, is not a sufficient condition for feasible disarmament negotiations. From Figure 9.1 it is clear that linear maximum force functions that originate with small positive levels and terminate at existing levels cannot lead to further reductions in armament. In some domain below the status quo force levels, for any given number of missiles desired by rival 1 the maximum it will allow rival 2 must be acceptable to rival 2 for the initial level of rival 1 force or more. Correspondingly, in some domain below the status quo force levels, for any given number of missiles desired by rival 2 the maximum it will allow rival 1 must be acceptable to rival 1 for the initial level of rival 2 force or more. Figure 9.2 illustrates the principle. If the U.S. proposes a level A'_a for itself the maximum U.S.S.R. force it will permit is R^{*1}. But the U.S.S.R. would permit A'_a if it were allowed only R^{*2}. Hence, the range R^{*1}-R^{*2} is a feasible bargaining range for a U.S. initial offer of A'_a. The feasible region is defined as that area captured between the functions in the domain A'-A" (R'-R").

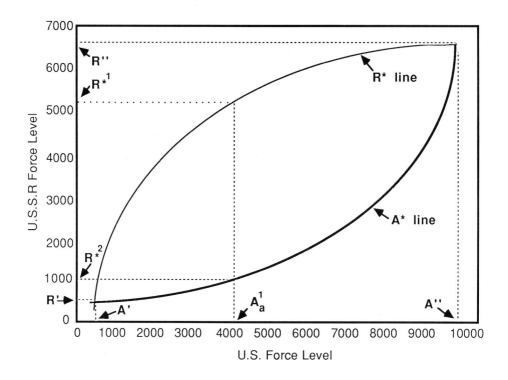

Figure 9.2: START Negotiation Set

This puts significant restrictions on the shape of the maximum force functions for a feasible region to exist. Both functions cannot be linear or near-linear, for example, as shown above. Because near-linearity may be a quite plausible form for the functions in the next phase of START, such negotiations may be fruitless without a change in functional forms. Further, both functions cannot be convex. This configuration of the functions implies that as own-force levels rise by equal increments a rival is willing to permit the other to have larger and larger responsive increments. Paradoxically, although such willingness indicates more liberal attitudes to rivals' postures, if both sides possess such willingness no feasible region will exist.

Within the feasible region, when it exists, what goals would the rivals seek in bargaining for a change in the status quo? I suggest that their objective functions would include three types of relative measures. First, they would be concerned in making their offers with the relative distances of such offers from the status quo force levels (I_a, I_r) to yield the first components, W_a and W_r, for their respective objective functions:

$$W_a = (I_a - A_a)/(I_r - A_r) \tag{9.5}$$

$$W_r = (I_r - A_r)/(I_a - R_a) \tag{9.6}$$

Each side has a goal of minimizing this component of its objective function, making the numerator as small as possible (that is for the proposed force level for itself to be as close to the status quo level) and the denominator as large as possible through bargaining.

A second goal is to compare the distance between their offers for rival force size and their maximum allowable force size to the distance of the opponent's status quo level from his proposed own-force size as indicated by the ratios:

$$X_a = (A_r - R^*)/(I_r - R_r) \tag{9.7}$$

$$X_r = (R_a - A^*)/(I_a - A_a) \tag{9.8}$$

Compared with the offered reduction in strength by the opposing rival, how much of the maximum allowable force for that rival is the other giving up? Considering these component goals only, each rival should seek to minimize the functions (9.7) and (9.8), making offers of other-rival levels as close to zero as possible.

Given only the goal components of equations (9.5)-(9.8) both rivals are driven to irreconcilable offers. The drive to achieve agreement, however, in the interest of both sides, leads them to temper these competitive goals with a cooperative one. The last component goal, therefore, is to seek agreement:

$$Y_a = \{[(A_a\text{-}R_a)^2 + (A_r\text{-}R_r)^2]/(I_r\text{-}I_a)^2\}^{.5} - 1 \tag{9.9}$$

$$Y_r = \{[(A_a\text{-}R_a)^2 + (A_r\text{-}R_r)^2]/(I_r\text{-}I_a)^2\}^{.5} - 1 \tag{9.10}$$

The parties have an interest in minimizing this function by moving their offers toward equality, when compared with the distance that initially separated them.

As an initial model, therefore, I suggest that their respective objective functions (Z_a, Z_r) might be written as a convex combination of these three components in (9.5)-(9.10), and that they seek to minimize these functions sequentially in the bargaining process:

$$\text{Min } Z_a = \alpha_a W_a + \beta_a X_a + \theta_a Y_a \tag{9.11}$$

$$\text{Min } Z_r = \alpha_r W_r + \beta_r X_r + \theta_r Y_r \tag{9.12}$$

$$\alpha_a + \beta_a + \theta_a = \alpha_r + \beta_r + \theta_r = 1 \tag{9.13}$$

$$A_a, A_r, R_r, R_a \geq 0 \tag{9.14}$$

Note that each rival is assumed to know only his own maximum force level function.

If the maximum force level functions (9.1) and (9.2) are everywhere convex or convex in the feasible region, Z_a and Z_r will be sequentially convex in that each rival will assume the other's offers are fixed and minimize with respect to its own decision variables. At each step of the negotiation, therefore, each rival will attain a global minimum. A "solution" is attained when $A_a=R_a$ and $A_r=R_r$, although it may be a preliminary agreement en route to a more satisfactory point to both parties.

Of course, the negotiation process will be much richer than this simple scheme can adequately portray, but this model permits one to focus upon the contributions to that process that a maturing rivalry can make. One would expect that θ_a and θ_r will grow as that occurs: the desire to achieve agreement should rise in importance relative to the achievement of the self-seeking goals. The second impact should be a greater willingness to grant rivals larger maximum forces for given own forces. That is, R^* and A^* should become more concave over time, enlarging the feasible region. Although this formally permits more uneven solutions to arise, the important practical result is the enlarging of the area in which smaller force levels for both rivals can be accepted.

9.6 Conclusions

The notion of mature rivalry is central to the process of disarmament. The very existence of ongoing disarmament processes is evidence that a posture of extreme political rivalry has tempered to the point that cautious cooperation is possible. As the process proceeds by stages, continued progress depends upon an intensification of those desires for cooperation if feasible regions for negotiations are to continue to exist. For that intensification to occur, which is to say, for a continuing maturation of the rivalry, certain preconditions discussed in Section 9.2 must intensify. The encouragement and acceleration of this development are important goals of the policy maker.

Footnotes

[1]See Kuenne (1988, 1989). For a full discussion of rivalrous consonance see Kuenne (1986).

References

Kuenne, R.E. (1986). *Rivalrous consonance: A theory of general oligopolistic equilibrium.* Amsterdam: North-Holland.

Kuenne, R.E. (1988). Conflict management and the theory of mature oligopoly. *Conflict Management and Peace Science*, 10, 37-59.

Kuenne, R.E. (1989). Conflict management in mature rivalry. *Journal of Conflict Resolution*, 33, 554-566.

Economics of Arms Reduction and the Peace Process
W. Isard and C.H. Anderton (Editors)
© 1992 Elsevier Science Publishers B.V. All rights reserved.

Chapter 10

WARS AND FAMINES:
ON DIVISIONS AND INCENTIVES

Amartya Sen

Lamont University Professor at Harvard University[*]

[Up to now, our analysis has pertained largely, if not entirely, to the problems faced by both developed and Eastern European countries. But most of the world's population resides in developing countries elsewhere, where the role and impact of military expenditures is significantly different. In the first of two papers relating to developing countries, Amyrta Sen asks the basic question: how does the preparation for and the execution of wars influence the ability of famine-prone countries to escape mass starvation --- a question of perhaps not much significance to highly developed industrialized market economies, but clearly of tremendous significance to developing economies. (eds.)]

10.1 Introduction

Famines have often been associated with wars. This historical link has re-emerged with remarkable force in the modern world. Famines have devastated war-torn countries in sub-Saharan Africa, such as Angola, Chad, Ethiopia, Mozambique, Somalia, Sudan, and many others. The association is not confined to sub-Saharan Africa, and there are terrible examples elsewhere as well, e.g., in Kampuchea. Sometimes, famines have also occurred in war time without being directly related to military actions, e.g., the Bengal famine of 1943 which occurred soon after the Japanese army moved into the neighbouring province of Assam and just after Calcutta was - rather slightly - bombed.

The relationship between wars and famines is a messy subject, and it would be hopeless to try to get a simple formulaic connection between the two types of phenomena. Nevertheless, there is considerable evidence that the preparation for and the execution of wars do often adversely influence the ability of famine-prone countries to escape mass starvation. Given the importance of the subject, it may be useful to attempt a preliminary sorting out of issues, dealing particularly with the different ways in which wars and war-like activities can weaken a poor country's defenses against famines.

I should begin with a couple of disclaimers. First, in this paper, I shall concentrate on the role of wars in the causation of famines, rather than the converse (i.e., the role of famines in the development of wars). It is indeed possible to argue that famines, in their turn, can contribute to the development of wars, but in this essay I shall not be directly concerned with that part of the possible linkage. This paper is about the different ways in which wars and military activities can - directly or indirectly - serve as causal antecedents of famines.

Second, the choice of focus in this paper is deliberately biased towards more indirect rather than direct links between wars and famines. The relationship between wars and famines has some simple and easily identifiable aspects. Wars destroy crops. They devastate the economy and ravage the stock of productive capital. They damage transport facilities and disrupt movements of food and other commodities. There do indeed exist clear and easily identifiable links between the two phenomena.

While these aspects of the relationship between wars and famines are undoubtedly important, they should not deflect us from investigating more complex and less obvious inter-connections between the two. This paper is concerned primarily with identifying some crucial but less direct connections between wars and famines.[1] The immediately destructive roles of wars have been noted often enough.[2] It may be useful in the present context to concentrate on the less straightforward interactions between wars and famines.

I shall argue that a central feature of the role of military activities in the causation of famines is the accentuation of economic and political divisions as a consequence - direct or indirect - of these activities. That accentuation can be analysed in terms of the economic and political incentives that influence actions and policies. Intermediation through social divisiveness is the primary focus of the approach explored in this paper.

It is not being claimed that this perspective captures most of the factors that causally link famines to wars. It is, however, *inter alia* a fruitful general connection to pursue - an associative linkage that is often missed in presentations that focus on the more immediate features of material destruction caused by wars. It is useful in this context to make use of what we do know about the causation of famines in general and see the contribution of wars in that over-all background.

10.2 Divisions and Incentives

Famines are caused by the inability of some sections of the population to command adequate food for survival. The vulnerable groups face starvation as a result of declines in their "entitlements" (i.e., the set of commodity bundles over which a family can establish operative control). Such an entitlement decline can happen in many different ways. The anticipation as well as the prevention of famines must take adequate note of the diverse ways in which entitlement failures may occur.[3]

A decline in food output can, of course, contribute to entitlement failures, even though it is not a necessary condition for such failures. A crop loss directly affects the food entitlements of peasants and share croppers, and indirectly makes it harder for others to command food in the market, especially through increased relative price of food. Famines have occurred, however, even without a decline in food output. Indeed, sometimes they have taken place in situations of "peak" availability of food in the economy.[4] No less importantly, even when famines take place in situations of reduced food availability, that availability decline can be one of many factors responsible for the inability of the famine victims to establish command over food.

Entitlement failures leading to famines can have many different causal antecedents. They can result, for example, from unemployment, leaving people without the economic means of commanding food. That connection, much explored in the recent literature on famines, was identified by Adam Smith himself.[5] Large-scale starvation can also result from severe declines of money wages in relation to food prices, making it hard for many to buy food, even when there is no job loss. Similarly, declines of exchange rates vis-a-vis food may erode the food-buying power of sellers of commodities such as services and craft products. There can also be other economic changes leading to sharp declines of the entitlements of particular groups of people in the society.

Famines are divisive phenomena. Typically they affect only a small section of the population - rarely more than five or ten percent of the people.[6] They have much more to do with the power to command food on the part of particular occupation groups than with the overall availability of food. Wars and military activities can disrupt the entitlements of vulnerable groups even without destroying crops or disrupting production or transport.

Divisiveness has two aspects - economic and political. The immediate links of famines are with economic divisions. With changes of relative prices and opportunities of transaction, the entitlements of different groups can move in sharply different ways. Sometimes the success of one group in commanding food can contribute to the failure of others to get enough for survival, with Lucifer taking the hindmost.

Economic divisiveness can, however, be moderated by political and legal processes. For example, if a country has unemployment insurance and minimal guarantees of income and food (for example, through poverty-related rights to assistance), then the "hindmost" groups will tend to be cushioned from falling below certain thresholds. These minimal guarantees are of crucial importance in preventing famines. This applies, incidentally, even to very rich countries. In the absence of these state-guaranteed rights, the means of commanding food enjoyed by the unemployed would be very meager indeed even in, say, Western Europe or North America. With an unemployment rate of around 12 per cent, there could easily have been widespread starvation in Britain or Belgium in the early 1980s, but for the protection of minimal entitlements provided by unemployment benefits and other poverty-relief programs.

In effect, these state-guaranteed supports serve as instruments of political correction of economic divisiveness. It is the absence of these protections in many war-torn economies in the Third World that makes the economic divisions take their full toll. Indeed, these political instruments of entitlement protection may, in fact, be further weakened by wars and by militarism (this issue will be taken up in section 10.5).

In understanding the relationship between wars and famines, we have to see how the political as well as the economic aspects of social divisions relate to war activities. Crucial to all this is the question of incentives. People's ability to command food in the market depends on what is supplied, what is produced, what is transported, and so on, and these economic activities are deeply influenced by the patterns of incentives operating in the economy. But incentives also have political aspects, in addition to economic ones. The willingness of the governments in power to moderate economic destitution by ensuring minimal guarantees depends on the political incentives the governments encounter to act that way. The effectiveness of such protective processes are deeply conditional on the nature of the operative political incentives.

10.3 Famine Mortality and Health Services

Wars not only destroy food output and productive capital, they also undermine social services. This is partly a result of the chaos and disruption of wars,[7] but also the consequence of governmental resources being taken away from social services to finance military build-ups.

One field in which such deflection is particularly important and immediate is that of health services. The role of public health measures in preventing famine deaths have often been underemphasized. Indeed, most people who die in a famine die from clearly identifiable diseases rather than from starvation as such.[8] Famines help the rapid spread of disease through the weakening of immunity systems, through population movements, through the breakdown of sanitary services, and through the attempts of the famine victims to eat whatever they can get (including discarded remnants of food picked from the garbage). The delivery of health care is an important part of famine prevention and relief.[9]

The underdevelopment and breakdown of health services can be among the important causal antecedents of large-scale famine deaths. There is, of course, no necessity to neglect health services in preparing for war, and indeed, as will be argued later on (in section 10.5), in a democratic country there are reasons to expect a considerable *intensification* of efforts towards widespread health care in war time. But health care, especially to deal with famine mortality, rarely receives the attention it deserves in highly stratified societies, with militaristic ruling classes.

10.4 Investment, Complementarity and Conflicts

The likelihood of wars also reduce private incentive to make long-run investments. It may not be frightfully smart to set up factories in a would-be battlefield, nor to invest much to improve the quality of cultivable land. One of the remarkable features of famines in sub-Saharan Africa is their association with stagnation and decline of productive abilities - not just in food production but also in other income-producing activities.[10] Because of the prevention of capital formation (going well beyond the destruction of the existing capital goods), the devastating effects of wars and war-like situations on productive abilities can be much more extensive and pernicious that is apparent from the statistics of capital loss.[11] In this area of economics as in others, "counterfactuals" are a central part of the analysis, and we have to contrast the actual condition with what could have been expected in a situation less ravaged by war-related uncertainties.

The adverse effects on productive abilities and economic opportunities can affect different groups in different ways. The occupation groups directly involved in activities that are shunned or curtailed do, of course, typically suffer most. But the process of economic linkages can adversely influence also the interests of other groups whose intitlements depend indirectly on these activities (e.g., on the use of transport facilities). Further, the reduction in the income of one group can adversely affect the incomes of others who produce commodities demanded by the former, and in this way destitution can "spread".

This feature of "complementarity" in the development of destitution can be contrasted with other interconnections that may have more "competitive" features. Different groups compete for the same supply of food and other vital commodities, and the prosperity of one group can adversely affect the ability of others to establish entitlement over those commodities. The incentives of the market can operate in the direction of deflecting food from one group to another. A war economy often brings about a rapid increase in the purchasing power of one group vis-a-vis another, and the *relative* decline of economic power of the latter group can result, as a consequence, in its *absolute* downfall in terms of the ability to command food and other vital commodities.

For example, the Bengal famine of 1943, in which it is estimated that about three million people died, was directly fed by the "war boom" in Bengal. That province in British India was close to the front line in the war with Japan, and served as a place in which a massive expansion of military and war-related civilian expenditures occurred at that time. The increased purchasing power of those favorably affected by the war boom (primarily located in Calcutta and some other urban areas) allowed them to take a considerably bigger share of the available food supply, leaving the rural masses (especially landless laborers) without the ability to compete in the "food battle".

Interestingly, that aspect of economic divisiveness was not moderated by political intervention in the Bengal of 1943. It was, in fact, exacerbated by governmental provision of subsidized rice for normal residents of Calcutta (through ration shops and "fair price" distribution centers), and those who had been favorably affected by the war boom in earning higher money incomes were *further* helped by the opportunity to buy food at lower prices.[12]

The political incentives the government had for giving priority to feeding Calcutta related to the fear of the British Raj that urban unrest could be very disruptive for the war efforts, whereas rural disquiet would be less articulate and less problematic. Deaths in the Bengal famine of 1943 were confined almost entirely to the rural population even though many died in the city of Calcutta after moving there in search of relief.[13] The economically divisive consequences of the war were, thus, magnified and strengthened by the political incentives operating on the government.[14]

In addition to damaging food crops, capital goods, transport services, etc., wars and war-like situations can prevent capital formation and disrupt economic opportunities, affecting the interests of some groups much more adversely than those of others. Massive war efforts can also cause economic shifts that sharply alter the balance of purchasing power against some groups, and if these groups are not crucial for war efforts, their predicaments may receive no governmental attention or remedy (indeed government action could worsen their predicaments). The last issue, viz., what the government has incentive to do or not do, is a more general question to which we now turn.

10.5 Political Incentives and Authoritarianism

Do wars make a country *more* politically divisive, or less so? Contrary to what was discussed in the last section, it may be thought that the answer may well be "less", since war efforts can contribute to generating a spirit of political solidarity in the nation. And national solidarity can be an important factor that contributes to attention being paid to the interests of the poor - thus working *against* the starvation and deprivation of vulnerable groups. There is some truth in this general expectation. Indeed, in an independent and democratic country the solidarity generated by war efforts can be effectively used to provide support for the more vulnerable sections of the community.

An example of this can be seen in the history of Great Britain during the World Wars. Both in the First and in the Second World War, the British government managed to provide more equal sharing of food and health care. Extensive public efforts were expended in looking after the interests of the worst off.

In fact, while the average availability of food declined in Britain during the Second World War, the incidence of clinical undernourishment also went down with a general improvement of the health conditions of the British population.[15] It is also interesting to note in this context, that the increase in life expectancy at birth in England and Wales was much faster in the two war decades (viz. nearly 7 additional years both in 1911-21 and 1941-51) than in the other decades of this century (life expectancy increased between 1 to 4 years in every other decade).[16]

Even the British National Health Service, which was born just after the end of the Second World War, was to a great extent helped by the war experience of sharing and caring. The pioneering development of a National Health Service to provide health care for all was greatly helped by the solidarity generated by Britain's war efforts.[17] There is a pattern here that is relevant to many countries in the world. But the situation is quite different in societies that lack a democratic system and in which the unequal sharing may be further consolidated by wars.

When a small group of military or civilian rulers, with direct links only with a relatively small section of the people, run a country, wars can strengthen the grip of these regimes and make them even less sensitive to the needs of others. Indeed, wars provide classic excuses for suppressing opposition parties, persecuting political opponents, and eliminating free and independent newspapers. The recent history of sub-Saharan Africa provides many illustrations of this tragic process.[18] With these changes, governments are less vulnerable to public criticism and can manage to survive extensive starvation caused by the entitlement failures of large occupation groups. Famines cuased by differential movements of economic power of different groups may, then, be left largely untouched, without an adequate attempt at recreating the lost entitlements through public support.[19]

Detailed studies of famine prevention in different parts of the world (including India and also such African countries as Botswana and Zimbabwe) bring out the fact that even in situations of severe decline of total food output and sharp reduction of market-based economic entitlements of particular sections of the population, famines can be altogether prevented by public policies aimed at protecting the vulnerable. This can be done in different ways. One effective means is through public employment for anyone who seeks them (and is ready to do a good day's work), thus providing a good channel of recreating the lost purchasing power of the potential famine victims.[20] Such a system has incentive advantages since the self-selection involved in the willingness to work can serve as an effective method of screening (separating out the really needy from those who would like to obtain governmental money without being in terribly dire situations).[21]

The ability to prevent famines exists widely across the world. However, it is remarkable how often this power is left unused. The governments may lack the political incentive to provide this protection if they feel unthreatened by the prospects of a famine. This invulnerability is itself fostered and strengthened by the authoritarianism (including the suppression of opposition parties and newspapers) that tends to go with war situations.

The political incentives are sometimes overlooked in trying to analyse famines in terms of purely economic parameters, but the nature of these incentives can be extremely important for understanding the prevalence or absence of famines.[22] It is a remarkable fact that while famines have occurred not only in market-based free-enterprise economies but also in interventionist socialist countries,[23] they seem to have never occurred in a democratic country which permits opposition parties and adversarial politics and does not suppress an independent press.[24] If the government has to go to the polls to secure reelection and has to withstand criticism in the media and in the legislatures, it would have good reasons to act quickly and effectively in preventing threatening famines. Indeed, efforts to avert impending crises and calamities can even lead to long-run improvements brought about by a war situation (e.g., as happened in Great Britain during the First and Second World Wars, discussed earlier).

The absence of famines in democratic politics applies not only to the richer countries, but also to those poor, developing countries which have a system permitting adversarial politics and critical journalism. Despite precarious food situations, famines can be effectively averted through public action in protecting the entitlement of potential famine victims.[25] Examples of successful protective action in situations of severely threatening famines can be found in India (in 1967, 1973, 1979 and 1985), Botswana (in 1982-87), Zimbabwe (in 1982-84), and elsewhere.[26]

The central issue here is the political incentive that operates on the government to prevent famines, and that incentive is particularly important since famines are almost always preventable through timely public action. One of the most pernicious effects of wars and war-like situations is a weakening of the opportunity of adversarial politics and social criticism. The excuse for suppressing opposition parties and independent newspapers has often been based on the alleged demands of war efforts, e.g., in many countries in sub-Saharan Africa.[27] The weakness of the democratic structure of many vulnerable economies and the accentuation of that weakness by wars and militarism are among the most important causal antecedents of famines in the modern world.

10.6 Concluding Remarks

The connection between wars and famines involve the operation of political as well as economic incentives, and the process can work through consolidating and aggravating divisions in the society with disastrous effects on the most vulnerable. It would be a mistake to concentrate *only* on the destruction of outputs and capital in causally relating famines to wars. The economic incentives governing production and distribution and the political incentives affecting public protection of the vulnerable can be the crucial features to look at in understanding how wars cause famines.

An ideal breeding ground for famines is provided by the "coupling" of (1) economic processes that make some sections of the population more vulnerable to starvation, and (2) political processes that make many governments more insensitive to the predicaments of the victims. I have tried to discuss how that "coupling" is fostered in many circumstances by the prevalence of war and militarism in the developing countries.

Wars can have diverse effects on political divisions depending on the circumstances. In some contexts, they can contribute to more national solidarity, which can in turn lead to public policies that result in a reduction of undernourishment and morbidity (as in Britain during the two World Wars). On the other hand, with a non-democratic political structure, led by authoritarian rulers, wars and military alerts can serve as grounds for further suppression of the news media and of the scope for adversarial politics in general. And with that the vulnerability to famines increases through the reduction of political incentives for undertaking preventive public action in a timely and adequate way.

The problem of famines is not, of course, confined to the war-affected economies. But the forces that foster the economic and political preconditions of famines can be particularly encouraged in some circumstances by militarism and war. A better understanding of the contribution of wars to famines calls for a closer examination of these political and economic linkages, and requires us to go well beyond the more obvious features of the destruction of outputs and capital stocks. The less apparent need not be any less potent.

Footnotes

*A paper prepared for a ECAAR/IIPS conference on "Economic Issues of Disarmament" at the University of Notre Dame, November 30 - December 1, 1990. An earlier version of the paper was presented in the seminar series on "Reconciliation, War and the State" at King's College, Cambridge.

[1] The analysis presented in this paper draws extensively on my monograph on famines, *Poverty and Famines* (Sen 1981) and on my joint book with Jean Dreze, *Hunger and Public Action* (Dreze and Sen 1989). Some of the empirical findings briefly referred to here have been discussed in greater detail in those works, and also in the collection of papers included in a three-volume series, *The Political Economy of Hunger* (Dreze and Sen 1990).

[2] It is also worth noting that wars and famines have often been temporally congruent even when the wars in question have led to relatively little destruction of crops or of productive capital.

[3] On this see Sen (1981).

[4] On this see Sen (1981) and Dreze and Sen (1989, 1990), among others.

[5] "Many would not be able to find employment even upon these hard times, but would either starve, or be driven to seek subsistence either by begging, or by the perpetration perhaps of the greatest enormities. Want, famine, and mortality would

immediately prevail in that class, and from then extend themselves to all the superior classes" (Smith 1776, pp. 90-1).

[6]On this see Sen (1981), chapters 6-9, and Dreze and Sen (1989), chapters 5-8.

[7]One of the worst examples in this respect is the disruption of health care and other social services in Mozambique due to the activities of rebels backed by - and partly based in - neighbouring South Africa.

[8]On this see Sen (1981: Appendix D), de Waal (1989), Dreze and Sen (1990).

[9]On the health-care aspect of famine mortality, see particularly de Waal (1989).

[10]See Dreze and Sen (1989), chapters 5-9.

[11]The actual and counterfactual destruction of capital applies not merely to the production of material goods (industrial and agricultural), but also to the economic basis of services, trade and finance.

[12]On this see Sen (1981), chapter 6.

[13]The relief offered in Calcutta was totally inadequate. The government refused to accept responsibility for feeding the destitutes, and indeed Governor Rutherford wrote to the Viceroy explaining why a famine had not been declared and the Famines Codes not invoked (see Sen 1981, pp. 78-83).

[14]Some of the specific policies undertaken by the government were also remarkably insensitive to the needs of particular occupation groups. For example, two of the hardest hit groups in the Bengal famine of 1943 were the fishermen and river transport workers, which had among the highest rates of destitution (see chapter 6 in Sen 1981). Along with other rural laborers, they too suffered from a general decline of competitive power via-a-vis urban dwellers, but in addition their economic opportunities were severely reduced because of the governmental requisitioning - and sinking - of all boats capable of carrying ten people or more, in the river-centered districts of Bengal. This "boat denial policy" was a fairly vague attempt to prevent the boats from falling in the hands of the Japanese army in case it reached there. In the event, the "boat denial policy" made no contribution to the war, but thoroughly decimated those whose livelihood depended on the use of those boats - fishermen and river transporters who had little political influence on the White Hall.

[15]On this see Hammond (1951). See also Titmuss (1950).

[16]On this question, see Dreze and Sen (1989), chapter 10. The measurement for the decade of the Forties relates to the period 1940-51, but the rates are not much modified by that variation.

[17]Richard Titmuss (1950) notes: "By the end of the Second World War the government had, through the agency of newly established or existing services, assumed and developed a measure of direct concern for the health and well-being of the population which, by contrast with the role of Government in the thirties, was little short of remarkable" (p.506). See also Winter (1986) dealing with public attitudes and state policies during the First World War.

[18]The consolidation of authoritarianism seems to have been a common feature, in these circumstances, of governments both of the right and of the left. In addition to the influence of local wars on national politics, sub-Saharan Africa has also suffered from the consequences of the international "cold war", which made the West as well as the Eastern block cultivate authoritarian regimes so long as they were, respectively, "allies". The weakening of the cold war in the recent years provides an opportunity of breaking that pattern.   The indirect encouragement to authoritarianism from abroad has been an important factor in the development of anti-democratic local politics - and thus of famines - in sub-Saharan Africa.

[19]Even in the Bengal famine of 1943, the war situation was cited as justification for the censorship of the local media, and criticisms voiced in that media had little impact anyway on decisions taken in London or by the Viceroy in New Delhi. Interestingly enough, the British Indian government was ultimately moved in mid-October (many months after the famine had started), only after Ian Stephens, the courageous editor of the British-owned Calcutta daily *The Statesman*, broke rank and published stinging attacks on governmental policy, which immediately led to questionings in Parliament in London (on this see Sen 1981).

[20]The economic problems involved in recreating the lost incomes of the potential famine victims is often exaggerated. A typical famine affects no more than, say, 10 per cent of the population (usually the famine victims constitute a much smaller fraction of the total population) and the share of the national income the famine victims would normally earn may be no more than 3 per cent or so (often much less). The total amount of resources needed for recreating their entire normal income would, therefore, be typically rather small (especially in comparison with the

proportion of the national income that is devoted to military and war-related expenditures). The additional food needed to recreate their entire normal food consumption would also be a relatively small fraction of the total food consumption in the economy. On these issues, see Sen (1981), chapters 6-9, and Dreze and Sen (1989), chapter 8.

[21]This tends to deal effectively with the newly deprived in a situation of a potential famine, even though it does not cover adequately those who are prevented from working as a result of chronic disability, age or other handicaps. But they too can be covered through a public distribution system that takes note of these identifiable characteristics. On these issues and related matters, see Dreze and Sen (1989), chapters 7 and 8.

[22]On this see Sen (1983) and Dreze and Sen (1989).

[23]Three examples are the Soviet famines in the Ukraine in the early 1930s, the Chinese famine of 1958-61, and the Kampuchean famine of the late 1970s. The Chinese famine led to an extra death of between 23 and 30 million people (on this see Ashton et. al. 1984 and Peng 1987) and is the most likely claimant to the distinction of being the largest famine of this century; on this see Sen (1983). See also Riskin (1987) and the paper by an anonymous Chinese scholar in Article 19 (1990).

[24]In the prevention of famines, an independent press has an adversarial role (in criticizing and pressuring) as well as a cooperative one (in providing early news of starvation and deprivation) vis-a-vis the government in power. On this see Sen (1983, 1984), Reddy (1988), Dreze and Sen (1989), Article 19 (1990), and Ram (1990).

[25]It should, however, be added that adversarial politics and free newspapers provide less protection against endemic undernourishment and deprivation, which are less photogenic and harder to politicize, and the responsibility for which is more difficult to assign. These issues have been discussed in Sen (1983, 1984), Dreze and Sen (1989), and Ram (1990).

[26]See Dreze and Sen (1989), and also the two papers by Jean Dreze on famine prevention respectively in India and in Africa, in Dreze and Sen (1990). I should explain, to prevent any possible misunderstanding, that it is not being claimed here that democracy is a *necessary* condition for such action, but only that there is considerable evidence in favor of its *sufficiency*.

[27]On this issue and related matters, see Sen (1983, 1984), Harrison and Palmer (1986), Kilongson (1986), Cohen (1987), de Waal (1989, 1990), Dreze and Sen (1989), Africa Watch (1990), Article 19 (1990), D'Souza (1990), among other writings.

References

Africa Watch. (1990). *Denying Sudan "the honour of living": a human rights disaster.* London: Africa Watch.

Article 19. (1990). *Starving in silence: a report on famine and censorship.* edited by Frances D'Souza, London: Article 19.

Ashton, B., et al (1984). Famine in China, 1958-61. *Population and Development Review,* 10.

Cohen, R., et al (1987). Censorship costs lives. *Index on Censorship.* 16.5.

de Waal, A. (1989). *Famine that kills.* Oxford: Clarendon Press.

de Waal, A. (1990). The Politics of Information: Famine in Ethiopia and Sudan in the 1980s. in Article 19 (1990).

Dreze, J., and Sen, A. (1989). *Hunger and public action.* Oxford: Clarendon Press.

Dreze, J., and Sen, A., eds. (1990). *The political economy of hunger.* 3 vols. Oxford: Clarendon Press.

D'Souza, F. (1990). "Preface," in Article 19 (1990).

Hammond, R.J. (1951). *History of the second world war: food.* London: HMSO.

Harrison, P., and Palmer, R. (1986). *News out of africa: Biafra to band aid.* London: Hilary Shipman.

Kilongson, M. (1986). Reports of famines are prohibited. *Index on Censorship.* 15.10.

Peng, X. (1987). Demographic consequences of the great leap forward on China's provinces. *Population and Development Review,* 13, 639-70.

Ram, N. (1990). An independent press and anti-hunger strategies: the Indian experience. in Dreze and Sen (1990).

Reddy, S. (1988). An independent press working against famine: the nigerian experience. *Journal of Modern African Studies,* 26, 337-45.

Riskin, C. (1987). *China's political economy.* Oxford: Clarendon Press.

Sen, A.K. (1981). *Poverty and famines.* Oxford: Clarendon Press.

Sen, A.K. (1983). Development: which way now? *Economic Journal,* 93, 745-62; reprinted in Sen (1984).

Sen, A.K. (1984). *Resources, values and development.* Oxford: Blackwell, and Cambridge, MA: Harvard University Press.

Smith, A. (1776). *An inquiry into the nature and causes of the wealth of nations.* republished, eds. R.H. Campbell and A.S. Skinner (Oxford: Clarendon Press, 1976).

Titmuss, R.M. (1950). *History of the second world war: problems of social policy.* London: HMSO.

Winter, J.M. (1986). *The great war and the British people.* London: Macmillan.

Economics of Arms Reduction and the Peace Process
W. Isard and C.H. Anderton (Editors)
© 1992 Elsevier Science Publishers B.V. All rights reserved.

Chapter 11

REGIONAL CONFLICT AND MILITARY SPENDING IN THE DEVELOPING COUNTRIES

Manas Chatterji

State University of New York at Binghamton

[In the paper that follows, we have desired to have a look at the problem of militarization and its growth in relation to economic development of poor countries from the perspective of a scholar who has grown up in such a country and is extremely sensitive to its needs. We have not asked for a critical evaluation of studies that have been done. Almost invariably these studies have used theories, methods and tools designed by scholars in advanced countries --- theories, methods and tools inappropriate for attacking problems of development or non-development in a great number of cultures so different from those of developed countries. The fact that so many contradictory and inconclusive findings are recorded in these studies already suggests the need for a completely fresh approach. Perhaps this paper by Chatterji may assist in meeting this need. (eds.)]

11.1 The Changing World Environment: Implications for Developing Countries

Drastic changes in the international scene have occurred over the last five years. The bipolar world with the United States and Soviet Union as two superpowers confronting each other in carving out their own area of influence no longer exists. the need of the so-called non-aligned countries to maintain a delicate balance, and when necessary to seek help from one superpower, has diminished.

Some of the effects upon European nations of the breakup of the superpower structure are well known. Others are being intensively studied. What are less known and being investigated on a much smaller scale are effects upon developing countries.

The breakup of the superpower structure and the increasing attention given by major industrialized powers to transition problems and regional conflicts in Europe have introduced new factors into the global situation. One of them is the diversion of economic aid to reconstruct the Soviet Union and Eastern Europe. Such will be at the expense of aid to the poor developing countries. This is likely to intensify the conflict situations within them. Less aid implies less control by a superpower.

Moreover, tension between countries in several regions of the world may increase significantly due to the absence of political pressure to cooperate. In Asia, Africa, and Latin America, U.S. - U.S.S.R. influence has declined and different types of geopolitical restructuring are and will be taking place. Should the U.S. abandon its bases in the Philippines, Korea, and Japan then China, Japan, and possibly Korea will emerge as regional powers with India dominating South Asia. One can only speculate what will happen in this and other major regions of the world since the political situation has been complicated by economic changes in Europe, as well as changes in international technological and production process of manufacturing industries.

Disarmament between superpowers will not necessarily decrease arms spending in the developing countries. If anything, it may remain at the same level or may even increase due to the growth of regional and internal conflicts and the greed of the developed countries to find new markets to support their economies.

Currently, there are no signs of reduced military spending in the developing countries. Most of the spending by the developing countries is on modern conventional weapons. Countries like India have more battle tanks than many western countries. India also has the third largest army and navy in the world and a significant number of combat aircraft. Vietnam, although suffering from economic problems, has more than one million men in its army with many aircraft and tanks. Indonesia, Malaysia and Singapore are jointly building up their defenses. Some countries in the Middle East and Vietnam have chemical weapons, in spite of their signing the 1972 treaty banning them. Several countries like Algeria, Egypt, and India have surface to surface missiles although they are obsolete. India, however, has been successful in modernizing its missile program. The most dangerous matter is the prospect of nuclear proliferation. Many countries, such as Israel, have refused to sign the 1972 nuclear non-proliferation treaty. India has not signed because it is apprehensive of the Chinese bomb; it has pressed for a world-wide ban.

Out of pure economic self-interest, countries such as North Korea, South Korea, Brazil, China, (and recently) Argentina, Brazil and Singapore have been and are quite active in arms supply. Israel has been busy selling arms for many years. Further, while the major powers have been active in controlling the spread of nuclear, chemical and biological weapons, in general they have not abated their high technology conventional arms sales to developing countries.

Even when a superpower or major industrialized nation intervenes to contain a regional conflict, it is not possible to generalize on the outcome, and on new militarization that ensues. Regional players are crucial, as has been seen in

Afghanistan, Cambodia and Angola. Cutting off of military assistance and sales of arms to the developing countries may not be a solution, even when accompanied by moral support from the United Nations and other international organizations.

11.2   Militarization and Economic Growth

Internal relations, superpower reconciliation, regional conflicts among and internal problems within the developing countries, and concern of these countries for economic development are all complexly interrelated. Nonetheless, we wish to focus on the effects of militarization upon economic development and the reverse relationship in poor countries. This paper aims to cover some of the findings of a limited number of studies. A subsequent paper will offer methodological improvements and suggest alternative procedures for analysis.

A considerable amount of the world's resource are spent on the development, production, and use of military equipment. The latest available figure for 1985 was $663 billion. In 1991, it can be estimated to be $1 trillion. Although eighty percent of the expenditure is incurred by the developed countries, the developing countries' share has consistently increased, from ten percent in 1950 to over twenty percent in 1984, as can be seen from Table 11.1. Their total spending was more than sixty billion dollars in recent years.

TABLE 11.1

Share of Third World in Global Security Expenditure,
According to Regions, 1950-1984 (in percentages)

Region/Country	1950	1955	1960	1965	1970	1975	1980	1984
Middle East[a]	0.5	0.5	0.9	1.2	2.5	6.9	7.3	7.1
China	0.5	2.9	5.7	8.8	10.3	7.3	7.6	5.6
Far East [b]	2.0	0.8	1.3	1.6	1.8	2.1	3.0	3.1
South Asia	1.2	0.7	0.7	1.2	1.0	1.0	1.2	1.3
Africa[c]	0.1	0.1	0.2	0.7	0.9	2.3	2.5	1.7
South America	1.3	1.0	1.1	1.1	1.1	1.7	1.8	1.0
Central America	0.5	0.2	0.3	0.3	0.3	0.3	0.4	0.5
All Developing	10.6	6.2	10.2	14.9	17.9	21.6	23.8	21.3

Source: Stockholm International Peace Research Institute, World Armaments and Disarmament SIPRI Yearbook, 1972, 1976, 1979, 1982, 1985 (Stockholm: Almqvist & Wiksell, 1972, 1976) and (London: Taylor & Francis, 1979, 1982, 1985).

[a]Includes Egypt.   [b]Excludes China.   [c]Excludes Egypt.

A first problem that arises in conducting empirical research on militarization is the classification of countries as developing or not. Usually, developing countries are thought to include most of those in the Far East, South Asia, Africa, South

America, Central America and Middle East. But the security situation is quite different in these countries. The Middle East is, of course, unique because of the inordinate amount of foreign intervention. In Africa, a large number of newly independent nations have emerged where previously there was no army. Although the growth rate of the military may appear to be high in these countries, the pre-existence of a zero base raises problems for analysis. In South Asia account must be taken of the India-Pakistan confrontation and war in Afghanistan. In Latin America, the interest of U.S. in the civil war of some countries cannot be ignored. In effect, if we group all these countries under the rubric of the "developing world," these considerations and others should be included appropri-ately in the model specifications. Although cross section analysis has many merits, in this area of investigation, cross section analysis should be supplemented by appropriate time series analysis for some countries, particularly large ones.

A second problem concerns sources of data, their measurement and reliability. A number of organizations publish data on military spending. Some reliable sources are (1) International Institute of Strategic Studies; (2) U.S. Arms Control and Disarmament Agency: *World Military Expenditure and Arms Transfer;* (3) Stockholm International Peace Research Institute: *World Armament and Disarmament Yearbook;* (4) *International Monetary Fund Government Finance Statistics;* and (5) United Nations: *U.N. Statistical Yearbook.* With respect to data on socio-economic variables, World Bank data and others compiled by individual scholars like Azar (1980) and Ruth Sivard (1983) are of importance. Another important source is Summers and Heston (1988). They present a set of international comparisons covering the period 1950-85 for 121 market and nine centrally planned economies. For each they estimate real per capita product and price level, gross domestic product, consumption, gross domestic investment, government expenditures, and population and exchange rates.

The accuracy and coverage of the available data leaves much to be desired. Many countries do not record all expenses, and data expressed in local currency is only of domestic interest. For comparability the data should be in constant prices or expenditures as a percentage of gross domestic product. However, exchange rates vary widely, and for some countries they are fixed unrealistically at a given point. The resulting data in U.S. dollars are thus questionable. Moreover, some economies are planned and others are open; money prices then do not reflect values in the same way in the two systems. For countries which have some kind of mixed economy this problem is less serious.

A third difficulty arises in measuring security expenditures. Ball (1984) presents five of the most common mechanisms used by governments to cover up this information: (1) double bookkeeping; (2) use of extra-budgetary accounts; (3) highly aggregated budget categories; (4) military assistance; and (5) foreign exchange manipulation.

Notwithstanding these difficulties, many scholars have addressed this topic. Since most studies start from the premisses of Benoit, who pioneered this area of study, it is useful to discuss his findings in some detail.

11.3   Benoit's Analysis and Findings

Benoit first presented his observations in his book, Defense and Economic Growth in Developing Countries (1973) and restated them in an article (Benoit 1978). In his words,

> It has usually been supposed by economists that defense expenditures reduce the resources available for investment and so slows down growth.. However, in a large study of less developed countries, an opposite pattern seemed to appear, and this finding was so unexpected and challenging that it seemed worthwhile exploring in detail... Contrary to my expectations, countries with a heavy defense burden generally had the most rapid rate of growth, and those with the lowest defense burdens tended to show the lowest growth rates." (Benoit, 1978, p. 271).

That military spending is able to stimulate growth can be explained as follows: "Defense programs of most countries make tangible contributions to the civilian economies by (1) feeding, clothing, and housing a number of people who would otherwise have to be fed, housed, and clothed by the civilian economy - and sometimes doing so, especially in LDCs, in ways that involve sharply raising their nutritional and other consumption standards and expectations; (2) providing education and medical care as well as vocational and technical training (e.g., in the operation and repair of cars, planes and radios; in hygiene and medical care; in construction methods) that may have high civilian utility; (3) engaging in a variety of public works - roads, dams, river improvements, airports, communication networks, etc. - that may in part serve civilian uses; and (4) engaging in scientific and technical specialties such as hydrographic studies, mapping, aerial surveys, dredging, meteorology, soil conservation, and forestry projects as well as certain quasi-civilian activities such as coast guard, lighthouse operation, customs work, border guard, and disaster relief which would otherwise have to be performed by civilian personnel. Military forces also engage in certain R&D and production activities which diffuse skills to the civilian economy and engage in or finance self-help projects producing certain manufactured items for combined civilian and military use (e.g., batteries and tires) which might not be economically produced solely for civilian demand" (Benoit, 1978, pp. 276-277).

Consider Benoit's methodology. The study examined growth rates, investment rates, foreign aid, defense spending, etc. from forty-four developing countries for the period 1950-65. It covered about seventy-five percent of the world's population, excluding mainland China. The aggregate study was followed up by case studies of India, South Korea, Mexico, Israel, the United Arab Republic and Argentina.

Benoit defined defense burden as the ratio of defense expenditure to the non-defense gross domestic product. He then correlated this with the growth rate of non-defense GDP, using Spearman's rank order correlation analysis, where the average of all values (at current prices) of the variables for available years between 1960 and 1965 was taken for each country. For a sample of n=44, the rank correlation coefficient of r=0.55 was found to be statistically significant with t=4.2 with a 1 in 1000 chance of it being accidental. The rank correlation coefficient analysis was confirmed by regression analysis with bilateral foreign aid, investment rate, and defense burden as independent variables and growth rate as the dependent variable. Sources for his data were the World Bank, Agency for International Development, and United Nations. Benoit's sample of nations included military dictatorships and as such may be considered overstating the association between defense burden and growth rate; hence he eliminated some countries from his sample, ran the regression and found the same result. Also, the correlation can be considered spurious should a third variable like foreign aid be responsible for the apparent correlation. However, based on a more refined and desegregated analysis with the bilateral foreign aid as an additional variable, he still found the defense burden to be a significant determinant of growth

Benoit next considered the direction of the relationship, namely, whether growth itself induces more defense spending. "No significant correlation was found between per capita income and defense burdens. Nor were tax revenues, total government expenditures, or the ratio of defense to total government expenditures closely linked to the rate of economic growth. And in multiple regression analysis economic growth did not emerge as a significant determinant of the defense burden" (Benoit, 1978, p. 275). Actual threats of war, incidence of war, and expectation of war were more important factors for the increase in defense expenditure.

Benoit's cross-sectional econometric study of forty-four countries was complemented by individual case studies of such countries as India, Mexico, South Korea, Israel, the United Arab Republic and Argentina. Analysis of the Indian situation is the most important since India is a big country with democratic institutions, a large population, an economic development program, potential sources of conflict with some neighbors, a strong manufacturing base with a large potential for weapons production, a large army, and a non-aligned foreign policy. After analyzing the Indian economy, economic policy, defense program, and the economic contents of the budget, he found, from a time series analysis, a positive correlation between growth and defense expenditures.

Benoit considered three types of unfavorable effects of defense expenditure on economic growth: (1) <u>Investment Effect</u>: the defense industry may absorb resources that might otherwise have gone into investment; (2) <u>Productivity Effect</u>: the defense and related government sectors are in general less productive and thus lower overall productivity; and (3) <u>Income Shift Effect</u>: higher defense expenditure means lower civil GNP. Benoit computed the impacts of these unfavorable effects on India. He then considered the stimulating effects of increased military expenditures and foreign aid (largely from the Soviet bloc as a result of India's border conflict with China). These effects were increased demand and employment, inflation, liberal monetary and fiscal policy, and the civilian type activities of the military, namely road building, modernization and nation building. He found an inconsistency between econometric and statistical analysis. The former showed a structural shift pointing to a slowdown in average growth associated with increased military expenditures. The latter revealed a significant positive correlation; the unfavorable effects of the increased military expenditures were counterbalanced by the favorable effects from the heavy inflow of foreign aid.

11.4   Critiques of Benoit

Subsequent to the publication of Benoit's book and paper, a number of articles were published criticizing his findings and offering alternative formulations. Ball (1983) objected to Benoit's definition of foreign aid and his interpretation of its relationship to economic growth and military expenditure. Benoit divided foreign flow into four main categories, namely: (1) economic aid; (2) long-term private investment; (3) military aid; and (4) military transfer payments (expenditure). However, he ignored foreign private investment, multilateral aid, and military assistance in his multiple regression analysis when he examined whether the defense burden or inflow of foreign resources was more closely associated with economic growth. His statement that a considerable amount of equipment and services (military aid) would not have been obtainable without the Military Assistance Program is not realistic in view of the trends in arms trade. After pointing out many other shortcomings in Benoit's study, especially his treatment of non-quantifiable effects, Ball concluded that Benoit's analyses fail to treat the existing diversity of forces and thus of questionable use for understanding the relation of defense to development.

Lim (1983) reexamined Benoit's result for the more recent period 1965-73 for twenty-one African, thirteen Western Hemisphere, eleven Asian and nine Middle Eastern and Southern European LDCs. His framework begins with a Harrod-Domar model

$$Y_g = f \text{ (IOCR, I/Y)} \tag{11.1}$$

where Y_g is the growth rate of real GDP, IOCR the incremental output-capital ratio, and I/Y the ratio of gross domestic investment to GDP. Allowing foreign capital inflow to affect the investment-defense expenditures tradeoff, he sets.

$$I/Y = f(D/Y, F/Y) \tag{11.2}$$

where D denotes defense expenditure and F foreign capital inflow. Replacing F/Y by the ratio F/S (S = gross national savings) which he considers more relevant in affecting the investment-defense expenditures tradeoff, he obtains by substitution of equation (11.2) into equation (11.1) the estimating equations

$$Y_g = f(\text{IOCR, D/Y, F/S}) \tag{11.3}$$

$$Y_g = f(\text{IOCR, D/GE, F/S}) \tag{11.4}$$

where equation (11.4) (an alternative to equation (11.3)) replaces D/Y with the ratio D/GE where GE is government current and capital expenditures. Using ordinary least square regression analysis, Lim finds that defense spending is detrimental to economic growth in LDCs," a conclusion opposite to Benoit's. However, there were important regional differences. The adverse effects that were marked in Africa and the Western Hemisphere were absent in Asia, the Middle East, and southern Europe." (p. 384).

Deger and Sen in a careful study for India (1983) did not find a positive impact of military expenditures on economic growth. For a set of industries which are especially susceptible to defense linkages, they did not find an important or significant effect, which "clearly demonstrates that the beneficial spin-offs generally discussed in the literature are much less than what is claimed." (p. 80).

Economic growth, according to Looney (1990), depends on socio-economic development. Conducting a factor analysis study of 110 developing countries over four year intervals - 1974, 1978, 1982, and 1986 - to detect the relationship between socio-economic development and military expenditure, he arrived at the following conclusions:

(1) Over time military expenditure per soldier became increasingly associated with non-defense per capita expenditure.

(2) Over time military participation became increasingly positively correlated with socio-economic conditions in Middle East countries, while for developing countries as a whole such positive correlation was fairly constant.

(3) Public non-defense expenditure became less associated over time with military participation rates for Middle East/South Asian countries but not for others.

(4) In countries with a high (low) level of militarization, the effect on socio-economic performance of the military participation rate declined (increased) over time.

In a study of eighteen Latin American countries over the period 1948-1979, Verner (1983) found no evidence that defense spending adversely affects educational expenditures.

For twenty-six African countries over the period 1967-1976, Nabe (1983) used factor and path analyses to observe signs of the path coefficients pairwise between the following variables: Military Expenditures; an Economic Development Factor (a composite of installed KW capacity, government expenditures except for health and education, and private expenditures), a social Development Factor (a composite of number of physicians, government expenditures on health, government expenditures on education and number of teachers) and GDP-manufacturing. Consistent with his hypotheses, he found that (a) the economic development factor has a positive relation with both GDP-manufacturing and the social development factor; (b) the social development factor has a positive relation with GDP-manufacturing; and (c) military expenditure has a negative relation with both the economic and social development factors, rejecting thereby Benoit's hypothesis.

Biswas and Ram (1986) used a Feder-type (1962) to sector model, the two sectors being the military and civilian. They concluded that there is no significant externality effect of the military sector on the civilian sector, and that a relative factors productivity differential across the two sectors is not statistically significant.

Most recently, Adams, Behrman and Bolden (1991) addressed Benoit's hypothesis for developing countries for the period 1974-86, dividing these countries into "low income" and "middle income." Distinguishing between military and non-military government spending in a Feder-type analysis, they conclude that neither of these components of government spending has a significant impact on private GDP, and that the bulk of the government impact on private GDP results from the inclusion of government sector production in the GDP accounts.

11.5   Some Summary Remarks

In summing up the literature, it is to be noted that the majority of the studies do in fact criticize and find fault with Benoit's analysis. However, some studies are supportive of Benoit such as: Whynes (1979) who using 1977 data finds for LDCs a correlation coefficient of +0.224 between defense burden and per capita income, the coefficient being -0.355 for the developed country sample; and Weidenbaum (1974) who cites a Rand Corporation Study of Latin America that suggests that nations with larger defense expenditures have greater economic growth.

However, the most recent studies, as they dig further and further into the subject, find that the factors involved are so numerous and difficult to express quantitatively and so much of a political and cultural nature that clear-cut relationships are not identifiable. Further, with the emergence in the 1980's of the developing countries' debt problem, new conflicting political and economic factors have come to play upon the relationship between defense spending and economic growth in these countries.   See Tables 11.2 and 11.3 for relevant magnitudes. These factors raise new challenges for the construction of more appropriate analytical models.

TABLE 11.2

The Third World External Debt, Selected Regions, 1982-90
Figures are in US $billion. (current prices).

Region	1982	1984	1986	1988	1990
Africa	121.4	133.0	171.3	199.8	206.0
Latin America and the Caribbean	331.2	358.2	383.6	402.7	417.5
Total debt	826.6	918.3	1086.7	1197.2	1246.3
Total debt-service payments	135.8	136.1	144.8	170.0	175.8

Source: International Monetary Fund, *World Economic Outlook*, Oct. 1989.

TABLE 11.3

Military expenditure and external public debt-service as shares of current
government revenue, selected Third World countries, 1987
(Figures are percentages)

Country	Military Expenditure	External Debt-Service	Military Expenditure Plus Debt-Service
Argentina	15.8	23.6	39.4
Colombia	14.5	50.7	65.2
Chile	22.0	25.6	47.6
Egypt	19.6	11.8	31.4
Indonesia	13.9	35.5	49.4
Israel	30.9	13.1	44.0
Jordan	48.9	36.2	85.1
Morocco	19.5	30.9	50.4
Pakistan	40.1	20.4	60.5
Philippines	15.5	48.1	63.6
Sri Lanka	30.7	24.2	54.9
Zimbabwe	22.5	23.5	46.0

Sources: World Development Report (World Bank: Washington, D.C.
1989);SIPRI data base; authors' calculations.

References and Selected Bibliography

Adams, G.F., Behrman, J.R., and Boldin, M. (1991). Defense expenditures and economic growth in the less developed countries: reconciling theory and empirical results. *Conflict Management and Peace Science*, 11, 19-35.

Azar, E.E. (1980). The conflict and peace data bank (COPDAB) project, *Journal of Conflict Resolution*, 24, 143-52.

Ball, N. (1983). Defense and development: a critique of the Benoit study, *Economic Development and Cultural Change*, 31, 507-524.

Ball, N. (1984). Measuring third world security expenditure: a research note. *World Development*, 12

Ball, N. (1985). Defense expenditures and economic growth: a comment. *Armed Forces and Society,* 11, 291-297.

Benoit, E. (1973). *Defense and economic growth in developing countries* Boston: D.C. Heath.

Benoit, E. (1978). Growth and defense in developing countries. *Economic Development and Cultural Change,* 26, 271-280.

Biswas, B. and Ram, R. (1986). Military expenditures and economic growth in less developed countries: an augmented model and further evidence. *Economic Development and Cultural Change*, 35, 361-372.

Boulding, K.E. (1974). Defense spending: burden or boon. *War/Peace Report*, 13, 19-20.

Chan, S. (1985). The impact of defense spending on economic performance: a survey of evidence and problems,*Orbis*, 29, 403-434.

Deger, S. (1981). *Human resources, government education expenditure and the military burden in less developed countries*, Discussion Paper No. 109, London: Birbeck College.

Deger, S. (1982). Does Defense Expenditure Mobilize Resources in LDCs? Paper presented at Annual Conference of Development Studies Association, Dublin.

Deger, S. and Sen, S. (1983). Military expenditure, spin off and economic development. *Journal of Development Economics,* 13, 67-83.

Deger, S. and Smith, R. (1983). Military expenditure and growth in less developed countries. *Journal of Conflict Resolution*, 27, 335-353.

Faini, R., Annez, P. and Taylor, L. (1984). Defense spending, economic structure, and growth: evidence among countries and over time. *Economic Development and Cultural Change,* 32, 487-498.

Feder, G. (1982). On exports and economic growth. *Journal of Development Economics,* 12, 59-73.

Frank, I. (1980). *Foreign enterprise in developing countries.* Baltimore: Johns Hopkins University Press.

Frederiksen, P.C. and Looney, R.E. (1983). Defense expenditures and economic growth in developing countries. *Armed Forces and Society,* 9, 663-645.

Frederiksen, P.C., and Looney, R.E. (1985). Defense expenditures and economic growth in developing countries: a reply. *Armed Forces and Society,* 11, 298-301.

Griffin, L. J., Wallace, M. and Devine, J. (1982). The political economy of military spending: evidence from the United States. *Cambridge Journal of Economics,* 6, 1-14.

Kaldor, M. (1978). The military in third world development. in R. Jolly (ed.) *Disarmament and World Development.* Oxford: Pergamon Press, pp. 57-82.

Kende, I. (1980). Local wars, 1945-76, in E. Eide and M. Thee (eds.) *Problems of Contemporary Militarism.* London: Croom Helm.

Kennedy, G. (1983). *Defense economics.* New York: St Martin's Press.

Kuh, E. (1959). The validity of cross-sectionally estimated behavior equations in time series applications. *Econometrica,* 27, 197-214.

Landau, D. (1983). Government expenditure and economic growth: a cross-country study, *Southern Economic Journal,* 49, 783-792.

Landau, D. (1986). Government and economic growth in the less developed countries: an empirical study for 1960-1980. *Economic Development and Cultural Change,* 35, 35-75.

Leontief, W. and Duchin, F. (1983). *Military spending: facts and figures, worldwide implications and future outlook.* New York: Oxford University Press.

Lim, D. (1983). Another look at growth and defense in less developed countries. *Economic Development and Cultural Change,* 31, 377-384.

Looney, R.E. (1990). Recent patterns of defense dxpenditures and socio-economic development in the Middle East and South Asia. mimeo.

Lotz, J.R. (1970). Patterns of government spending in developing countries. *The Manchester School,* 38.

Luttwak E. (1968). *Coup d'etat .* London: Allen Lane.

Moll, K.D. and Luebbert, G. M. (1980). Arms race and military expenditure models. *Journal of Conflict Resolution,* 24, 153-85.

Mahalanobis, P.C. (1963). *The approach of operations research to planning in India.* Bombay: Asia Publishing House.

Maizels, A. and Nissanke, M.K. (1986). The determinants of military expenditures in developing countries. *World Development,* 14, 1125-1140.

Mariano, R.S. (1990). Defense expenditures and economic growth in the Philippines: a macrosimulation analysis. mimeo.

Nabe, O. (1983). Military Expenditures and Industrialization in Africa, *Journal of Economic Issues,* 17, 575-587.

Neuman, S.G. (1978). Security, military expenditure and socio-economic development: reflections on Iran. *Orbis,* 23, 569-594.

Palma, G. (1978). Dependency: a formal theory of underdevelopment or a methodology for the analysis of concrete situations of underdevelopment? *World Development,* 6, 881-924.

Ram, R. (1986). Causality between income and government expenditure: a broad international perspective. *Public Finance/Finances Publiques,* Vol. XXXXI/XXXXIieme Annee, No. 3, pp. 393-410.

Richardson, L. (1960). *Arms and insecurity.* Chicago: Quadrangle.

Rubinson, R. (1976). The world-economy and the disribution of income within states: a cross-national study. *American Sociological Review,* 41, 638-659.

Scholing, E. and Timmermann, V. (1988). Why LDC growth rates differ: measuring 'unmeasurable' influence. *World Development,* 16, 1271-1294.

Sen, A. (1983). Development: which way now? *Economic Journal,* 93, 745-762.

Sivard, R.L. (1983). *World military and social expenditures.* Washington, DC: World Priorities.

Smith, R.P. (1977). Military expenditure and capitalism. *Cambridge Journal of Economics,* 1, 61-76.

Smith, R.P. (1980a). Military expenditure and investment in OECD countries 1954-1973. *Journal of Comparative Economics*, 4, 19-32.

Smith, R.P. (1980b). The demand for military expenditure. *Economic Journal,* 90, 811-820.

Summers, R. and Heston, A. (1988). A new set of international comparisons of real product and price levels estimates for 130 countries, 1950-1985. *The Review of Income and Wealth,* Series 34, Number 1.

Sunkel, O. (1973). Transnational capitalism and national disintegration in Latin America. *Social and Economic Studies*, 22, 132-176.

Terrell, L.M. (1971). Societal stress, political instability, and levels of military effort. *Journal of Conflict Resolution,* 15.

Verner, J.G. (1983). Budgetary trade-offs between education and defense in Latin America: a research note. *Journal of Developing Areas,* 18, 77-91.

Weidenbaum, M.L. (1974). *The economics of peacetime defense.* New York: Praeger.

Whynes, D. K. (1979). *The economics of third world military expenditures.* London: Macmillan.

Chapter 12

DO ARMS RACES LEAD TO PEACE?

Jean-Christian Lambelet

University of Lausanne
Département d'économétrie et d'économie politique (DEEP/HEC),
and Graduate Institute[*]

[The last contribution to this book brings to bear on the subject the perspective of a European, a resident of a "neutral" country, who over the years has conducted some of the most rigorous analysis of arms races. The significance of the question he asks needs no comment. (eds.)]

12.1 Introduction

From the standpoint of arms race analysis the *end of the cold war* would appear to be readily explainable in terms of the extended Richardsonian model which dominates the field, the explanation being roughly as follows.[1]

Given some underlying initial conflict, two or more countries embark on a competitive military build-up involving weapons as well as manpower. This process is not open-ended: because of economic constraints, it will eventually converge towards some dynamic equilibrium in which each participant spends a higher fraction of its resources on defense than if there were no race.[2] This will be at the expense of consumption and/or investment.[3] If consumption is curtailed, current economic welfare is reduced whereas future welfare is undermined if defense outlays crowd out investment.[4] But all participants suffer from the arms race which is seen as a globally suboptimal process.

There is no such dynamic economic feedback in Richardson's original model.[5] Most models of the second and later generations however include a more or less detailed supply side along the preceding lines.[6]

All participants in an arms race do not necessarily have the same economic resources at their command. A competitor with a smaller economic base will generally have to allocate a higher fraction of its output to defense, and hence will suffer more. To the extent that investment is crowded out, growth will be impeded and the defense burden will become correspondingly heavier over time - until that burden and the associated welfare loss become too heavy to bear, and the country gives up.

Seen in that light, the arms race between the Soviet Union and the U.S. - or, more broadly, between East and West - has apparently come to an end, and global peace has seemingly been established after more than forty years of confrontation, essentially because of the superior staying power of the United States and its Allies. Supposedly, the East-West race has thus ended with the U.S. *et al.* being the *economic* victors.

Granting for a moment that this is what really happened, it can be interpreted as meaning that arms races may - and sometimes actually do - lead to peace. Richardson, who was writing with the pre-1914 and pre-1939 competitions in mind,[7] thought it practically axiomatic that unstable (ie. real) arms races had to end in war.[8] Most analysts who worked immediately after Richardson probably shared this basic view although the issue of the link between arms races and the outbreak of war was practically never addressed explicitly.

In 1975 however this writer published a short essay on that question in which he argued that "*(...) the historical record suggests that unilateral disarmament or a failure to keep up with the other side may at times increase the odds of a war breaking out. Similarly, there are also cases of arms races which increased the stakes so much that an open conflict became less likely.*"[9] Ten years later the argument was pushed one step further in a paper which argued that peace science in general and arms race analysis in particular needed to be complemented by a normative theory, just as welfare economics complements positive economics. It was proposed that some arms races could be viewed as "good things", for example when a fundamentally peaceful country acts in self-defense against a basically aggressive power. As a result, it is no longer sure that an arms race always makes up a globally suboptimal process, even when it leads to war and, possibly, defeat.[10] Put differently, an arms race entails lower economic welfare, but not necessarily lower *overall* welfare because it may, under some circumstances, genuinely enhance external security.[11] By the same token, motivations and attitudes (peacefulness vs. aggressiveness) have to be explicitly integrated in the analysis and the nature of the underlying conflict has to be examined, a complicating factor being that there may be a feedback process from the arms race itself to the underlying conflict and to the runners' motivations.[12]

The apparent end of the cold war now suggests that the analysis should be pushed still one step further. The East-West arms race may have been - indeed, probably was - asymmetric, in that one side was more aggressive than the other, particularly in the later stages of the confrontation.[13] It may also have increased the stakes so much that open nuclear warfare has been effectively deterred.[14] But, on top of all that, it is now arguable that, because of unequal economic strength, this most important of all races has finally brought about genuine global peace, ie. something fundamentally different from the more or less precarious state of neither-war-nor-peace which existed since the aftermath of World War II till about 1989.[15]

This writer is however not at all certain that this explanation of the end of cold war, which emphasizes economic factors, is wholly or even partially correct for it is open to a number of more or less obvious counter-arguments, to which we now turn.

12.2 Objections and Competing Views

The first thing to be noted is that even if it is true that the United States has won the cold war because of its superior economic staying power, it still has had to pay a heavy price for it. Insufficient private and public investment, the ensuing ageing of the stock of private and public equipments, insufficient and possibly deteriorating human capital, lasting public deficits which are financed by borrowing abroad - all this and more of the same may be due at least partly to the heavy defense burden which the U.S. has had to bear for several decades.[16] The arms race with the Soviet Union may have finally led to peace, but its consequences are probably going to be felt in the U.S. for a long time to come, and it would of course have been much better if there had been no race at all, obvious though this may sound. The real winner of the arms race may thus have been some third party, some *tertius gaudens* such as Japan and, to a lesser extent, Western Europe.[17] It is not impossible that in the years to come this state of affairs will lead to serious and lasting international tensions of a different sort. The cold war may have died, but it has left a heavy legacy, or so it can be argued.

On a more fundamental level, it is debatable whether the Soviet Union's "surrender" in the cold war has been due wholly or even mainly to an increasingly crushing defense burden. As a first competing view, one might argue that the Soviet Union has actually given up because of *general* economic bankruptcy, which in turn followed from the nature of its economic system.

In that context it may be worth recalling the so-called "socialism controversy" which was very much in the news in the 1930's, at least inside the economics profession. A number of sometimes very prominent and mostly left-leaning economists[18] were then arguing that in terms of economic efficiency a highly centralized economic system could and would lead to the same results as a perfectly functioning market economy while being decidedly superior on other counts such as income distribution and social equity. On the opposite side of the political spectrum, other equally prominent economists[19] replied that such a system would likely run into insurmountable problems of incentives and information transmission. At the theoretical level the controversy then subsided, till it was revived in the seventies in the context of the "principal-agent" problem, the general conclusion then being that any highly centralized economic system was indeed likely to be incompatible with a performing system of *individual* incentives. To be sure, enthusiasm, devotion to the common good, the will to create a "new man" and the like can for a while substitute for individual incentives, as they probably did for some time in the early stages of the "Soviet experiment".[20]   But enthusiasm, devotion and the like can last only that long.[21] True, Soviet planners did try to set up an alternative incentive system stressing access to higher education and to the perks of the "nomenklatura", not to mention negative incentives (penalties of various kinds), but such a system was bound to be a very inferior second-best. As a result, the general performance of the Soviet economic system started declining at an accelerating rate in the seventies and eighties, the resulting bankruptcy making it impossible for the Soviet leadership to sustain the arms race with the West in general and the United States in particular.

A second competing view stresses the role of changing political and social attitudes inside the Soviet Union and its satellites. As anyone travelling in the East during the sixties and the seventies could not fail to notice, there was a steady erosion of the Communist/Socialist creed. People went on paying lip service to it but "true believers" were becoming ever scarcer. This may have been due to improved information[22] or to natural doctrinal erosion. True, the resulting vacuum was not necessarily filled with other values. And to the extent that it was filled, it was not only filled with "Western values" (democracy, human rights) as there also was a resurgence of old attitudes ("Great Russian" nationalism, "Slavophilism"). Nevertheless these changes generally meant that the West was less and less seen as a threat, as a natural enemy, as something to be kept at bay, guarded against and justifying a strong military establishment. These changes in perceptions and attitudes may have been reinforced by the inferior, indeed deteriorating performance of the economy; and they may have in turn contributed to the economic deterioration, according to the preceding explanation. But, from the perspective of this paper, the important thing is that to a large extent these changes may have been and probably were autonomous, i.e., unconnected with the arms race. This third competing explanation is particularly relevant if it is true that the East-West arms race, while it lasted, was mainly driven by Soviet "self-stimulation", which is indeed what was found empirically by Lambelet-Luterbacher-Allan in a 1979 study.[23]

12.3 A Research Agenda

We thus have (at least) three competing explanations for the end of the cold war and the East-West arms race. The Soviet Union gave up (1) because, having the weaker economic base, it could no longer bear the economic burden of the arms race; (2) because of general economic bankruptcy; (3) because changing attitudes and values, particularly vis-à-vis the West, made it ever more difficult to justify a large defense establishment by reference to a serious external threat from a different and hostile social system.

These three explanations are not mutually exclusive and all three may have been at work, the question then being that of their respective importance. Our guess, for what it's worth, would be that the specific economic burden of the arms race was a contributing factor, but that the principal explanation is the second one (general economic collapse due to the nature of the system).

But the question certainly deserves being looked into more carefully and systematically. One way to that end would be to take as a starting point the latest (1987) Lambelet-Luterbacher model[24] and to use it for simulation purposes. This model is made up of three submodels: a resource allocation (or arms race) sector; a "diplomatic" conflict submodel accounting for changing motivations and attitudes; and a war-peace submodel. Consequently the whole apparatus would appear to lend itself to such an investigation. However it would have to be modified or completed on a number of counts, of which we now discuss the two main ones.

First, the purely economic sector is too rudimentary. On both sides GNP or rather its trend values are taken as exogenous. The consumption-investment-defense allocation problem would thus have to be modelled explicitly and, on top of that, GNP growth should be endogenized (which is quicker said than done). Second, the war-peace submodel would probably have to be modified. Because this submodel consists of a differential game where the actors only have the choice between continuing to deter or engaging in war, the security level variables which are at the heart of the submodel are subject to sudden changes - from 0 to 1 or vice-versa, for instance, which corresponds to full-scale war breaking out or peace being concluded.[25] The nice thing about this approach is that it could account for the relative suddenness with which the cold war ended. However it is not clear that two states only (war or peace) are adequate in this context as it might be more realistic to distinguish a third state (no open warfare but no real peace either, i.e. the cold war).

Clearly, estimating such a model and using it for simulation purposes would be no small task. For one thing, data problems mean that many parameters would have to be chosen on apriori, plausibility grounds. For another thing, it is not immediately clear how some possibly important factors should be modelled and tested (e.g. autonomous changes in attitudes). Yet, we feel that the enterprise is probably feasible and that it would yield interesting and possibly novel insights given the necessary time and resources.

12.4 Peace For Our Time?[26]

In the preceding discussion the end of the cold war, the de-escalation of the East-West arms race and the Soviet Union's "surrender" were taken as incontrovertible *facts*, the indications to that effect being sufficiently clear, numerous and consistent.[27] However this does not mean that the millennium has finally arrived and it should be no ground for euphoria. No one knows what shape and course the former Soviet empire will take in the future, the huge Soviet nuclear arsenal still exists, and it is surely not impossible that some configuration will ultimately emerge in the East which would constitute a threat to peace in the region and quite possibly to world peace.[28] Besides there are and will be other threats to the stability of the international system, the Gulf Crisis and War being a timely reminder to that effect. The demise of the cold war has certainly made the world a saf*er* place, but that does not mean that it is as yet a perfectly safe place.

The possibility of a positive feedback loop from the arms race process to the underlying initial conflict and back to the arms race is one of the themes of post-richardsonian peace science. Motivations and attitudes are then seen as partly endogenous: as the arms race escalates, the competitors may more or less lose sight of the original conflict and the piling up of arms by the other side becomes the main motive of anxiety. There is good historical evidence to the effect that such a feedback loop is more than just a theoretical possibility.[29]

In principle there is nothing which should prevent this effect from working in reverse, that is in a de-escalating context too. As the arms race winds down, mutual confidence gains ground, old conflicts are re-assessed and possibly solved, etc. The effect would be to accelerate the de-escalation of the arms race and to hasten the transition to genuine peace. On the face of it this would seem to be all for the good. The question we however would like to raise here is whether this amplification effect could not possibly go *too far* and whether, under some circumstances, it might not ultimately and paradoxically lead again to a dangerous world. A historical precedent may help make clear what we have in mind.[30]

It can be argued that it was America's 1917 intervention which decisively tipped the scales in favor of the Allies at the end of World War I. History cannot be rewritten, but it is a fair guess that if the United States had remained neutral France and England would not have been able to contain Germany's offensive in the spring-summer of 1918 after Russia's collapse had allowed it to transfer large numbers of troops from the Eastern to the Western front.[31] Germany would then have achieved the decisive breakthrough in the West which it had been seeking since the fall of 1914.

If that was so, it meant that the United States could not but have a great influence and responsibility in shaping the new post-war international order even though France and England had contributed much more, in terms of blood and money, to the war effort against the Central Powers. Of course, President Wilson was very aware of this and it was because the United States had such a strong hand that the Versailles Treaty ended up by embodying neither a peace of reconciliation nor a truly carthagenian peace,[32] but something in between the two. As the allied country which had suffered most, France and particularly Clemenceau and Foch wanted a harsher peace, but they gave in substantially to the American views, partly on the understanding that afterwards the United States would actively guarantee the new international order in the shaping of which it had had such an important part.

As everyone knows, history took a rather different course. In 1917 and while the war lasted, the bulk of the American people had wholeheartedly and even enthusiastically supported America's intervention in Europe. But soon after the actual fighting had stopped the mood in the United States started to change towards isolationism, an evolution which can be interpreted in terms of the reverse feedback effect mentioned above. In November 1919, the Senate refused to ratify the Versailles treaty, the United States remained outside the League of Nations and more generally withdrew almost completely from the international scene or at least from Europe. This was not the only factor which, after a "twenty-year armistice",[33] led to World War II, but it was an essential one. And even then, it was only after an open, direct and major aggression on the U.S. had occurred that the bulk of the American people finally saw that their country simply could not stay aloof from the rest of the world.[34]

"*Comparaison n'est pas raison*", as the French say. I.e., it is surely not foreordained that, like what happened after World War I, the end of the cold war will lead to excessive psychological demobilization in the West. But, as we see it, the danger does exist, the Gulf Crisis being an indication to that effect, paradoxical though this may seem at first. To be sure, the Gulf Crisis came to a happy ending, at least as seen by those who thought that the *Anschluss* of Kuwait was something absolutely intolerable from the point of view of international law and rights.

However, the really significant thing may not be so much that action was finally taken to redress that intolerable wrong and that it was done so efficiently, but rather the hesitations, the "without-me" attitudes, the mental self-torturing which beforehand afflicted a large fraction of Western public opinion[35] - whereas the simple, plain and ascertainable truth was that Saddam Hussein *was* (is) a sort of Hitler, although with a different ideology and also, fortunately, without the same economic and military resources at his command.

On a more general and theoretical level, it would certainly be interesting to have a closer and more rigorous look at the question of whether or under what circumstances the reverse feedback effect under discussion could end up, if it is strong enough, increasing the odds that war will break out. Again, this could presumably be done - given the necessary time and resources - with the help of the latest Lambelet-Luterbacher model, and it could probably be done on a purely theoretical level (ie. without having to quantify the model's various parameters).

Footnotes

[*]Heartfelt thanks are due Walter Isard who supplied the moral stimuli which led to this short essay.

[1]By the "extended" Richardsonian model we mean all arms race models where there is not only mutual stimulation but also a supply side.

[2]Of course this fraction need not be constant over time.

[3]This ignores foreign help which can be quite important for smaller countries (e.g. Israel). For the big powers (United States, Soviet Union) and even for medium-sized powers (France, United Kingdom, Germany) direct foreign financing is largely negligible.

[4]We know of no scientific study specifically addressing the question as to whether defense expenditures crowd out investment more than consumption or vice versa (but this may just indicate how limited our knowledge is). In those arms race models which include an economic sector, consumption is usually some function of income; this means that defense expenditures tend to crowd out investment.

[5]In Richardson's specification the change over time in country X's defense effort is a positive function of the level of country Y's effort and a negative function of its own level: $dX/dt = aY - bX + c$, where a, b and c are positive parameters. The term $-bX$

can be interpreted as a supply constraint (or as a "fatigue" effect) in a static context only (no economic growth). See Richardson (1960) and for a discussion see Lambelet and Luterbacher with Allan (1979), particularly pp. 50-51.

[6]For an early example, see Lambelet (1971), particularly the simulations on pp. 160 *et seq.*

[7]This does not mean that the events preceding World War I are perfectly clear-cut. For example, the Anglo-German naval competition lost most of its momentum following the 1912 Haldane mission to Berlin - see this writer's three pieces on the Anglo-German naval rivalry published in 1974, 1975 and 1976 in the *Papers of the Peace Science Society (International)*, particularly the first one: "The Anglo-German Dreadnought Race 1905-1914".

[8]This is clearly so in Richardson's main work (*op.cit.*, especially chapters I-III) which came out in book form in 1960 although it was written before 1947 at the latest. In 1951, however, Richardson published a short note on the link between arms races and the outbreak of war - see: "Could an Arms-Race End Without Fighting?", *Nature*, Sep. 29, 1951, pp. 567-568. In that note Richardson acknowledged the theoretical possibility that an arms race could end without a war, only to dismiss it as unrealistic - to wit: "But could events really happen thus? As far as I know, they never yet have done so". This is confirmed in a later comment by M.R. Horne in *Nature*, Nov. 24, 1951, p. 920.

[9]See Lambelet (1975b). For various attempts to formalize the approach proposed in this article, or something akin to it, see a series of papers by Brito-Intriligator and Intriligator-Brito, for example: Intriligator and Brito (1984). At the time, i.e., around 1975, the views expressed in our paper were not well received - not to say violently attacked - by those who make no distinction between the scientific analysis of arms races and related issues, on the one hand, and short-sighted naive peace activism, on the other.

[10]See Lambelet (1985). The volume that this paper is in is full of errors, some of which make it impossible to understand what the various authors meant (they were given no opportunity for proofreading). Anyone interested in a readable version of our contribution to this volume will receive a clean version on request (DEEP/HEC, BFSH1, CH-1015 Lausanne-Dorigny, Switzerland).

[11]As to the possibility of defeat and utter destruction, "better die fighting than live as slaves" is certainly a justifiable choice for which there is no lack of historical evidence.

[12]For a formal general model of conflicts, arms races and war which includes such a feedback loop, see Lambelet and Luterbacher (1987).

[13]In the paper cited in note 10 it was argued that the partial occupation of Afghanistan and, even more so, the building of a blue-water navy, complete with aircraft carriers, meant that the Soviet Union had evolved over time from a basically defensive posture, along the lines of Kennan's classical characterization, to a clearly expansionary attitude, as has often been the case historically with ageing empires.

[14]Of course, sheer luck may also have had something to do with it.

[15]Seen in that light, the title of the present paper is a natural choice.

[16]To the extent that the American "twin" (public and foreign) deficits are at least partly the result of heavy military spending, it could be argued that Japan, Western Europe and other foreign lenders willy-nilly did bear part of the U.S. defense burden. There is however a fundamental difference between acquiring interest- or dividend-bearing U.S. assets, on the one hand, and financing defense expenditures "*à fonds perdus*", on the other.

[17]It is striking that the World War II victors (the U.S., the Soviet Union, Britain), who were in charge of global security after 1945, all face serious economic problems today whereas the losers (Japan and Germany, also Italy and France to some extent) all enjoy economic health and strength. This is probably more than just a coincidence.

[18]Such as O. Lange, A. Lerner, E.M.F. Durbin, F.M. Taylor, and others.

[19]Foremost among which were F.v.Hayek and L.v.Mises.

[20]For two impressive eye-witness accounts of the role played by enthusiasm and devotion in the early stages of the centralized stalinistic economic system, see: Robert Byron, *First Russia, Then Tibet*, originally published in 1933 and reissued by Penguin Books in 1985, especially the prescient discussion around page 38; and E.

Maillart, *Parmi la jeunesse russe*, originally published in 1930 and reissued by Editions 24-Heures, Lausanne, 1989.

[21]As has been shown times and times again - for example, think of R. Owen and New Lanarck.

[22]It was striking to see that, at least in the cities, Eastern people generally tended to be quite well informed about world affairs, that they were familiar with the information and analyses about their own countries which circulated in the West, and that very many regularly listened to the BBC, the Voice of America, etc.

[23]See note 5. For a criticism or rather self-criticism of this study, see Lambelet (1986), especially note 9.

[24]See note 12.

[25]See the discussion on page 97.

[26]It appears that the exact words used by Chamberlain in 1938 were: "Peace *for* our time", and not "Peace *in* our time".

[27]Some important indications being: the Soviet Union's wellnigh complete withdrawal from the Middle East, Ethiopia and other places; its attitude during the Gulf War; its letting go of Eastern Europe in 1989; its general courting of the West; the course taken by various arms reduction negotiations; and so on and so forth.

[28]For example, one could image that Russia proper and possibly some outlying areas such as Kazakhstan and Siberia will eventually come to form a new, non-communistic but strongly nationalistic nuclear-armed state permanently at odds with most of its immediate neighbors, ie. the other new states which would have arisen on the ruins of the late empire.

[29]See our 1986 survey mentioned in note 24, especially pp. 8-10.

[30]What follows is largely based on the work and analyses of Pierre Renouvin.

[31]It was not only or even primarily a question of additional manpower and material resources, but a question of morale: France and England knew that help - and what help! - was on its way.

[32]As Keynes pretended at the time.

[33]As Marshall Foch had put it in 1919 or 1920.

[34]Even so, some historians wonder what would have happened if Nazi Germany had not declared war on the U.S. a few days after Pearl Harbor. In fairness, it must be added that the Roosevelt Administration or a good part of it had a clearer vision of where the interests of the United States lay, but the problem was precisely American public opinion.

[35]With - to be sure - large variations between individual countries.

References

Intriligator, M.D. and Brito, D.L. (1984). Can arms races lead to the outbreak of war? *Journal of Conflict Resolution*, 28, 63-84.

Lambelet, J.C. (1971). A dynamic model of the arms race in the Middle East, 1953-1965. *General Systems*, 16, 145-67.

Lambelet, J.C. (1974). The Anglo-German dreadnought race. *Papers, Peace Research Society (International)*, 22, 1-45.

Lambelet, J.C. (1975a). A numerical model of the Anglo-German dreadnought race. *Papers, Peace Research Society (International)*, 24, 29-48.

Lambelet, J.C. (1975b). Do arms races lead to war?" *Journal of Peace Research*, 4, 44-66.

Lambelet, J.C. (1976). A complementary analysis of the Anglo-German dreadnought race, 1905-1916. *Papers, Peace Research Society (International)*, 26, 219-66.

Lambelet, J.C. (1985). Arms races as good things? in U. Luterbacher and M.D. Ward (eds.) *Dynamic Models of International Conflict*. Boulder, CO: Lynne Rienner Publishers, Boulder (Colorado), 1985, pp. 161-174.

Lambelet, J.C. (1986). The formal ('economic') analysis of arms races: what - if anything - have we learned since Richardson? *Conflict Management and Peace Science*, 9, 1-18.

Lambelet, J.C. and Luterbacher, U. with Allan, P. (1979). Dynamics of arms races: mutual stimulation vs. self-stimulation. *Journal of Peace Science*, 4, 49-66.

Lambelet, J.C. and Luterbacher, U. (1987). Conflicts, arms races and war: a synthetic approach. in C. Schmidt and F. Blackaby (eds.) *Peace, Defence and Economic Analysis*. New York: St. Martin's, pp. 85-103.

Richardson, L.F. (1960). *Arms and insecurity*. Pittsburgh: Homewood.

Economics of Arms Reduction and the Peace Process
W. Isard and C.H. Anderton (Editors)

Chapter 13

KEY DIRECTIONS FOR RESEARCH

Walter Isard and Charles H. Anderton

Cornell University
and
College of the Holy Cross

13.1 Introduction

We now wish to provide some evaluation of the peace economics literature -- in particular, to identify gaps in it and topics that are given insufficient attention, as we point up key directions for research. It cannot be said that the survey presented in Chapter 1 and the choice of topics in the subsequent chapters are unbiased. Certainly, the authors' perspectives have been involved, even though these perspectives reflecting outlooks several generations apart and different social backgrounds, are not similar. We trust that critical comments by colleagues and reviewers of this book will help suggest a more rounded view of peace economics.

13.2 The Urgent Need for Developing Country Studies

Recall Arrow's contribution. He limited his discussion of the different ways suggested by economic theory for estimating the economic effect of major U.S. arms reduction (ways also relevant for any major increase). What he had to say by way of analytical methods could be claimed to relate to such reduction in most, if not all, developed and industrialized countries. He was careful to avoid any reference to the problem in developing countries. Yet, impact of changes in military expenditure in developing countries is an extremely important topic for study, and is recognized to be so by many scholars and policy analysts.

Recall the little and inconclusive results of studies on this topic from Benoit (1973) on. Chatterji identified several reasons for this state of affairs: (1) problems in defining and classifying a developing country; (2) severe data gaps and inadequacies; and (3) problems in the measurement of security expenditures. More urgent is the need to replace the set of theories, methods and tools constructed for analyzing developed country economies with a fresh, more appropriate set. In all probability this can and should come about from many more historical and case studies which identify key qualitative attributes and proxy measures of them (such as the qualitative concept of economic welfare for developed countries and GNP as its measure). Clearly such attributes would be sensitive to unique characteristics of internal politics and ethnic conflicts, to language and other cultural differences within a country and to specific factors such as a populace's view of militarization purely and simply as a job-creating process or as a way to develop a market for the product of domestic firms --- a way to spark industrialization --- without any thought given to the negative (or positive) externalities imposed on other countries.

13.3   Need for a More Rigorous General Conceptual Framework and its Further Development

As indicated in Chapter 1 several general conceptual frameworks have been developed for a multi-nation system with explicit military sectors and functions --- in line with Hirshleifer's contention that most national economies are geared simultaneously to war and peace. These frameworks, however, need serious improvement. One direction would involve further development of the interconnection of the micro and macro aspects of an economy and set of economies. Others would involve the incorporation of disequilibrium aspects into some, if not many, of the diverse economic processes covered, some recognition of forms of irrational/rational behavior and strategy, a more satisfactory consideration of the play of expectations (rational or not) and uncertainty, and the encompassing of political economy factors to be discussed in the next section. These frameworks should be extended to permit more effective study of how different technologies (military and other) and institutions can promote cooperation and restrict conflict, and how models of potential high level violence (wars) can be extended to cover situations of low level conflict (crime, street warfare and perhaps even rent-seeking).

13.4   Need for Better Defined and More Comprehensive Political Economy Studies

Arrow pointed out in his chapter the need to examine the effect on economic impact analysis of "public choice in a dynamic context and about increasing returns to scale in the political field" (p.), also having in mind feedback effects.

It is fair to say that the peace economics literature has, by and large, failed to deal adequately with non-economic factors, especially those of a political nature. In various analyses (as noted in Isard 1990), there is scant attention, if any, paid to current and time changes of: (1) the underlying motivation of nations, whether to reduce insecurity and maintain a balance of power, to retaliate for the insecurity caused by actions of one's opponents to achieve a balance of terror, to counteract the ambition of one's opponents (or one's power-driven elite), to assume a position of strength (greater strength) when negotiations on arms control is expected, or some like factor; (2) the underlying communications and perceptual situation (structure), whether the protagonists mutually perceive threat from the mere existence of military capabilities, or have misperceptions regarding the intentions and myopic-nonmyopic behavior of their rival, or possess extreme attitudes (such as religious fanaticism, or unbounded-unfounded optimism), and so forth; (3) the underlying policy of the nations involved, whether to prepare for war (or some form of aggression), to prevent war (such as in deterrence efforts), or to conduct a surrogate war (for example, an economic war designed to exhaust the resources of an opponent) -- or whether it is some combination of these and other possible policies (including competitive and complementary civilian policies).

At more specific levels, some of the political economy and related factors to which economists have paid scant attention are (as indicated in Isard 1990):

(1) the effectiveness of military and other foreign aid in achieving one's security goals;

(2) the positive effects that expenditures on military programs have on public opinion through creating new jobs when a state of unemployment exists;

(3) the current public concern, support, approval, or disapproval of military expenditures per se;

(4) the possibility of (a) internal unrest when too little goods remain for distribution to the nation's populace, or the less-fortunate fraction of that populace and (b) shifting attention away from internal problems by focusing on external threats generated (exacerbated) by military expenditures;

(5) the particular point of a current year in an electoral cycle, or an economic planning cycle;

(6) the outstanding grievances both recent and accumulated that a nation has with its rival;

(7) the ambition that a nation has for dominating its rival, or its propensity for submissiveness;

(8) the hostility (friendliness) and distrust (trust) that a nation has with regard to its rival;

(9) the need for the nation to serve in a "balance-of-power" capacity with regard to other nations;

(10) the existence or nonexistence of a state of war mobilization in one or more nations.

Still other factors and relationships pertain to (1) the composition of threatening and nonthreatening weaponry possessed by its rival, (2) a nation's expectations regarding future technology and rate of obsolescence of existing weaponry and weaponry under production, (3) the stocks of diverse weaponry of its allies and the allies of its rival, (4) the uncertainty associated with the effectiveness of one's efforts at maintaining secrecy regarding military structure and capability and the adequacy of one's intelligence efforts, (5) the decision-making structure of and organizational politics within a nation, (6) the nation's specific view of what is optimal behavior on its part and that of its rival, and (7) time lags in diplomatic and other reactions and in build-up and build-down of weapon stocks.

Admittedly study of many of these variables is much closer to the core of political and other social sciences than economics. Yet, if economists are to examine arms races and the broad range of conflict situations and try to understand them, as they should since economic variables are key to many of them, they must take into account these political economy-type variables.

We have already noted that a few economists are starting to examine some of the above factors -- such as Polachek and Seiglie in the use of COPDAB data in their research reported on in this book. There should be more extensive use of such data, improvement in their gathering and processing, and exploitation of voting and other data in use by non-economists. Moreover these data should be disaggregated, reorganized and supplemented by collection of new data to allow an analyst to identify better some of the general and key factors already noted. For example, in a military expenditure function, could we have a variable relating to the ambition (anti-status quo) of a nation and thus its propensity to arm for attack, a second variable to indicate the desire of a nation to see and thus contribute to a balance-of-power (mutual deterrence) situation, a third variable to measure the extent of hostility (friendliness) of a nation toward a rival (or other nations), and a fourth variable measuring internal unrest within a nation (and its consequent aggressiveness toward other nations). The COPDAB data (even when updated) would then need to be disaggregated and enormously supplemented, often by data to be collected on a continuing basis, to be able to treat several variables of this nature.

13.5 Need for Development of Contextual Game and Coalition Analysis

In providing an evaluation of the game theory literature, Shubik (1987), as already noted, stresses the need for analyzing both capacity-constrained rationality and context-rational behavior, the latter term being "a reminder that behavior must be assessed in the context of the situation at hand and it warns against spurious generality" (p. 57). It is with reference to coalition analysis, the part which falls within the realm of game theory and the part that does not, that his statement that "experiments are needed to study the differences and causes of differences in situations where the game or other theoretic situation is the same, but the briefing or setting of context, the players (their training and background), and organizational structure and time pressures are varied" (p. 80, words in italics are our own).

As one observes the way coalitions form and disrupt, the back and forth negotiations in forming governments (in a multi-party system or the equivalent) and policies (in a multi-interest group situation or the equivalent), one cannot help but be impressed on the one hand with the critical importance of the coalitions that are formed and policies realized and on the other with the extreme dearth of analytic knowledge of the process involved. We know game theory has very little to say about the solution to an active coalition process. Here a base of experiments of the sort urged by Shubik, let alone historical case studies, is required. One of the key questions upon which these experiments and studies can cast light is: how identify the effect upon the coalition process of the hierarchical structure of parties involved. This question goes beyond the question raised by Shubik: "Who are the players?" (p. 62). It involves not only numbers of parties directly and indirectly involved, but also their relationship to each other, including the relationship among the behaving units which each party may represent. This last consideration raises of course the question of how aggregate the preferences of the units represented by each party, even if only a ranking of a limited number of joint actions (coalition arrangements) is sought, let alone determine the importance ranking of each of the subparties.

A second key question upon which experiments and historical studies can cast light is: what are the effects of different information flow and communication-network structures on: (a) the coalition process; (b) more specifically, the probabilities for the formation of different coalitions and their disruption; (c) parties' perceptions and misperceptions in general and of such specific items as threats and motives of others. Closely related is the analysis of changes in the information-communication structure as the process proceeds, experience is gained, parties invest in the accumulation and processing of information and in the establishment of new communication links (all perhaps with costs and anticipated gains in mind); and so forth.

Still another key question concerns how the asymmetries of the engaged parties affects the coalition process---asymmetries in their stocks of knowledge, personalities (such as aggressiveness), value systems, attitudes, perceptions and misperceptions, resource bases, and in the pressures exerted upon them by their constituencies and in what they consider to be relevant and fair practices.

13.6   The Need for Conflict Management Procedures With Greater Politico-Economic Feasibility and Analytical Significance

Closely related to coalition formation is the area of conflict management. The formation of an effective coalition typically involves a compromise that resolves (successfully copes with) the conflict among the objectives, behavioral propensities, proposals, etc. of the parties involved. And, conversely, the attainment of say a peace treaty where there have existed conflicts among the objectives, behavioral propensities and proposals on issue treatment represents, broadly conceived, the formation of an effective coalition --- disrupted of course when a party breaks the treaty.

As has already been reported, there have been abstract contributions by game theorists on processes by which to reach a solution to certain kinds of conflict. At the other extreme, there have been seminal contributions by international lawyers, social psychologists and others employing nonmathematical and nonquantitative analyses who advance procedures to manage conflicts. In between have been some economists such as Boulding and Schelling, who have drawn upon more than one discipline and professional field in analyzing approaches and have suggested, implicitly or explicitly, ways to cope with conflict. However, such analyses and suggestions have not come anywhere near what is required for today's major conflicts.

Isard (1988) has noted that qualitative (nonquantitative) conflict management procedures set forth by international lawyers, social psychologists and political scientists often fail to resolve a conflict, and in many cases could be fruitfully complemented with probing quantitative analysis --- particularly with regard to economic variables and the problem of estimating significant feedback effects. To be specific, consider the situation where side payments are relevant. What levels and composition of side payments are possible and what are their tradeoffs with the extent and number of agreements on several issues of conflict? Or consider the question of different levels and weapons composition of disarmament. In a noteworthy U.N. study, Leontief and Duchin (1983) considered three disarmament scenarios, each one being optimal for one of the three groups of nations involved and thus being an extreme, politically infeasible scenario from the standpoint of all three groups. The middle ground, wherein might lie a set of politically feasible scenarios was not explored since Leontief was not interested in this problem. Yet, from the standpoint of world welfare, the "middle ground" of conflict situations must be explored for acceptability and implementability. In the world input-output framework of Leontief this cannot be done without an economic analyst capable of estimating direct and indirect impacts of the different middle ground scenarios for each of the several parties involved and jointly determining with others the middle ground scenarios to be examined.

In certain conflict situations, whether with regard to arms control, trade, or environmental issues, the Klein LINK model or an extended CGE model to embrace many or relevant groups of countries may be the core tool for economic analysis. An economic analyst, capable of operating such a model and fully aware of its virtues and limitations, would need to be actively involved in identifying middle ground scenarios to be inputted.

Perhaps, as the world moves into an explicit and full consideration of impending man-made environmental catastrophes --- which will add to the set of already major conflictual areas --- an even more extensive and comprehensive issue complex problem will be confronted requiring an economist's active and central role. For example, consider an issue complex involving: (a) control of emissions of greenhouses gases or other environmental pollutants (a concern of such nations as Germany, Japan and Sweden); (b) control of arms exports to Middle East countries, or ethnic cultural entities, or other political and cultural units capable of aggressive behavior, or to all (a concern of such nations as the United States and Britain); and (c) financial aid to developing countries. In using existing and designing (inventing) new conflict management procedures to identify scenarios whose direct, indirect and feedback implications are to be investigated necessarily with world models (whether crude or sophisticated), how can an economic analyst not be actively involved? In turn, it becomes essential for economics to conduct research at least on the design of existing and new conflict management procedures, or their properties, that are suitable for examining with (inputting into) world models or other comprehensive frameworks for economic analysis.[1]

13.7   Other Needed Research Directions

Clearly there are other important directions for research that the authors have failed to perceive or appreciate. Some scholars will undoubtedly consider key: (1) work with several types of improved models on the impact of arms expenditures on macromagnitudes, especially investment and GNP growth in developed countries, mixed economies, and totalitarian regimes, (2) further examination of the effect of military expenditures on trade directly and on levels of hostility among nations and thus indirectly upon trade, and on how trade affects the level of political conflict and thus indirectly arms expenditures, (3) investigations of the possibility of developing a defensive capability without attack potential, of developing a non-threatening weaponry system (4) work on different perceptions of the costs and gains of war, (5) analysis of mature political leadership drawing upon cumulated duopoly and oligopoly doctrine, (6) empirical and case studies on the impacts of military R&D, (7) theoretical and empirical work on the economics of terrorism and guerrilla warfare, (8) investigation (such as that of Hansen, Murdoch, and Sandler, 1990) of the possibilities for and practice in burden sharing especially if one anticipates that the operations of a U.N, police force will mount significantly in the future, and so forth.

In brief, one can easily conclude that there is almost unlimited research to be done in the newly developing field of peace economics.

Footnotes

[1]See Isard (1990) for a conceptual framework that involves feedbacks of the climate and ecologic systems on a multi-national world economy.

References

Benoit , E. (1973). *Defense and economic growth in developing countries,* Lexington, MA.: Lexington Books.

Hansen, L., Murdock, J.C., and Sandler, T. (1990). On distinguishing the behavior of nuclear and non-nuclear allies in NATO. *Defense Economics*, 1, 37-56.

Isard, W. (1990). Progress in global modeling for world policy on arms control and environmental management. *Conflict Management and Peace Science*, 11, 57-94.

Leontief, W. and Duchin, F. (1983). *Military spending: facts and figures*. New York: Oxford University Press.

Shubik, M. (1987). The uses, value and limitations of game theoretic methods in defense analysis. in C. Schmidt and F. Blackaby (eds.) *Defense and Economic Analysis*. New York: St. Martin's Press.